POLITICAL CRIME IN
CONTEMPORARY AMERICA

CURRENT ISSUES IN
CRIMINAL JUSTICE
(VOL. 4)

GARLAND REFERENCE LIBRARY
OF SOCIAL SCIENCE
(VOL. 863)

CURRENT ISSUES
IN CRIMINAL JUSTICE

GENERAL EDITORS
Frank Williams III
Marilyn McShane

POLITICAL CRIME IN CONTEMPORARY AMERICA
A Critical Approach

Edited by
Kenneth D. Tunnell

GARLAND PUBLISHING, INC. • NEW YORK & LONDON
1993

Library of Congress Cataloging-in-Publication Data

Political crime in contemporary America : a critical approach / edited by
Kenneth D. Tunnell.
    p. cm. — (Garland reference library of social science ; vol. 863.
Current issues in criminal justice ; vol. 4)
    ISBN 0-8153-0928-7
    1. Political crimes and offenses—United States. I. Tunnell,
Kenneth D. II. Series: Garland reference library of social science ;
v. 863. III. Series: Garland reference library of social science. Current
issues in criminal justice ; vol. 4.
HV6285.P65 1993   92-45728
364.1'31'0973—dc20   CIP

Printed on acid-free, 250-year-life paper
Manufactured in the United States of America

Table of Contents

FRANK WILLIAMS III AND MARILYN MCSHANE

Series Preface

This work represents the fourth volume in Garland Publishing's Current Issues in Criminal Justice series. The series is generally devoted to readable, scholarly work in criminal justice and, in particular, work that breaks new ground or fills in existing gaps in knowledge. The editor of this anthology, Ken Tunnell, has met all of these criteria. Each of the articles in this volume has been hand-picked by Tunnell, and the authors are recognized scholars who have agreed to contribute their thoughts to a unique anthology. We believe that readers will be stimulated and challenged by the arguments for this alternative criminological approach.

The topic of political crime is one that has been largely ignored in criminology yet has profound implications for definitions of crime and the interplay between power and law. The issue of harm is indeed a critical one for criminology, as Leslie Wilkins has so cogently argued in his *Consumerist Criminology*. Allowing a one-sided political definition of crime to govern research and theorizing has long been problematic for the disciplines of criminal justice and criminology. Under our current paradigm of legalistic crime, it is clear that much of the harm inflicted upon society is beyond the "proper" province of our studies.

The writing in Tunnell's "Prologue" to this book is equally as powerful as the individual contributions. In it he makes an appeal for wider recognition of not only harms by the state but also of the validity of values in *doing* criminal justice and criminology.

Clearly, values are an integral part of our work and it seems more appropriate to recognize their presence than to perpetuate our current "value-free and objective" scientific stance. From crack mothers to chicken factory foremen, emotional scenarios of human behavior set the stage for the production of law. Throughout the traditional interactions of criminal and victim, we have to be reminded that the state has been a major player in these dramas either through its intervention or its absence. We invite readers to explore, in this book, the world of value-oriented scholarship and decide for themselves if our legalistic paradigm should experience a mild revolution.

Acknowledgments

While attending the annual meeting of the Academy of Criminal Justice Sciences in Nashville, Frank Williams and I talked about a Political Crime panel for which I had served as the discussant. When asked if I would be interested in proposing a political crime anthology as part of Garland Publishing's Current Issues in Criminal Justice, I was delighted, for political crime, a long overlooked yet fundamental issue in criminology and criminal justice, had been an ongoing interest of mine for some time. Soon afterward, I began the slow, arduous process of contacting various individuals who I realize had and continue to have very busy lives, hectic demands, and research agendas for the next several years, yet individuals who I was confident could make invaluable contributions to such a work. As the potential authors were contacted, I was more often pleased than disappointed by their responses. Bob Bohm, Gregg Barak, Wayman Mullins, and Drew Humphries were some of the first individuals contacted who agreed to contribute to the work. Later, and often through introductions from friends, Kim Cook, Ray Michalowski and Judy Aulette, Sue Caulfield and Nancy Wonders, and Jeffrey Ross agreed to contribute chapters. These individuals represent some of the most important thinkers, researchers, and writers in the area of political crime and I am delighted to have their work as part of this reader.

Each of the contributors has approached this anthology with all the seriousness that an editor could hope for. As a result, each contributed a first-rate chapter on the various issues pertinent to political crime. I am especially grateful to the authors for their willingness to contribute, their diligence in producing such outstanding scholarship, and their patience with me as an editor. Obviously, this work would not have been possible without their generous contribution and to each, I offer a heartfelt thank you.

I am especially grateful to Frank Williams III and Marilyn McShane for their willingness to oversee this needed series in Criminal Justice and for offering me the opportunity to compile this anthology. Frank and Marilyn have been wonderful series editors by providing sound advice and moral support. Thank you both, Trey and Marilyn.

I also am grateful to the kind folks at Garland Publishing, especially Phyllis Korper, for giving me the opportunity to assemble such a reader and for their unwavering support for this project.

Thanks yet again to Ilona Leki for her moral support, confidence, comradery, love, and sound advice.

This book is dedicated to peoples' struggles everywhere.

KENNETH D. TUNNELL

Prologue

The State of Political Crime

More than likely, it comes as no surprise that crime, as an act, and the social reactions to it, are political constructs. After all, crime is a violation of legal norms legislated by a political body as criminal deviance. Likewise, the consequences of such—the systemic reaction by the criminal justice system—represent both normative and political reactions by agents of the State entrusted with prescribing and dispensing punishment for politically defined deviance. This conceptualization of crime, in and of itself, is probably not foreign to most readers and, in fact, is one that more than likely is widely agreed on. For simply stating that crime is a political act does not neglect the seriousness of those actions currently defined as criminal and those actions that typically come to the public's mind when thinking of crime. For criminologists of both the left and the right would agree that violent crime represents actions that cause both personal and social harms and are just those acts that deservedly are labeled crimes. Likewise, there is broad agreement that certain property crimes, such as armed robbery and burglary, are appropriately labeled criminal, since they result in both personally and socially harmful consequences. Yet, as widely accepted as a political construction of crime undoubtedly is, it receives very little attention in criminological literature. Given the criminological community's scant treatment of political crime as both a theoretical concept and an empirical phenomenon, the state of political crime is wanting.

Prologue

The term "political crime" itself suffers from a lack of clarity, for as a concept, it has been defined in a variety of ways; some definitions explicate the abstract qualities of the concept while others severely limit its application and explanatory power. For example, political crime typically is treated rather narrowly, limiting its definition to illegal acts committed by politically or ideologically motivated individuals whose objective, while violating the law, is to effect social change or to rebel against unfair laws and governments. These crimes are considered altruistic and committed by "convictional criminals" (Schafer, 1974). However, rarely do we witness the explication of the ideology and political agenda of "convictional" offenders and how their actions may effect social change. Little attention is given to the alternative/progressive positions of those contracultural individuals who engage in criminal misconduct as a means to their greater goal—objective social change.

As an illustration of the scant attention given to political crime, a recent analysis of criminal justice and criminology introductory texts (which undoubtedly contain widely recognized and accepted tenets about crime, criminals, and their treatment) shows that political crime in any form gets very little coverage (Tunnell, 1993). Although the sociology of law implicitly contains political explanations for what is and what is not defined as deviant, *political* explanations for crime are seldom articulated (even those widely accepted explanations). Likewise, critical queries of socio-political relationships and their contribution to socially harmful behavior receive little coverage in widely disseminated texts. This absence of political explanations and conceptualizations of what is and is not legislated as crime is disturbing, since any analysis of the sociology of law, selective criminalization, and selective enforcement is implicitly political.

Selective Criminalization

No doubt lawmaking is a selective process, since various acts are included in the rubric of crime while others are excluded. The rationale for inclusion and exclusion is often unclear because law criminalizes various social harms while leaving many significant social harms untouched by the criminal label (see, e.g., Chambliss 1979; Reiman, 1990). Throughout the history of the United States, various social acts have been pronounced illegal, and for whatever reason, suddenly no longer criminal. For example, sedition is rarely recognized as crime. Likewise, laws aimed at controlling the Communist party in the United States (Communist Control Act of 1954) and laws restricting labor's efforts at organizing and mobilizing the rank and file have appeared and then disappeared, as have the post-Civil War black codes and Jim Crow laws. Such laws were enacted to preserve a socio-economic order at a particular juncture in history, although dissident groups and progressive criminologists continuously have posed the question, "Whose order?" (e.g., Turk, 1982). Individuals whose relationships with the law are characterized as oppressive rather than as protective have little access to the means of communication, have found they are unable to speak out, and in fact often are unable to articulate their oppression in any formalized manner (e.g., Turk, 1982). Thus, their voices are largely absent from political and criminalization processes.

The State's control of social harms, especially those resulting from the socio-economic order itself, has been much slower coming to fruition than the control of politically defined "undesirables." The criminological community (and nonacademic progressive groups) have consistently called for politically initiated controls on acts of commission and omission that result in innumerable social harms and costs, yet with little success. Doubtless, civil rights, affirmative action, and some environmental laws of the 1970s represent political and social victories for progressives yet, despite their continued efforts, few significant inroads have been accomplished beyond these measures. Far-reaching social harms, such as corporate transgressions and transgressions resulting from the symmetrical relationships between corporate America and the State remain largely unchallenged. Criminalizing such activities is considered, by state managers and politicians, actions that would significantly threaten social relationships and the political-economic order. Yet, failure to act in such a way to protect the populace from such social harms can be treated as a form of crime—political crime. For political decisions are made to ignore such activities and their consequences. Likewise, the State's failure to remedy various social problems (e.g., poverty, unemployment) when it is in the State's power to do so has been treated as State crime—a form of political crime (e.g., Barak, 1991; see also Bohm's chapter in this anthology). And, evidence suggests that the worst crimes— physically, economically, and in terms of civil rights violations— indeed have been carried out by the State and its agents who are free from the law as a form of social control (Friedrichs, 1992).

The criminal justice and criminology communities mostly ignore the broader and fundamental issues of political crime and selective criminalization. Left unexplored are political decisions by the State that fundamentally restrict individuals' rights and freedoms (including freedom in reproductive choices); acts of hate by one group toward another solely on the basis of race or ethnicity; acts committed by the State that, although not defined as criminal, result in widely harmful social consequences; social problems that, although abhorrent, are left unresolved by a State that possesses the means to alleviate such harms; and acts, not defined as criminal, conducted by corporations that cause physical, economic, and environmental harm to countless individuals. By focusing on these broader misdeeds, the political nature of actions that cause wide-scale social harm is better revealed. Furthermore, the social relationships that contribute to such a criminogenic environment become clarified. A broader conceptualization of political crime implicitly includes such acts of commission and omission that result in grave social harm. Addressing such issues is an area that remains unexplored and one in desperate need of sound scholarship.

The Political Economy of Political Crime

The State as a political body that acts, reacts, and fails to act, as well as the broader political economy within which it functions, are essential to a critical examination of political crime. After all, political crime (defined broadly to include the State's omissions described above) takes its particular shape in the United States due largely to the political economy of U.S. society and no doubt assumes quite different shapes in states with different political economies. The political economy of the United States plays a significant role in determining which acts are defined as criminal (although not necessarily harmful) and which are excluded from the purview of the criminal law and criminal labels (often acts with quite harmful consequences). For the widely accepted role of the State and its managers is to maintain order while preserving the dominant mode of production. Actions conceivably threatening to this economic order and its culture are not only made criminal, but are those activities that the State and its repressive arm, the criminal justice system, police in a variety of ways. For example, with the influx of technological developments of recent years, information-gathering now plays a fundamental role in combatting threats to the political economy of the United States. Likewise, infiltration of antisystemic groups is conducted by the FBI, the CIA, and other agencies entrusted with preserving such order. For example, the FBI's admitted infiltration of CISPES, the State's persecution of the Sanctuary movement, and the selective and in fact inhumane incarceration of individuals defined as "political threats" illustrate this point (see, e.g., Korn, 1988; Zwerman, 1988). Perhaps even more telling, in recent years Americans have witnessed the erosion of their own personal liberties and civil rights. During the Reagan/Bush administrations, we have witnessed the reversal of laws once designed to preserve our individual liberties. Although these reversals allegedly have been aimed at the "criminal class," the law makes no distinction between criminals and noncriminals. For example, the State has given carte blanche to its agents of control in a variety of ways; by reversing the exclusionary rule, by making

greater use of the military for domestic law enforcement, by
limiting court appeals, by allowing juveniles and the mentally
retarded to be executed for capital offenses, by allowing employers
in a variety of professions to test their employees for casual drug
use, by escalating anti-labor initiatives by assailing the National
Labor Relations Board to further dilute the solidarity of the
working class, by continuing to engage Native Americans in one
court battle after another over their land (including their sacred
burial grounds) and its mineral rights, and by enacting increasingly
punitive measures aimed at controlling minorities and the
dispossessed through mandatory and longer prison sentences and
for a variety of new crimes (viz., drug laws) (e.g., Austin and Irwin,
1990; Jenkins, 1992; Matthiessen, 1991). These changes are
indicative of the political economy of the United States at a
particular epoch in history—no doubt a particularly conservative
time and one characterized by an erosion of any semblance of
community and a promotion of increasing state control, increasing
corporate profits, and symbolic lip service to the reactionary right.
The State's criminalization of various activities that restrict
individuals' choices and freedoms, while widening the ever-
increasing net of social control, are indicative of political decisions
made to preserve both a particular economic system and a culture
that reproduces its citizens' assumptions about what is legitimate,
illegitimate, socially harmful, and criminal.

Political Crime and the Responsibility of Criminologists

Three decades ago, Alvin Gouldner (1962) challenged us as
social scientists and thinkers to reconsider the growing trend in our
discipline—value neutrality—a form of false consciousness. He
encouraged us to resist the efforts of those who espouse the
necessity of a value-free sociology (and by extension, criminology
and criminal justice). He considered value neutrality a cop-out for
those who choose to "live off sociology rather than for it" and who
use neutrality as a springboard for selling their skills and professions
on the free market (Gouldner, 1962: 204). Gouldner raised

rhetorical questions for the sociological community—a group that undoubtedly is committed to understanding social conditions. For example, should we be indifferent to the moral implications of our work? Should we express feelings for or against something that we study? Should we or should we not inform laypersons about troubling social conditions and their antecedents? As a guide post for answering such questions, Gouldner reminds us that the recognized originator of the value neutrality doctrine, Max Weber, acknowledged that objectivity was not synonymous with moral indifference. And in fact, Gouldner admonishes us to not be morally indifferent, but rather to "take sides." By so doing, we as social scientists can contribute to a critical understanding of various social phenomena, including political crime, the selective process of criminalization, the criminogenic environment implicit in monopoly capitalism that displaces countless individuals and forces them to live on the margins of society, and the crimes of omission carried out by the State—that institution presumably committed to protecting its citizenry. And by doing so, perhaps our work coupled with our position-taking will contribute to making this a saner, safer, and more humane society within which to live.

Of course, Gouldner has not been alone in shaking up this professional dogma. Just five years after his address, Becker (1967) characterized the issue of whether sociologists ought to "have values" as a false and imaginary dilemma. Becker reminds us that "there is no position from which sociological research can be done that is not biased in one way or another" (1967: 245). Having values is not the question, but rather how do we use them, or using Becker's words, "Whose side are we on?" Perhaps in a way more guarded than Gouldner's, Becker calls on sociologists to be aware that there are "sides" and that each side has its own interests, ideologies, and agendas. And before Gouldner and Becker, Marx explicitly wrote of taking sides—by committing ourselves to the criticism of oppressive social and political arrangements.

Nothing prevents us therefore from starting our criticism with
criticism of politics, with taking sides in politics, hence with
actual struggles, and identifying ourselves with them (Marx,
September 1843, letter to Arnold Ruge, reprinted in Selsam, *et
al.*, 1970).

Thus, the alternative voices from beyond the mainstream offer
a dilemma. Not one of whether to investigate the social with our
values in check, but rather how best to use them—whether in
research, in the dissemination of our findings, or in analyses of
political and social arrangements as starting points for
understanding crime, social problems, and the roles of the State.
Thus, one mission for a committed social science community is to
impart a critical awareness to others, be it our students, colleagues,
or world neighbors. A critical awareness of the firmly entrenched
political and economic forces at work will further explicate the logic
of individuals who violate the law because of their political
convictions as well as individual victims of vast social harms
currently tolerated by the managers of political and economic
forces. We must be mindful that such harms are not impossible to
alleviate; the political economy simply needs to work differently by
benefitting humanity rather than a minority of wealthy and
powerful individuals. Our mission should be not only to clarify
political crime as a useful and analytical concept, but also to use it
to point to socially injurious behavior condoned by a State that fails
to alleviate such socially injurious behavior and fails to adequately
address issues of inequality, racism, sexism, homelessness, and
unemployment, to name only a few mammoth social problems
(and that are treated as political crimes in this anthology). We can
work toward these objectives, in effect, only by continuing to "take
sides" as we articulate the various dimensions of what is and what is
not defined as crime and who is and who is not defined as criminal.
Such issues are implicitly political and are deserving of continued
critical inquiry and explication.

REFERENCES

Austin, James and John Irwin. 1990. *Who Goes to Prison?* San Francisco: National Council on Crime and Delinquency.

Barak, Gregg. 1991. *Crimes by the Capitalist State.* Albany: State University of New York Press.

Becker, Howard S. 1967. "Whose Side are We On?" *Social Problems* 14: 239–247.

Chambliss, William J. 1979. "On Lawmaking." *British Journal of Law and Society.* 6 (2): 149–171.

Friedrichs, David O. 1992. "Governmental Crime: Making Sense of the Conceptual Confusion." A paper presented to the Academy of Criminal Justice Sciences, Pittsburgh, March.

Gouldner, Alvin W. 1962. "Anti-minotaur: The Myth of a Value-free Sociology." *Social Problems* Winter:199–213.

Jenkins, Philip. 1992. "Fighting Drugs, Taking Liberties: The Effects of the Drug War." *Chronicles* May: 14–18.

Korn, Richard. 1988. "The Effects of Confinement in the High Security Unit at Lexington." *Social Justice* 15: 8–19.

Matthiessen, Peter. 1991. *In the Spirit of Crazy Horse.* New York: Penguin.

Reiman, Jeffrey. 1990. *The Rich Get Richer and the Poor Get Prison* (3rd. ed.). New York: Macmillan.

Schafer, Stephen. 1974. *The Political Criminal.* New York: The Free Press.

Selsam, Howard, David Goldway, and Harry Martel. 1970. *Dynamics of Social Change: A Reader in Marxist Social Science.* New York: International Publishers.

Tunnell, Kenneth D. 1993. "Political Crime and Pedagogy: A Content Analysis of Criminology and Criminal Justice Texts." *Journal of Criminal Justice Education* 4 (1): forthcoming.

Turk, Austin T. 1982. *Political Criminality: The Defiance and Defense of Authority.* Beverly Hills: Sage.

Zwerman, Gilda. 1988. "Special Incapacitation: The Emergence of a New Correctional Facility for Women Political Prisoners." *Social Justice* 15: 31–47.

Overview

This anthology gives little coverage to more widely acceptable tenets about crime, its legislation, and the reaction of the criminal justice system. Rather, the focus is on those issues typically excluded from discussions and debates about the political nature of crime and, as a result, goes beyond mainstream discussions of crime and politics by raising fundamentally critical queries about crime and its politicization. Issues typically omitted from discussions of political crime are just those given a forum here. For example, the issue of social harm has been raised time and time again by progressive social scientists and particularly by criminologists who suggest that those acts that cause grave social consequences are those that are excluded from the criminal label and should be those crimes that the criminal justice system controls. An unresolved issue for criminologists is an acceptable definition of crime that does not simply rely on statutory law. The chapter by Robert Bohm addresses these issues by focusing on political omissions by the State, or the State's unresponsiveness to vast social problems that result in social harms; inequitable distribution of wealth, homelessness, poverty, unemployment, underemployment, hunger, racism, sexism, and intentional and negligent killings (e.g., industrial accidents). These actions, while not criminal, "arguably should be." In this context, Bohm considers such omissions political crimes because the State and its managers are those who consistently refuse to act, although evidence suggests that humane and political action could indeed alleviate and eliminate some of these problems that have such tantamount social consequences.

Related to Bohm's work, two chapters focus specifically on the consequences of political decisions by State managers and politicians within the current politically conservative era.

The chapter by Drew Humphries debunks some widely held beliefs about crack-using mothers, their children, and the political nature of criminalizing their pregnancies. Specifically, Humphries focuses on recent state policies and punishments aimed at controlling activities pertaining to women only. Crack-using pregnant women and the increasing public and political attention they received during the conservative 1980s are treated as yet another myth in the war on drugs that when first made public functioned to distract the American people from the drug war's failures. In fact, conservative politics (and ensuing state policies) have made good use of symbolic communication by portraying crack-using pregnant women as minority, welfare dependent, or that which corresponds to conservative appraisals of everything that is wrong with America. Humphries debunks widespread assumptions about the numbers of crack-using pregnant women, the physiological effects on newborns, and the recovery trends of such babies. We discover that the problem is not as widespread as we have been led to believe and in fact, that crack use is a rather minor part of America's drug problem. At the heart of this issue is the State's omission for failing to address the socio-economic conditions of urban America, where the majority of crack-using pregnant women reside, as well as failing to provide adequate prenatal care, housing, ongoing health screening, and postnatal care for these women and their children. Such omissions arguably are crimes, but are not legislated as such. Rather, the pregnancy itself is considered criminal and in fact, some women have been incarcerated for using illicit drugs while pregnant, charged with distributing drugs to minors.

Kim Cook's contribution is an analysis of recently enacted punitive state policies, particularly those aimed at punishing and controlling women who seek control of their reproductive choices. An examination of the punitive elements of anti-choice legislation, her chapter debunks and unmasks the "pro-life" agenda and analyzes it as a form of punitive control. Recent legislation that chips away at women's constitutional rights to abortion is viewed as part of the growing "law and order" movement, which also supports capital punishment. In fact, Cook's analysis, which focuses on punitive states and their anti-choice legislation, shows that those states with very punitive policies (e.g., capital punishment) are those also working to enact some of the most restrictive and punitive abortion laws in the United States. Cook situates these recent developments within a new conservatism that has swept the United States in the past decade and treats such movements of life-style political groups as implicitly political as they attempt to impose strictures on, and in fact criminalize, a constitutional guarantee.

The issues raised in the chapter by Susan Caulfield and Nancy Wonders complement the work of both Humphries and Cook. Caulfield and Wonders offer a political analysis and explanation of personal violence against women. More specifically, they suggest that the State contributes to violence against women by failing to criminalize and enforce various personal harms against women. Thus, they explain such crime as implicitly political. The state is complicitous, they argue, both by allowing a culture of violence toward women to permeate American social life and by failing to protect women by tolerating various acts specifically against women. The State has failed, in effect, by design, and as a result is guilty of engaging in political crime based solely on gender.

The chapter by Jeffrey Ian Ross describes a form of political crime that often comes to mind when thinking of political crime—oppositional crime, or what Ross labels "oppositional political terrorism," which is carried out by antisystemic groups or individuals (to use Schafer's term, "convictional criminals") who desire to effect social change. Ross does a service to scholarship by critically reviewing the literature in this area. His criticisms are appropriate given that political crime is often recognized as the oldest form of crime, yet rarely appears in the volumes of literature published annually in sociology, criminology, and political science.

Ross's chapter points toward new directions essential for sound scholarship in this area and for critical inquiries into political crime.

Wayman Mullins's chapter describes a form of political crime—domestic terrorism carried out by members of the far right against minorities—and what we now recognize as hate crimes. Mullins criticizes the criminological community for failing to consider such activities as political crimes and raises issues about the State's slow response rate to these acts that threaten and harm society, and especially minorities. He gives considerable coverage to detailing the various hate organizations, their ideologies and objectives, and the various modes by which they function. His work further describes the dynamics of hate crime organizations by focusing on a particularly troubling recent development—the recruitment of the young. Mullins's treatment of these organizations, their recruitment, activities, and agendas, are treated as political crimes with grave social consequences that escalated within a particular political climate—the conservative 1980s in the United States.

Judy Root Aulette and Ray Michalowski make use of the recently emerging concept state-corporate crime by describing their recent case study of the Imperial Chicken Processing Plant fire in Hamlet, North Carolina. Aulette and Michalowski treat this fire as state-corporate crime, and show that it occurred due to the State's failure to act, although legally entrusted to do so, in protecting worker safety. This fatal state-corporate crime is explained as the result of a series of social decisions made by various agencies and institutions of the public and private sectors. Specifically, Aulette and Michalowski explain this crime by situating it within several social realms—"societal" (i.e., North Carolina's industrial regulation history), "institutional" (i.e., Imperial's own industrial relations), and "control" (i.e., regulatory agencies' failure at containing, what proved to be, Imperial's fatal legal violations). By using such an analysis, they show how this "crime," while far from an aberration, was the result of a cooperative relationship among agents of the State and Imperial's management.

The chapter by Gregg Barak details political crimes by the capitalist State—crimes of both omission and commission. Related to the former, Barak, like Bohm, reminds us as a criminological community to pay heed to the State's policy of economic noninterventionism regarding the human suffering of unemployment and homelessness. Barak questions why there are no legally guaranteed rights to work and to housing and treats the State's omission as criminal. Political crimes of commission by the State include intentional, premeditated (and often legally supported) acts such as slavery, genocide, and the investigation, infiltration, and destabilization of insurgent groups and "threatening" political parties. Further examples of the State's commission include wiretapping, surveillance of political undesirables, and state-supported terrorism. While admonishing us as a criminological community that these are the social harms pertinent to criminology, Barak suggests that the study of such may prove difficult due to the resistance of the publicly powerful and our own discipline's reluctance to consider State criminality a legitimate part of criminology and criminal justice.

These eight chapters represent the most recent thoughts on political crime. Beyond that, they encourage us to reevaluate our conceptualizations of just what is "political crime," how it is defined, and how we, as social thinkers and as members of the world community, can raise the social consciousness about those acts that indeed cause and have caused immeasurable social harm.

POLITICAL CRIME IN
CONTEMPORARY AMERICA

Social Relationships That Arguably Should Be Criminal Although They Are Not: On the Political Economy of Crime

From time to time, but less frequently of late, criminologists engage in intramural debate over the appropriate definition of crime. Most criminologists today act as if the debate is settled in favor of a "legal" definition. However, the debate is not settled, nor will it ever be until quiescent criminologists address the political economy of crime and recognize that "political crimes" are committed regularly and with impunity because they are not defined legally as crimes or the laws prohibiting them routinely go unenforced. After providing a brief history of the debate over the appropriate definition of crime, this chapter describes some of the aforementioned "political crimes" and shows how they are related to the current political economy of the United States.

On the Appropriate Definition of Crime

The modern debate on the appropriate definition of crime was initiated by Edwin Sutherland on December 27, 1939, with his presidential address to the American Sociological Society. In his speech, Sutherland argued that "white-collar crime" was real crime even though it generally was responded to by regulatory agencies and administrative (civil) law rather than by the agencies of criminal justice and statutory (criminal) law. Sutherland's remarks were revolutionary for several reasons, not the least of which was his persuasive challenge to the then accepted myth that poverty was the major cause of crime. Poverty obviously could not be a cause of white-collar crime. Sutherland's speech was published in 1940 and was followed five years later by another article on the same subject.

In 1947 the debate was joined by Paul Tappan who asserted that crime is a violation of the criminal law, and that people who have not been convicted of a crime (i.e., a violation of the criminal law) are not criminals. Thus, Tappan did not consider as criminals persons who had been convicted of administrative law violations. Sutherland, of course, disagreed and countered that, because of Tappan's strict criterion, poor people were overrepresented among convicted criminals.

The Sutherland-Tappan debate drew some additional attention in the next few years but seemingly was resolved in favor of Tappan's position. Nevertheless, the debate was critically important because Sutherland, perhaps for the first time, raised questions about the scope and biases of the legal definition of crime.

For the next twenty years, there was a lull in the debate. Then, in 1970, Herman and Julia Schwendinger published a powerful critique of legalistic definitions of crime and in the process expanded the scope of Sutherland's position. While the Schwendingers acknowledged Sutherland's contribution of showing the error in defining crime by reference to violation of only the criminal law (and not the civil law), they criticized him for restricting his definition of white-collar crime to violation of legal precedents, whether criminal or civil. Anticipating an argument developed in this chapter, the Schwendingers asked, "If ruling classes and powerful interest groups are able to manipulate legislators to their own advantage, isn't it possible that there are instances of socially injurious behaviour which have no legal precedents?" (Schwendinger and Schwendinger, 1975:126).

The Schwendingers (1975) maintained that any definition of crime is informed, either implicitly or explicitly, by moral standards, a position roundly rejected by all "value-free" social scientists.[1] They identified the moral standards governing their definition of crime as human rights or, more specifically, the right of human beings to realize their human potential. Thus, a criminal, for the Schwendingers, is any person who denies other people the right to realize their human potential. Not only are individuals criminal in this way, but so are social relationships and social systems. According to the Schwendingers, "If the terms imperialism, racism, sexism and poverty are abbreviated signs for theories of social relationships or social systems which cause the systematic abrogation of basic rights, then imperialism, racism, sexism and poverty can be called crimes according to the logic of our argument" (1975:137). The Schwendingers admitted that their definition of crime is not necessarily a satisfactory one, but only that it is preferable to a legal definition that consigns criminologists who adopt it to a position of subservience to the State.

Tony Platt (1975:103) reiterated the Schwendingers' call for a human rights-based definition of crime but, in doing so, couched his definition within an explicitly socialist context:

> . . . a radical perspective defines crime as a violation of politically-defined human rights: the truly egalitarian rights to decent food and shelter, to human dignity and self-determination, rather than the so-called right to compete for an unequal share of wealth and power. A socialist, human-rights definition of crime frees us to examine imperialism, racism, capitalism, sexism and other systems of exploitation which contribute to human misery and deprive people of their human potentiality.

Similarly, in 1977, Richard Quinney, who had been struggling with the issue of the political nature of crime since the early 1960s (see, for example, Quinney, 1964), proposed a typology of crime that included "crimes of domination." Among these crimes were (1) "crimes of control" (e.g., violation of civil liberties through various forms of surveillance, use of provocateurs, and illegal denial of due process); (2) "crimes of government" (e.g., crimes of warfare and the assassination of domestic and foreign leaders); (3) "crimes of economic domination" (e.g., corporate crimes, like price-fixing and pollution of the environment); and (4) "social injuries" (e.g., denial of basic human rights resulting in racism, sexism and economic exploitation.) Like Platt, Quinney viewed crime in the United

States as integrally tied to the political economy of advanced capitalism.

Finally, William Chambliss (1976:101–2) perhaps best summarized the political part of the thesis advanced in this chapter:

> Crime is a political phenomenon. What gets defined as criminal or delinquent behavior is the result of a political process within which rules are formed which prohibit or require people to behave in certain ways. It is this process which must be understood as it bears on the definition of behavior as criminal if we are to proceed to the study of criminal "behavior." Thus to ask "why is it that some acts get defined as criminal while others do not" is the starting point for all systematic study of crime and criminal behavior.

In sum, a fundamental problem with the present way that crime is legally defined, a problem common to the critiques of Sutherland, the Schwendingers, Platt, Quinney, Chambliss, and others (e.g., Barak, 1991; Black, 1979; Liazos, 1982; Michalowski, 1985; Reiman, 1979), and the focus of this chapter, is: Some social relationships[2] arguably should be criminal although they are not (or the laws prohibiting some social relationships should be enforced although they routinely are not). Because crime is political,[3] many dangerous and harmful acts of commission or omission are not defined as crimes and, therefore, are not considered or addressed as crimes, while many less dangerous and less harmful acts are defined as crime and treated accordingly.[4] As this chapter shows, ultimately what is or is not defined as crime is the result of political choice—decisions made by human beings for human beings.

However, political decisions, including the criminalization process, do not take place in a vacuum. They are shaped by the material conditions and by the goals and values considered legitimate at particular stages in a society's development. Under the dominant modes of production and distribution in the United States today a primary goal (indeed, a necessity of life) is the accumulation of capital (wealth). Achievement of this goal is motivated primarily by the popularly accepted values of individualism, competitiveness, and materialism.

There is nothing inherently wrong or criminogenic with the goal of capital accumulation. Theoretically, increased capital could be used to satisfy the needs and to enhance the standard of living of the world's population. However, when the goal is motivated primarily by individualistic, competitive, and material values, the means by which capital is accumulated and the way in which it is distributed can be problematical. Indeed, nearly all crime in the United States today, including the "political crime" described in this chapter, is a product of the individualistic, competitive, and materialistic pursuit of capital.

The goal of capital accumulation is pursued both as an end-in-itself and as a means of achieving another highly valued goal—political power. As noted above, it is political power that ultimately determines what is or is not defined as criminal. Thus, those individuals/groups who have achieved the greatest success in the accumulation of capital and political power can control to a considerable extent what types of social relationships are or are not defined legally as crime. Under these circumstances and within historically contingent bounds, it is unlikely that most of the methods by which capital is accumulated by highly successful individuals will be criminalized even when they are exploitative of the rest of the population. There are limits however, and the most blatantly outrageous forms of capital accumulation, particularly those that jeopardize the capital accumulation efforts of other wealthy people, often are criminalized (or controlled by civil law).

This chapter, then, is another entry in the debate over the adequacy of a legal definition of crime. It is unabashedly value-laden, as all social science, and especially criminology, must be.[5] Theses of this chapter are: (1) most of the social relationships described below, although not defined legally as crime, are in fact "political crimes," and (2) failure to prevent the "crimes" when they are preventable also is "political crime."

Six social relationships have been selected as representative of the kinds of crimes (although they are not legally defined as such) that are particularly important because of the many other dangerous and harmful behaviors (i.e., crimes) to which they contribute (cf. Currie, 1985:Chaps. 5 and 7; Elias, 1986:Chap. 4; Gordon, 1971; Michalowski, 1985; Simon and Eitzen, 1990:38). The social relationships are the grossly inequitable distribution of wealth in the United States, poverty, hunger, institutionalized racism, institutionalized sexism, and intentional or criminally negligent killings that are not treated as such. The group is not exhaustive; there are other "crimes" that could have been included, e.g., homelessness (cf. Barak, 1991; Barak and Bohm, 1989).

The Grossly Inequitable Distribution of Wealth

The basis for most crime in the United States today and, as argued here, a "political crime," is the grossly inequitable distribution of wealth. Note that the "crime" is *not* unequal wealth, which is probably an unobtainable, however laudable, ideal. The crime is the grossly inequitable distribution of wealth, its maintenance, and its destructive consequences.

Inequity in the distribution of wealth in the United States increased at an unprecedented rate during the 1980s. By the end of the decade, excluding the value of private homes, the top one-half of one percent of the population of the United States owned 45 percent of the country's wealth (Brouwer, 1988). In 1983, the top one-half of one percent of the population (approximately 420,000 households) owned 35 percent of the country's wealth (Drinkard, 1986). Prior to 1983, the previous highest level of disparity was in 1929, just before the Depression, when the top one-half of one percent owned 32 percent of total wealth (Drinkard, 1986). In 1963, by contrast, the same group held slightly more than 25 percent of total wealth (Drinkard, 1986).

At the top of the top one-half of one percent are the 400 richest people in the United States. According to *Forbes* magazine, in 1990 the richest 400 people in the United States had an average economic worth of $681.9 million and, together, they had approximately $272.5 billion (Seneker, 1990)—approximately the size of the 1991 federal budget deficit. In 1990 the United States could boast 66 billionaires, five fewer than the previous year (Seneker, 1990). The richest person in America in 1990 was John Kluge whose estimated wealth was $5.6 billion (Seneker, 1990).

Wealthy people typically are admired because of the exemplary characteristics presumed to be associated with the accumulation of great fortunes. Hard work, education, and deferred gratification are often suggested as qualities that lead to riches. However, the great fortunes of this country were made by the "robber barons" who acquired their wealth at least partly through illegal activity. As for Horatio Alger stories, they are often myth. For example, six of the top fifteen richest Americans in 1990 gained their fortunes by inheritance (Seneker, 1990). (This is not meant to imply that inheritance of any type is undesirable, only inheritance that is superfluous.)

The next one-half of one percent of the population averaged $1.7 million in assets in 1983; the next nine percent averaged $419,000; and the remaining 90 percent of the population averaged just under $40,000 in assets (Drinkard, 1986). Altogether, the top ten percent of households in the United States hold nearly 72 percent of the nation's net privately owned assets, while the bottom 90 percent of households (actually the bottom 65 percent of households, see below) hold only 28 percent of privately owned assets (Drinkard, 1986). The bottom 25 percent of the population (higher according to some estimates, see next section) holds virtually no assets; most of them are in debt.

Although the aforementioned distribution of wealth in the United States had remained relatively constant since 1910 (Kolko, 1962; Simon and Eitzen, 1990), at least until the 1980s, the last years during which economic inequality among Americans declined were 1977 and 1978 (Ehrenreich, 1986). Since then, in a sharp reversal of the equalizing trend that had been under way since shortly after World War II, the gap between rich and poor has grown further apart (Ehrenreich, 1986). Between 1979 and 1987, for example, the standard of living for the poorest fifth of the population fell by 9 percent, while the living standard of the top fifth rose by 19 percent (Passell, 1989).

Here is not the place to tackle the thorny questions of what disparities constitute gross inequity and how those disparities can be reduced. Blueprints for wealth redistribution abound. Before any change is planned, however, it is important first to recognize the crime.

The grossly inequitable distribution of wealth in the United States affects all Americans and, for that matter, all people of the world—for a relative few, positively, and for most others, negatively. Some of the attendant "criminal" problems associated with the grossly inequitable distribution of wealth are discussed in the following sections of this chapter. Before turning to the next section, however, consider one psychic benefit of wealth. According to a 1986 survey conducted for *Money* magazine, wealth makes people happy. There is a positive linear relationship between how happy people claim to be and their household incomes (Ward, 1986). This finding contrasts sharply with the frequent media portrayals of the unhappiness visited upon the rich and the powerful. While it is true that happiness and unhappiness are subjective states that all people experience to varying degrees, it also is likely that wealth enhances a person's subjective state of happiness and ameliorates his or her state of unhappiness.

Poverty

A direct product of the grossly inequitable distribution of wealth and another "political crime" is the existence of poverty, especially in a country with so much wealth. According to 1988 government statistics, 13.1 percent or approximately 32 million people in the United States were poor (Scanlan, 1989). In 1988, the official government poverty level for a family of four was $12,092 (Scanlan, 1989). Government statistics, however, are notorious for underestimating the poverty problem (see Beeghley, 1984). According to a recent report by The Families USA Foundation and the Center on Budget and Policy Priorities

("Poverty Said To Be Rising," 1990), 44.6 million people in the United States (and not the official 32 million) live in "real life" poverty. The report noted that more than 12 million working Americans are desperately poor even though they earned incomes that put them above the government's official poverty line.

Furthermore, contrary to popular stereotypes that portray the typical poor person as a lazy but physically able adult derelict, half the nation's poor in 1988 were children under 18 or elderly over 65 (Scanlan, 1989). Indeed, 20 percent of all children, more than 48 percent of black children, and 25 percent of all preschoolers lived in poverty in 1988 ("Children No. 1," 1989). Also contrary to popular stereotypes: (1) only 10 percent of poor children are urban, black, and living with a mother on welfare ("Study Debunks Myths," 1991); (2) Hispanics are the fastest growing group of poor children with 1 in 3 poor; (3) nearly two-thirds of poor families in 1989 included at least one worker; (4) 40 percent of poor children live in families with the father present; (5) nearly two-thirds of all poor families are small with only one or two children; (6) and nearly one-third of poor children live in urban areas although poverty in the suburbs, where 25 percent of poor children reside, is growing at a faster rate ("Bleak Findings," 1991). Poverty in the midst of plenty and the forces that maintain it are "criminal" in their own right, but poverty also causes a variety of other serious problems ("crimes").

Hunger

Hunger is still a widespread American reality and, according to the Physician Task Force on Hunger in America, the problem of hunger is getting worse, not better (Daly, 1985). Available evidence indicates that as many as 20 million citizens may be hungry at least some period of time each month (Daly, 1985). According to a 1985 *New York Times Magazine* report, more free-meal distribution centers are serving more people in the United States than at any time since the Depression (Lelyveld, 1985). During the 1980s, there was a steep annual rise in the tonnage of outdated, unsalable

or surplus food that was channeled by food companies to the needy
through private "food banks" serving thousands of "food pantries"
(Lelyveld, 1985).

Like the poor, far from matching the stereotype of social
deadbeats and down-and-outers, more than two-thirds of the
recipients of private food aid in a recent New York survey were
children (Lelyveld, 1985). An even more recent national survey
showed that 12.5 percent of children in the United States (about
5.5 million children) go hungry ("5.5 Million Children," 1991).
The study found that these children were "more likely to suffer
from infections, fatigue, an inability to concentrate and higher rates
of school absenteeism" ("5.5 Million Children," 1991).

What is particularly distressing about the problem of hunger in
America is that it is not caused by a lack of food. According to the
Physicians Task Force report, the cause of hunger in the United
States is the "clear and conscious policies of the federal
government" (Daly, 1985). For example, from 1982 to 1985,
$12.2 billion was cut from federal food stamp and child nutrition
programs (Daly, 1985). That the money was diverted primarily for
the purchase of unnecessary military hardware makes the problem
even more troubling. In any event, not feeding the hungry,
particularly when the means are readily available, is a "political
crime," even if it is not legally defined as such.

Institutionalized Racism

Racism takes many forms, but the type of racism described here
is economic. Although great strides have been made in race
relations in the United States,[6] between 1950 and 1988, nonwhite
family median income was approximately 56 percent of white
family median income.[7] Before 1950 the disparity was greater. For
a time, the economic situation of blacks in relation to whites was
improving. For example, between 1939 and 1951, the income of
male black wage and salary workers rose from 37 percent to 62
percent of the income of male white wage and salary workers (Piven
and Cloward, 1979). However, between what has turned out to be

the acme of black prosperity, in 1951, and the early 1960s, male black wage and salary income fell from 62 percent of white male income to approximately 53 percent (Piven and Cloward, 1979).[8] Piven and Cloward (1979) argue that the widening gap in economic disparity between 1951 and the early 1960s played a key role in the black civil rights movement. The movement, they maintain, was not only about political rights but economic rights as well. As noted, the black-white disparity in median family income currently has settled around 56 percent.

While it is true that laws now protect individuals from racial discrimination in employment (as well as discrimination in housing and other areas of public life), the law does not prohibit the type of institutionalized economic racism described above. Moreover, when individuals are discriminated against as, for example, when two employees with similar qualifications and tenure doing the same work are paid differentially solely because of their race, the individual discriminated against must be proactive in addressing the situation. That is, the victim of discrimination must hire an attorney and be prepared to engage in costly and protracted litigation, with no guarantee as to the outcome. Since in most cases the litigant will have lost his or her job, he or she also must be prepared to exhaust any savings or other resources during the legal battle. Many people, particularly those who have families to support, will be dissuaded by these difficulties from attempting to legally redress the racial discrimination that they have experienced. Also, with the increased difficulties associated with filing class action suits, resolving the problem of economic racial discrimination has become even more formidable.

Institutionalized economic racism exists at least in part because of the important role it plays in capital accumulation. Not only are profits (and capital) increased by not having to pay workers their fair share in wages, but stratifying workers by pay and race obscures their common interests (by placing them in competition with each other) and thus makes it less likely that they will unite to seek better wages and working conditions. Paying workers higher wages and improving working conditions allegedly reduces profit margins and the flow of capital to the wealthy.

Some of the consequences of institutionalized economic racism already have been described in previous sections of this chapter; others are discussed in subsequent sections. Here, however, consider only one of the consequences, albeit a very important one. The income disparities described above both directly and indirectly affect people's health and life chances. According to a recent report issued by the U.S. Public Health Service ("Health: A Dual Society," 1990), "by most indicators—life expectancy, infant mortality, heart disease, stroke and cancer—whites are getting healthier, but minorities are doing worse." Specifically, "black males, whose life expectancy is 65, will live an average of seven years less than white men. Black women, expected to live to be 74, will live five years less than white women" ("Health: A Dual Society," 1990). Additionally, "the infant mortality rate for black babies is 17.9 deaths per 1,000 live births, more than twice the white rate. The homicide rate for young black men was more than seven times the rate for white males in 1987" ("Health: A Dual Society," 1990). The gap between white and minority health care is widening.

The continued existence of institutionalized ecomomic racial discrimination and the consequences it produces is a "political crime." That it typically is not considered crime is criminal as well.

Institutionalized Sexism

Like racism, sexism takes many forms, but the type of sexism described here is institutionalized economic sexism. Between 1960 and 1987, women's earnings have been approximately 60 percent of men's earnings (this is for year-round full-time workers) (U.S. Bureau of Census, 1989:2).[9] In 1988, 1989, 1990, and the first three months of 1991, the percentage of women's earnings compared to men's has been, respectively, 66 percent, 68 percent, 71 percent, and 73 percent ("Women's Pay," 1990; "Women's Pay Gaining," 1991).

The disparity between men and women's earnings, moreover, varies by age. According to statistics for 1986 compiled by the U.S. Department of Labor, women under 20 earned approximately 92 percent of what men of the same age group earned; women 21–24 earned 86 percent of what was earned by their male counterparts; women 25–34 earned 78 percent; women 35–44 earned 64 percent; women 45–54 earned 61 percent; and women 55 or older earned 61 percent of what men in the same age group earned (Loeb, 1986). These figures, incidentally, do not include underpaid and undervalued housework which is another major source of women's economic inequality.

Factors contributing to the disparity in male and female incomes include: (1) "the historical concentration of women in traditional low-paid 'female' jobs such as clerical work and low-skilled service jobs,"[10] (2) "women, due to recent entry in the labor force in large numbers, [not having] time to work their way into the best-paid jobs," (3) "women [losing] seniority by taking time out to have children," (4) "until recently, women [not taking] the graduate studies and special training necessary for the highest-paid fields," and (5) "*lingering outright discrimination and unequal pay*" ("Gender Bias," 1990, emphasis added). The first and fifth factors listed above are directly related to the capital accumulation process and function in much the same way as does institutionalized discrimination by race (see discussion in previous section).

As noted with regard to institutionalized racism, individual women are protected by laws from discrimination in employment (and elsewhere), but like with institutionalized racism, victims must be proactive in their defense, which is unlikely given the formidable obstacles. Laws that prohibit sex discrimination do not protect women as a group from the institutionalized economic sexism described above. The continued existence of institutionalized economic sexism and the consequences it produces is "political crime."

Intentional and Criminally Negligent Killing

The "political crime" examined in this section includes (1) intentional or criminally negligent killing that is not prohibited by the criminal law, and (2) nonenforcement of criminal law prohibiting killing. As legally defined, relatively few people in the United States are killed illegally each year. According to the FBI's "uniform crime reports" for the past several years, approximately 20,000 murders and nonnegligent manslaughters are committed annually in the United States. With a well-armed population of approximately 250 million people, many more murders of this type reasonably might be expected. Nevertheless, many thousands more people than the FBI's 20,000 are killed intentionally or through criminal negligence each year, even though the deaths generally are not responded to as crime or counted by the FBI. A major reason for treating these "unofficial" killings with impunity is that to do otherwise would impede the accumulation of capital by the already wealthy.

For example, each year in the United States medical doctors kill approximately 10,000 people by unnecessary surgery, 20,000 people by making errors in prescribing drugs, and another 20,000 people by spreading diseases in hospitals. While most of the deaths are truly accidents, making a legal response inappropriate, a small but significant number probably are intentional or criminally negligent (see Green, 1990:188).

Regarding unnecessary surgery, a Cornell University study found that in approximately 20 percent of the cases in which a second opinion was sought, the second doctor recommended against the proposed surgery (Coleman, 1989:113). Based on findings of the study, "a House subcommittee investigating the medical profession calculated that there were 2.4 million unnecessary surgical procedures a year, which cost the public $4 billion and resulted in the loss of 11,900 lives" (Coleman, 1989:113; also see Green, 1990:181–2; Liazos, 1982:282; Reiman, 1979:73). Indirect evidence of the effects of surgery on the death rate in a community is provided by a natural experiment that occurred when doctors in Los Angeles went on strike in 1976. During the strike, the death rate in Los Angeles declined weekly; however, in the first week following the end of the strike, when surgeons were back at work, the death rate in Los Angeles increased from 14 to 26 deaths per 100,000 people (cited in Liazos, 1982:282). As for errors in prescribing drugs, in a study conducted by Dr. Sidney Wolfe of the Health Research Group, antibiotics prescribed in American hospitals were found to be unnecessary in 22 percent of all cases; at that rate, approximately 10,000 potentially fatal adverse reactions could be produced" (Coleman, 1989:113; also see Reiman, 1979:74).

Perhaps the most telling evidence that doctors in the United States often allow their financial interests to supersede the interests of their patients is from comparisons of patients insured by Blue Cross, which compensates doctors on a fee-for-service basis, and patients who belong to health maintenance organizations (HMOs) that pay doctors a flat salary regardless of how many procedures they perform. A study sponsored by the former Department of Health, Education and Welfare found that people covered by Blue Cross had twice as much surgery as those people who belonged to HMOs (Coleman, 1989:113–14). A similar study of Medicaid patients found that patients who went to doctors in private practice were operated on twice as often as patients who had prepaid health plans (Coleman, 1989:114). In short, it appears that the more money that can be made from a medical procedure, the more often it is performed (Coleman, 1985:114).

Many doctors readily admit that they are not sure "what really helps their patients or what is useless or even harmful" ("Doctors Admit," 1990). Dr. David Eddy, Director of the Duke University Center for Health Policy Research, states, "We don't know what we're doing in medicine" ("Doctors Admit," 1990). According to the Institute of Medicine, "perhaps one-quarter to one-third of medical services may be of little or no benefit to patients" ("Doctors Admit," 1990). Dr. Dennis O'Leary, President of the Joint Commission of Health Care Organizations, maintains that "uncertainty about the most effective diagnostic and therapeutic approaches is pervasive" ("Doctors Admit," 1990). The Congressional Office of Technology Assessment reports that "the link between the process of care and patient outcomes has been established for relatively few procedures" ("Doctors Admit," 1990). And Dr. Donald Berwick, Vice President of the Harvard Community Health Plan, adds that "the embarrassment of our ignorance about the efficacy of health care practices is both hard for us to admit and hard for our clients to accept" ("Doctors Admit," 1990). Medical malfeasance is not without its costs, both human and financial: "At least 20% of the nation's health bill—$125 billion last year . . . is wasted on unnecessary, inappropriate or downright dangerous treatments" ("Doctors Admit," 1990).

Rarely are doctors severely sanctioned by their profession or legally punished for their crimes. According to data from 1971 to 1974 compiled by the Federation of State Medical Boards, "of the approximately three hundred and twenty thousand physicians in the United States, sixteen thousand are believed to be incompetent or unfit, but on the average only seventy-two licenses are revoked each year" (Coleman, 1989:155; also see Mesce, 1985). The number of doctors charged legally with murder is unknown. Coleman (1989:155) reports that "the single most common cause for revocation of a license for disciplinary reasons is not fraud or malpractice [or murder], but narcotic law violations, which usually involve either an addicted physician or one who supplies drugs to addicts." According to a report delivered at the 1986 meeting of the New York State Society of Anesthesiologists, as many as 75 percent of the 2,000 or more anesthesiology-related deaths in the United States each year are the result of malpractice or mistakes by doctors (Raeburn, 1986). In sum, although doctors infrequently kill their patients intentionally or by criminal negligence, when they do kill them, they do so with relative impunity.

Many more Americans are killed annually by industrial disease or accident than by doctors. Estimates indicate that each year some 100,000 lives are lost to industrial disease and 14,000 to industrial accidents (Coleman, 1989:7; Reiman, 1979:65 and 67). Consider, for example, the industrial disease and deaths caused by asbestos.

The dangers of asbestos were discovered as early as the Roman Empire, and modern medical science confirmed the danger decades ago (Coleman, 1989:1 and 35). Yet, major asbestos producers have fraudalently denied the dangers, have kept secret studies that expose the danger, and have funded studies to "prove" that asbestos is safe (Coleman, 1989:1 and 35; Liazos, 1982:296). Additionally, company doctors often failed to inform workers that their lung problems probably were caused by exposure to asbestos (Coleman, 1989:1 and 35). It is estimated that "of the half-million living workers who have been exposed to significant doses of asbestos . . . one hundred thousand will die from lung cancer, thirty-five thousand from mesothelioma (a rare cancer of the linings of the lungs and stomach), and thirty-five thousand from asbestosis" (Coleman, 1989:36). These estimates do not include the probable asbestos-related deaths of tens of thousands of people who have not worked directly with asbestos but who have been exposed to it (Coleman, 1989:1). Put differently, the former Department of Health, Education and Welfare estimated that 67,000 Americans will die each year for the next thirty [now 20] years from asbestos (cited in Liazos, 1982:296).

As for industrial accidents, according to a recent report by the National Safe Workplace Institute, "U.S. workers are nine times more likely to be killed on the job than a Briton, and more likely to be seriously injured than a two-pack-a-day cigarette smoker is to contract cancer" ("Worker Safety," 1989:9A). Consider two examples from the mining industry:

> In 1981 . . . an explosion in a Colorado mine killed fifteen workers. Since 1978, that mine had received 1,133 citations and fifty-seven orders for immediate correction of known dangers from federal inspectors, but the owners did nothing. . . . Over a number of years, the Utah Power and Light Company had been cited for thirty-four safety violations in one of its coal mines. Disaster finally struck in 1984, when an underground fire killed 27 miners. Nine of the violations previously cited and ignored were linked directly to the ignition and spread of the fire (Simon and Eitzen, 1990:136).

No one knows how many of these deaths legally are crimes, but "data from Wisconsin indicate that 45 percent of the industrial accidents in that state result from violations of state safety codes" (Coleman, 1989:7). In addition, "Inspectors from the Occupational Safety and Health Administration [OSHA] have found violations of health and safety codes in 75 percent of the firms investigated" (Coleman, 1989:8). The National Safe Workplace Institute, in a 1988 report, estimated that OSHA's failure to enforce laws protecting American workers has "resulted in more than nine thousand avoidable workplace fatalities since 1981" (Green, 1990:132; Simon and Eitzen, 1990:137).

That people die from industrial disease or accident, when those deaths are preventable, is criminal. Culpable are the CEOs of industry who, after unsafe working conditions have been exposed, opt for profits over safety of employees.[11] Also culpable are the bureaucrats of government who are employed to protect American workers from unsafe working conditions but fail to do so. When the deaths are preventable, the "crime" is a political one. (See the Aulette and Michalowski chapter in this edition for further explanation of this political crime.)

Tens of thousands of lives are lost annually to environmentally caused cancer, and approximately 30,000 to lethal industrial products (Coleman, 1989:8; Simon and Eitzen, 1990:117). According to the National Cancer Institute, "as much as 90 percent of all cancer may be environmentally induced, and cancer is now second only to heart disease as the leading cause of death in North America" (Coleman, 1989:8; also see Reiman, 1979:74 and 76). One of the major causes of environmentally induced cancer, as well as other health problems, is tobacco smoking which is estimated to kill 346,000 Americans annually (Simon and Eitzen, 1990:123). Ironically, even though over 30,000 studies have documented the health hazards associated with tobacco smoking, and "no medical group or scientific group in the world has disputed the conclusion that smoking is very injurious to health," the tobacco industry continues to deny the evidence against smoking and to aggressively market its products (Simon and Eitzen, 1990:123; also see Reiman,

1979:79–81). As noted, when these deaths are preventable but not prevented, the failure to prevent death is "political crime."

Regarding lethal industrial products, according to the National Commission on Product Safety:

> Manufacturers have it in their power to design, build, and market products in ways that will reduce if not eliminate most unreasonable and unnecessary hazards. . . . [However] competitive forces may require management to subordinate safety factors to cost considerations, styling, and other marketing imperatives (quoted in Simon and Eitzen, 1990:118).

Probably the most notorious example of corporate disregard for human life is Ford Motor Company's duplicity in the production and distribution of 1971 through 1976 Pintos and Bobcats (Coleman, 1989:41; Green, 1990:129; Simon and Eitzen, 1990:118–19). According to a Ford internal memorandum obtained through the Freedom of Information Act, Ford executives knew in advance that the aforementioned automobiles were unsafe because of problems with the car's gas tank (Coleman, 1989:41; Green, 1990:129; Simon and Eitzen, 1990:119–20). According to the National Highway Traffic Safety Administration, the problem was that "low to moderate speed rear-end collisions . . . produce[d] massive full tank leaks due to puncture or tearing of the fuel tank and separation of the filler pipe from the tank" (Coleman, 1989:41). The Ford executives not only failed to make changes for economic reasons, but repeatedly denied that there was anything wrong with the cars. Even when the problem was made public, Ford continued to deny that there was a problem. In the end, Ford was held legally responsible and was required to pay well over $100 million in damages. However, the money did little good for the more than 50 people who died as a direct result of automobile accidents involving Pinto or Bobcat gas tank ruptures (Coleman, 1989:41). That no Ford Motor Company executive was convicted of murder is a "political crime."[12]

Another more recent example of corporate malfeasance involved General Motors (GM) and their "X-cars" (Buick Skylark,

Chevrolet Citation, Oldsmobile Omega, and Pontiac Phoenix). These cars had problems from their beginning in 1980 and were subject to numerous recalls. The most serious problem was a brake defect that presumably contributed to the deaths of 13 people (Coleman, 1989:40).[13] According to documents obtained by the House Commerce Committee, the National Highway Traffic Safety Commission knew about the problem long before it was made public (Coleman, 1989:41; Simon and Eitzen, 1990:120). The Commission allegedly concealed the results of its study because of pressure from GM—the United States' largest private employer (Coleman, 1989:41). As was the case with the Ford Motor Company, no GM executives or, for that matter, no bureaucrats of the National Highway Traffic Safety Commission, were convicted of murder—a "political crime."

Each of the examples described in this section illustrates a willingness to sacrifice innocent human life for the goal of capital accumulation and increased wealth. Such disregard for the lives of American citizens, or for that matter any person, is a "political crime" even though it may not be considered so legally.

Conclusion

The appropriate definition of crime remains one of the most critical unresolved issues in criminology. As long as a narrow legal definition is used, the political economy of crime will be underexamined by criminologists and unaddressed by the agencies of criminal justice. Largely ignored will be social relationships that arguably should be criminal although they are not.

To say that some social relationships should be criminal and others not is clearly a normative statement, a question of values. Indeed, "crime" is political (and economic) precisely because only the values of some people (sometimes a sizeable majority but not always) are enacted into law. Regarding the political, as Chambliss and others have argued, "What gets defined as criminal or delinquent behavior is the result of a political process within which rules are formed which prohibit or require people to behave in certain ways" (1976:101).

A reasonable question is who should be held legally responsible for the "political crimes" described in this chapter? As noted in the previous section, when the crimes involve the conscious decision to sacrifice innocent human life in order to produce increased profits (and capital), the responsibility lies with the professionals involved (as in the case of doctors), CEOs of offending companies, and the government bureaucrats who are employed to protect American workers and consumers but fail to do so.

Also culpable are politicians or their agents who are responsible for the creation of criminal laws and, to a large extent, the legitimation of particular social relationships. While it is true that politicians generally support the dominant goals and values in society and are responsive to the monied interests (i.e., capital accumulators) that support their political campaigns, such support and response is not required, especially when it is destructive of the well-being of the vast majority of the population. Politicians should be held responsible for their acts of commission or omission and, if they were, it is likely that the socially destructive relationships described in this chapter would be defined legally as criminal.

How responsibility is to be determined or apportioned and what social response is appropriate are other important questions that space limitations preclude addressing here.

Few, if any, of the ideas presented in this chapter are novel. What is new are the recent examples that show what Sutherland found in the 1930s, and what the Schwendingers, Platt, Quinney, and others observed in the 1960s,1970s, and 1980s, still exist in the 1990s. The message continues to fall on deaf ears. Until there is a pervasive awareness of its political-economic nature, little progress will be made in the reduction of all types of crime in the 1990s and beyond.

NOTES

1. For a critique of the "value-free" position in criminology, see Black, 1979; Bohm, 1981.

2. Legal relationships, e.g., offender and victim, are but one type of social relationship. Thus, crime is both a social and legal relationship.

3. If "crime" is defined as violation of criminal law, then all crime is "political crime" because criminal law is produced by political process: "political power determines the precision of the definition and the measurement of the phenomena" (Schwendinger and Schwendinger, 1975:122).

4. This is not to argue that all dangerous, harmful, and intentional acts of commission or omission ought to be crimes. For example, treatment of cancer with chemotherapy is a dangerous, harmful, and intentional act, but given its potential benefits to the victim it can hardly be considered a crime. Thus, the effects of actions or inactions on a victim is a way of distinguishing crimes from merely dangerous and harmful intentional acts of commission or omission.

5. Black (1979:20) writes that "'crime' is not merely a matter of fact; it is also an evaluation," while Galliher and McCartney (1977:10) provide a particularly powerful analogy to make the same point:

> If sociology makes no moral judgement independent of criminal statutes, it becomes sterile and inhumane—the work of moral eunuchs or legal technicians. . . . If moral judgements above and beyond criminal law were not made, the laws of Nazi Germany would be indistinguishable from the laws of many other nations. Yet the Nuremberg trials after World War II advanced the position that numerous officials of the Nazi government, although admittedly acting in accordance with German laws, were behaving in such a grossly immoral fashion as to be criminally responsible. . . . In the Nuremberg trials, representatives of the Allied governments—France, England, the Soviet Union, and the United States—explicitly and publicly supported the idea of a moral order and moral judgments independent of written law. . . . The claim was that . . . the defendants had committed atrocities against humanity. . . . The example of Nuremberg shows that moral judgements by students of crime can be made independently of particular cultural definitions of crime.

6. Some would argue that race relations in the United States of late have been regressing.

7. Data for 1950 through 1964 are from U.S. Bureau of Census, 1966:340; data for 1965 and 1970 through 1981 are from U.S. Bureau of

Census, 1982:432; and data for 1982 through 1988 are from U.S. Bureau of Census, 1990:450. Data were not available for 1966, 1967, 1968, 1969, and 1983. Data are in current dollars. Between 1950 and 1988, the proportion of black family median income to white family median income ranged from 51% in 1958 to 62% in 1975.

    8. Note the change in the level of analysis from family median income to income of wage and salary workers. Based on the former, the acme of black prosperity was in 1975 (62%), not in 1951 (53%). In 1988 the proportion of black family median income to white family median income was 57%.

    9. The range is from 57% in 1973 and 1974 to 65% in 1985 and 1987.

    10. However, even female doctors made only 62.8% of what their male counterparts earned in 1988 ("Female Doctors," 1991).

    11. Green (1990:96–7) argues that "organizations [also] are liable for crimes committed by their employees through the modern legal theories of 'identification' . . . 'imputation' . . . [and] 'collective knowledge'."

    12. Although it was ultimately acquitted, the Ford Motor Company was charged in Indiana with criminally negligent homicide involving the Pinto (Coleman, 1989:146; Green, 1990:4 and 129). However, in 1985, three Film Recovery Systems Corporation executives were the first corporate executives in the United States to be convicted of murder "for having 'knowingly created a strong probability of death' by allowing employees to work around highly toxic chemicals used to recover silver from film" (Green, 1990:4). Corporations also have been charged with involuntary manslaughter in worker-related deaths (Coleman, 1989:146; Green, 1990:4).

    13. According to Simon and Eitzen (1990:120), there were 15 deaths.

REFERENCES

Barak, Gregg. 1991. *Gimme Shelter: A Social History of Homelessness in Contemporary America.* New York: Praeger.

———— (ed.). 1991. *Crimes by the Capitalist State: An Introduction to State Criminality.* New York: State University of New York Press.

Barak, Gregg and Robert M. Bohm. 1989. "The Crimes of the Homeless or the Crime of Homelessness? On the Dialectics of Criminalization,

Decriminalization, and Victimization." *Contemporary Crises* 13:275–88.

Beeghley, Leonard. 1984. "Illusion and Reality in the Measurement of Poverty." *Social Problems* 31:322–333.

Black, Donald. 1979. "Common Sense in the Sociology of Law." *American Sociological Review* 44:18–27.

"Bleak Findings." 1991. "Bleak Findings: 1 in 3 Hispanic Kids Are Poor." *The Charlotte* [NC] *Observer* (June 3).

Bohm, Robert M. 1981. "Reflexivity and Critical Criminology." In Jensen, Gary F. (ed.) *Sociology of Delinquency: Current Issues.* Beverly Hills: Sage, pp. 29–47.

Brouwer, Steve. 1988. *Sharing the Pie: A Disturbing Picture of the U.S. Economy in the 1980s.* Carlisle, PA: Big Picture Books.

Chambliss, William J. 1976. "The State and Criminal Law." Pp. 66–106 in W. J. Chambliss and M. Mankoff (eds.) *Whose Law What Order?* New York: Wiley.

"Children No. 1." 1989. "Children No. 1 On Poverty List, Report Shows. *The Charlotte* [NC] *Observer* (October 2).

Coleman, James W. 1989. *The Criminal Elite: The Sociology of White Collar Crime,* Second Edition. New York: St. Martin's.

Currie, Elliott. 1985. *Confronting Crime: An American Challenge.* New York: Pantheon.

Daly, Christopher B. 1985. "Physician Task Force Says Hunger 'An Epidemic'." *The Anniston* [AL] *Star* (February 27).

"Doctors Admit." 1990. "Doctors Admit They're Flying Blind." *The Charlotte* [NC] *Observer* (February 4).

Drinkard, Jim. 1986. "Statistics Show Rich Even Richer." *The Anniston* [AL] *Star* (July 25).

Ehrenreich, Barbara. 1986. "Will Economics Divide America into Two Parts?" *The Anniston* [AL] *Star* (September 14).

Elias, Robert. 1986. *The Politics of Victimization: Victims, Victimology and Human Rights.* New York: Oxford University Press.

"Female Doctors." 1991. "Female Doctors Have Low Status, Pay, Report Says." *The Charlotte* [NC] *Observer* (September 10).

Galliher, John F. and James L. McCartney. 1977. *Criminology: Power, Crime, and Criminal Law.* Homewood, IL: Dorsey.

"Gender Bias." 1990. "Gender Bias Still Hurts Women's Careers, Pay." *The Charlotte* [NC] *Observer* (April 23).

Gordon, David M. 1971. "Class and the Economics of Crime." *The Review of Radical Political Economics* 3:51–72.

Green, Gary S. 1990. *Occupational Crime.* Chicago: Nelson-Hall.

"Health: A Dual Society." 1990. "Health: A Dual Society: Whites Do Better, Minorities Suffer." *The Charlotte* [NC] *Observer* (March 23).

Kolko, Gabriel. 1962. *Wealth and Power in America: An Analysis of Social Class and Income Distribution.* New York: Praeger.

Lelyveld, Joseph. 1985. "Hunger in America." *The Anniston* [AL] *Star* (September 11).

Liazos, Alexander. 1982. *People First: An Introduction to Social Problems.* Boston: Allyn and Bacon.

Loeb, Karen. 1986. "Younger Women Close Wage Gap." *USA TODAY* (September 11).

Mesce, Deborah. 1985. "Group Wants Incompetent Doctors Disciplined." *The Anniston* [AL] *Star* (August 29).

Michalowski, Raymond J. 1985. *Order, Law, and Crime: An Introduction to Criminology.* New York: Random House.

Passell, Peter. 1989. "Social Forces Dig a Deeper Hole for Poor." *The Anniston* [AL] *Star* (July 21).

Piven, Frances Fox and Richard A. Cloward. 1979. *Poor People's Movements: Why They Succeed, How They Fail.* New York: Vintage.

Platt, Tony. 1975. "Prospects for a Radical Criminology in the USA." Pp. 95–112 in I. Taylor, P. Walton, and J. Young (eds.) *Critical Criminology.* London: Routledge & Kegan Paul.

"Poverty Said To Be Rising." 1990. "Poverty Said To Be Rising: U.S. Statistics Hide Problem, Study Says." *The Charlotte* [NC] *Observer* (July 19).

Quinney, Richard. 1964. "Crime in Political Perspective." *American Behavioral Scientist* 8:19–22.

———. 1977 *Class, State, and Crime: On the Theory and Practice of Criminal Justice.* New York: David McKay.

Raeburn, Paul. 1986. "Study Finds Many Deaths Unnecessary." *The Anniston* [AL] *Star* (December 14).

Reiman, Jeffrey H. 1979. *The Rich Get Richer and the Poor Get Prison: Ideology, Class, and Criminal Justice.* New York: Wiley.

Scanlan, Christopher. 1989. "Poverty Rate Nearly Unchanged." *The Charlotte* [NC] *Observer* (October 19).

Schwendinger, Herman and Julia Schwendinger. 1975. "Defenders of Order or Guardians of Human Rights?" Pp. 113–146 in I. Taylor, P. Walton, and J. Young (eds.) *Critical Criminology.* London: Routledge & Kegan Paul.

Seneker, Harold. 1990. "The Richest People in America." *Forbes* (October 22):1–397.

Simon, David R. and D. Stanley Eitzen. 1990. *Elite Deviance,* Third Edition. Boston: Allyn and Bacon.

"Study Debunks Myths." 1991. "Study Debunks Myths about Child Poverty." *The Charlotte* [NC] *Observer* (June 3).

Sutherland, Edwin H. 1940. "White-Collar Criminality." *American Sociological Review* 5:1–12.

———. 1945. "Is 'White-Collar Crime' Crime?" *American Sociological Review* 10:132–39.

Tappan, Paul. 1947. "Who is the Criminal." *American Sociological Review* 12:96–102.

U.S. Bureau of Census. 1966. *Statistical Abstract of the United States: 1966.* (87th edition.) Washington, D.C.

———. 1982. *Statistical Abstract of the United States: 1982.* (103d edition.) Washington, D.C.

———. 1989. *Money Income of Households, Families, and Persons in the United States: 1987.* Current Population Reports, Series P-60, No. 162. U.S. Government Printing Office, Washington, D.C.

———. 1990. *Statistical Abstract of the United States: 1990.* (110th edition.) Washington, D.C.

Ward, Sam. 1986. "Taking Our Financial Pulse." *USA TODAY* (October 23).

"Women's Pay." 1990. "Women's Pay Up to 68% of Men's: Household Income in '89 Rose, But 31.5 Million People in Poverty." *The Charlotte* [NC] *Observer* (September 27).

"Women's Pay Gaining." 1991. "Women's Pay Gaining." *The Charlotte* [NC] *Observer* (May 14).

"Worker Safety." 1989. "Worker Safety Slips in U.S." *The Charlotte* [NC] *Observer* (September 4).

DREW HUMPHRIES

Crack Mothers, Drug Wars, and the Politics of Resentment

Crack/cocaine is widely understood to be dangerously addictive, to have reached epidemic proportions, and to require massive institutional intervention. While this paper is not about the crack epidemic *per se*, it focuses on a category of crack user, women of child bearing age, and looks closely at the way "crack mothers" have been represented.[1] Cultural images defining crack mothers merit attention for several reasons. First, the public representation is based largely on distortion and thus the resulting myths require remedial contrast with reality-based images. Second, myths about crack mothers have helped justify the War on Drugs and distracted public attention from the War's failures. And third, crack mothers combine the very targets that reflect what conservatives, the New Right and the Evangelical Right, believe is wrong with America.

Crack Mothers: Myth and Reality

"Crack mother" refers to a standard set of claims about one part of the crack problem, maternal drug use and its adverse effects on pregnancy and child rearing. Some claims fall into the category of social myths, representations that distort reality and have been used for political ends. Underneath the myths, however, lies a painful and difficult reality. Women of childbearing age are using crack—this no one would deny; and crack, along with poverty and inadequate prenatal care are responsible for the addition of avoidable risk to pregnancy, newborns, and older children.

31

Magnitude of the Problem

Numerically speaking, the annual figure—375,000 drug-affected U.S. births, has been used as the best estimate of the problem (Chasnoff, 1988, 1987). Considerable confusion, however, surrounds the meaning of this estimate. As stated it refers to drug-affected births, which includes crack as well as a variety of other illicit drugs, although it is frequently, but erroneously cited as estimating the number of crack-affected births. A second problem concerns the sample on which the estimate was based and the indicators of crack use. The survey sampled urban hospitals in which crack use would have been high. It mixed self-reported illicit drug use with the results from positive urine screens from either the mother or the newborn. And it failed to differentiate between crack and cocaine. Nonetheless, survey results have been widely used as the estimate of crack use among pregnant and delivering women.

Even if this figure were correct, which it is not, it would still have been difficult to assess whether the 375,000 drug affected births represented an extremely large problem or whether the births constituted a relatively minor one. One appropriate method for making the assessment is to determine how important crack/cocaine is to the drug problem, and then how important maternal crack use is to the crack/cocaine problem. Official data have consistently shown that the drugs constituting the drug problem include, in rank order of use, alcohol, tobacco, marijuana, and then at much lower use levels, cocaine and crack (NIDA, 1989a:30–32, 67–72; 1991a:19). In 1990, only between one and two percent of the population, depending on age, had used cocaine in the last month (NIDA, 1991a:28–31), and even fewer, less than one percent, had used crack in the last month (NIDA, 1991a:51). Monthly prevalence figures suggest that cocaine and crack were not major contributors to America's drug problem. This coupled with the twenty-year decline in drug use raises serious questions about the epidemic proportions of crack/cocaine. And yet from 1985 to 1989 official sources showed an increase in weekly and daily use for cocaine (as reported in Akers, 1991:51; see also Somerville, 1989:4;

Cimons, 1989:1). This upsurge in weekly and daily use was cause for concern, especially when cocaine-related deaths and cocaine-related admissions to emergency rooms were also high (as reported in Akers, 1991:51).

Shifting from cocaine use to the monthly prevalence of crack, official data, as indicated above, provide the information required to estimate the number of women of childbearing age who might have used crack. In 1990, 0.2 percent of the population had used crack in the previous month, but assuming that the Household Survey would underreport crack use, we use a working percentage figure of 0.5 percent. The latter percent suggests that there were approximately one million crack users in the United States in 1990. If just under half of the one million crack users were women—many of whom would have been of childbearing age, then there could have been no more than 500,000 potential crack mothers in the population. Actually the 1988 National Household Survey on Drug Abuse found that the number of women who used crack in the year was just 474,000, or less than 1 percent of the childbearing population (NIDA, 1989b: 59; see also Gieringer, 1990). Of these potential crack mothers, only a portion would be pregnant in any one year. The source document for President Bush's War on Drugs placed the number of crack babies delivered each year at 100,000 (See Kusserow, 1990).

Crack-Exposed Babies

While it may be difficult to make the case that crack mothers as a category of drug user contribute greatly to the drug problem, it is the case that the high-risk pregnancies associated with crack use have inflicted avoidable harm on newborns. The statement is however by no means an affirmation of stereotypes that define "crack babies." It is easy to conjure up the stereotype. Crack babies are underweight, often premature infants, who, according to frequent television news reports, suffer horribly from crack withdrawal and face a half-life of neurological impairment. Visualized as severely impaired, crack babies serve as a standing indictment; their crack-related risks and actual deficits become the measure of their mothers' willfully inflicted injury or wanton disregard for their well-being.

Early in the crack panic, the list of crack-related problems was long (Chasnoff, 1988, 1987). It included among other things miscarriage, premature labor, intrauterine growth retardation, all of which contribute to low-birth weight babies which are at risk for life-threatening complications (Chasnoff, 1986). Following delivery, newborns exposed to crack are at risk for withdrawal, stroke, respiratory ailments, urinary tract difficulty, and, some suggested, Sudden Infant Death Syndrome (Chasnoff, 1988). The crack babies were described as irritable, difficult to care for, and requiring expensive medical and dedicated emotional attention. Long term consequences of cocaine-exposure included emotional disorders, learning disabilities, and sensory-motor difficulties.

Critics raised questions about crack's causal role in pre-and post-natal complications. For one thing, it is impossible to trace neonatal outcomes to crack or any other single drug because the crack mothers often drank, smoked cigarettes, and used other illicit drugs (Chasnoff, 1987, 1986). In addition, poverty, poor nutrition, and inadequate prenatal care are all associated with poor neonatal outcomes. And on this last point, screening procedures for identifying maternal drug use in hospitals have been shown to single out the population in which infants with low birth weight present a problem: poor, minority women (Chasnoff, 1991).

Questions about crack-related risks come also from allegations of bias in the presentation of research findings. Koren et al. (1989) reported that of 58 abstracts on fetal outcomes following exposure to cocaine that were submitted for presentation at the Society of Pediatric Research conference, nine reported no effects and 28 reported adverse effects. Only one of the abstracts reporting no effects was accepted for presentation, despite the fact that these studies verified cocaine use and used control cases more often than the other studies. Reviewers, however, accepted over half of the abstracts reporting adverse effects. Researchers concluded that there may be a "distorted estimation of the teratogenic risk of cocaine" (Koren et al., 1989:1440).

In subsequent research, Sudden Infant Death Syndrome along with urinary tract difficulties were removed from the list of cocaine related conditions. Those that remained—intrauterine growth retardation, miscarriage, premature labor, and preterm delivery—all contribute to low birth weight and may indeed pose life-threatening risks. But despite these risks, most crack babies were found to escape the ill-effects of the drug. Gierginger reports, for instance, that the U.S. Department of Health and Human Services estimates that over 2 out of 3 crack-exposed babies suffered no adverse consequences at birth (1990, see also Kusserow, 1990). Prenatal care has been shown to improve the outcome for drug-exposed newborns (Chasnoff, Griffith, Murray, 1992). And finally, predictions about permanent neurological impairment have been shown to be erroneous. Dr. Chasnoff's longitudinal study of crack babies suggests and continues to suggest that they develop within normal ranges. Prenatal care combined with post-natal interventions have been shown effective for maintaining normal development in children who have been exposed to drugs (for a discussion see Humphries et al., 1992a, 1992b).

Crack-Using Mothers

The media portrait of crack mothers as minority, poor women is consistent with the demographic profile supplied by official sources. The 1988 NIDA survey found that crack use was more prevalent in Black and Hispanic populations. Among women, prevalence was highest among 18 to 25 years old, and in this age group, Hispanic women have higher use rates than Black or white women. Field studies reported a disproportionate concentration of crack users in inner-city poor, Black, and Puerto Rican neighborhoods in New York City, San Francisco, and Miami (see discussion Akers, 1992; Inciardi, 1992). As widely reported, crack emerged in inner-city neighborhoods which had already suffered poverty, disorganization, and job loss.

During the crack scare, *The New York Times* published an article suggesting that the "addictive" power of crack was great enough to destroy women's "maternal instinct" (Hinds, 1990:A8). "The maternal instinct gets blocked out," a treatment center director was quoted as saying, "because the only thing that matters is the addiction" (Hinds, 1990:A8). The missing "maternal instinct" was indicated by crack mothers' willingness to abandon their babies, leaving them to be cared for as foster children or boarder babies. With no "maternal instinct" to speak of, experts warned that crack use among the mothers who kept their babies placed the babies at risk for further abuse. The power of crack to destroy maternal instinct took on its core meaning in the context of debates over the "duty of care." The "duty of care" argument suggested that at some point in the pregnancy, women had an obligation to protect the fetus, and if and when they failed in fulfilling the duty, women were legally liable for the consequences. The duty of care was but one legal argument for holding crack-using pregnant women responsible for poor neonatal outcomes, but this and other arguments rested on unusual ideas that motherhood was instinctual.

The idea that women are genetically endowed with the motives, skills, and techniques for modern motherhood is as ludicrous as the idea that drugs can destroy such instincts. Mothering is a social construct, it involves expectations about what caretakers are required to do for children and it includes internalized identities based on one's ability to fulfill those expectations. Available research indicates that drug use does not necessarily or irrevocably destroy one's ability to parent. In *Women on Heroin*, Rosenbaum made plain that mothering is a positive force in the lives of heroin users (1981). Heroin users know and work hard to meet social expectations for good mothering. Mothering is often the only legitimate status left open to heroin using women. When heroin use threatens to interfere with their capacity to mother, these women may seek treatment or place their children with more responsible relatives.

Interim results from research on crack and mothering are consistent with findings for heroin (Murphy and Rosenbaum, 1990; Murphy, Kearney, and Rosenbaum, 1992). Crack-using mothers face the enormous obstacles of single-parenthood and poverty in raising children, but they nonetheless strive to fulfill expectations about good mothering. Strategically, crack mothers meet expectations by segregating their drug use from mothering. They take care to keep drug money separate from the monies necessary for maintaining the household and children. They manage time and child care so that the children are not exposed to their mothers' drug use. And if these women lose control over their crack use, they may voluntarily place their children with responsible relatives.

The discussion thus far suggests that the crack use is a relatively minor part of America's drug problem, that crack use among poor, minority women of childbearing age produced at the height of the so-called epidemic about 100,000 crack babies, that most of these babies, 2 out of 3, escaped the drug's adverse effects, and that the development of adversely affected children fell within the normal range in follow-up studies. While stereotypes of bad mothering abound, research paints a picture of women struggling against poverty, inadequate health care, and cutbacks in social services to meet required conditions of good mothering. When they fail, it is difficult to attribute that failure to crack use, when so many of the conditions in inner-city neighborhoods are beyond the control of any of its inhabitants.

The War on Drugs

Myths about crack mothers are not simply the residue of premature or faulty research efforts; they have all been enlisted with dramatic effect in the War on Drugs. That innumerable crack mothers are responsible for the widespread suffering of innocent newborns has been used to help forge the moral consensus in support of the War on Drugs; and the punitive reaction that these myths promoted helped detract from failures of the War. The 1986

Anti-Drug Abuse Act, enacted under President Reagan, was intended to reduce the demand for a range of illicit drugs and to halt their illegal importation. Monies appropriated under this Act financed prison construction at home and interdiction efforts abroad. It created a federal task force headed by the vice-president, provided for employee-drug testing programs, and supported the "Just Say No" campaign to address domestic demand for drugs.

Three years later, President Bush announced a second initiative in the War on Drugs, the 1989 Omnibus Anti-Drug Abuse Act. In his speech announcing that 8 billion dollars would be allocated for drug prevention, treatment, education, and law enforcement, he singled out crack/cocaine as the most dangerous drug, and identified maternal crack use as a major problem. Drug czar William J. Bennett assumed command of the War and oversaw the assistance to state law enforcement, implementation of stiffer penalties for drug users, renewed interdiction efforts, including the engagement of U.S. troops, and investigation of money laundering.

In the hands of President Bush's speech writers, crack became the symbol for what was wrong with America. It was the most addicting drug in America. It was destroying youth, both born and unborn, and it had reached the moral and political center of the nation. President Bush, holding up the vial of crack for all America to see, explained that it had been purchased just across the street from the White House. While the purchase had been engineered by Secret Service agents, the symbolism attached to crack, the enemy that threatened the family and had come within striking distance of the capital, resonated with war imagery associated with dispatching U.S. military troops to destroy the cocaine laboratories in producer countries.

The War on Cocaine proved, according to most commentators, to be a losing proposition (see Akers, 1991). The supply lines used by crack/cocaine smugglers have not been interrupted by interdiction efforts. Supplies available to domestic users have remained the same or actually increased during the War. Further, most criminologists cite the counterproductive effects of the new tougher drug laws (Walker, 1985; see also Isikoff and Thompson,

1990: C1). While stiff sentences have failed to deter crack use or trafficking, they are nonetheless responsible for court backlogs that have pushed civil matters off court calendars and for the explosion in the prison population (Pitt, 1989; Egan, 1990; *New York Times*, 1989). Moreover, the fact that prohibitory laws promote the profitable black markets, including their attendant violence, is firmly established (see Inciardi, 1992). Tough laws serve to enrich organized crime (see, e.g., Brooke, 1991; Isikoff and Robinson, 1989). And finally, the undercover character of drug enforcement exposes citizens to entrapment, night time raids, and police informers (Manning and Redlinger, 1983; see, e.g., Kotlowitz, 1991).

While crack helped launch the war, "crack mothers" became the collective scapegoat for its failures. In the late 1980s, pregnant drug users came under prosecutors' scrutiny. At the outset, pregnant drug users were, like Brenda Vaughn, detected following arrest. Brenda Vaughan, an African-American woman, was charged with and convicted of second-degree theft for check forgery in Washington, D.C. Although probation is the normal sentence for first-time offenders like Vaughan, the judge decided to imprison the pregnant woman after she tested positive for cocaine. "I'm going to keep her locked up until the baby's born," said Judge Peter Wolf at the time of sentencing (Churchville, 1988:A1). No drug charges were brought against Vaughan nor did the prosecution seek a trial on possession or use of illegal drugs.

More frequently, pregnant drug users were like Jennifer Johnson, another African-American woman, detected when they entered the hospital to deliver babies. Johnson was charged with and convicted of two counts of delivering drugs to a minor on the grounds that she had passed cocaine to her newborn child through the umbilical cord after the baby was delivered but before the cord was cut (Curriden, 1990). A Florida court gave Johnson fifteen to twenty-four years probation, mandatory drug rehabilitation, drug and alcohol prohibitions, and required her to report subsequent pregnancies to her probation officer and to enter a court-approved prenatal care program (Curriden, 1990; Sherman, 1989).

Prosecutors argued that pregnant women who used drugs were breaking the law and should be arrested, prosecuted, and convicted. Incarceration was intended to send a message of general deterrence[2] to would-be pregnant drug users. In addition it was designed to provide the bargaining point for forcing the women into treatment. Programs incorporating these goals sprang up around the country, and like the one in Charlotte, North Carolina, relied on hospital administered screens to identify and forward suspected crack mothers for prosecution or diversion. Prosecutions, oddly enough, have not been concentrated in the urban areas where official and field sources suggested the problem occurred. North Carolina, New Mexico, and Michigan have produced celebrated prosecutions, while Washington, D.C., and Los Angeles are the few major urban areas represented on the list. The geographical discrepancy suggests that local prosecutors have simply taken advantage of an exploitable issue to make a name for themselves. The publicity surrounding the crack prosecutions has focused on a handful of prosecutors who have made crack mothers their cause. But there is another explanation. One cynical urban prosecutor suggested during an interview that prosecutors in outlying districts are the only ones with room in their jails for crack mothers.

To date, such programs have resulted in over 70 criminal prosecutions, many of which are on appeal. Defense attorneys have successfully appealed convictions on grounds that drug-trafficking laws were intended to prohibit the exchange of controlled substances between adults, not between a mother and her newborn (Paltrow, 1990). But the prosecutions are open to criticism on other grounds. The fact that the prosecutions target poor women of color is a reflection of hospital-based screening biases: women from all backgrounds use drugs, but poor minority women are singled out for drug testing (Chasnoff, 1990). And finally, feminists see the prosecutions as a way of placing the interests of the unborn above those of the mother, a precedent which threatens the right to privacy and turns women into "incubators" unable to control pregnancies or maintain bodily integrity (Pollit, 1990).

The Politics of Resentment

The capacity of "crack mothers" to orchestrate punitive reactions has to be understood in relation to the politics of resentment. The politics of resentment refer to the sense that one's group has declined in importance as other groups have enjoyed an upsurge in prestige or in material well-being. Secondly, the politics of resentment refers to various efforts on the part of declining groups to recapture power or prestige. Lastly, resentment finds expression in punitive reactions to groups perceived as responsible for another's relative decline. Such politics have a long history in the United States, have been widely studied (Lipset, 1970; Hofstader, 1965), and have been applied to the gender issues involved in maternal drug use (Faludi, 1991:426ff). But to understand crack mothers fully, one has to understand how the symbol appeals to different sorts of resentments.

Conservatives in contemporary political context have justified traditional claims on class, race, and gender privileges, but the justifications are indirectly, frequently symbolic. Willie Horton, the ad campaign which exploited racial fears and helped to elect George Bush president in 1988, provides one example of negative symbols that entrench traditional privileges. Crack mothers provides a more complex example since it draws on class, race, and gender resentments.

An Assault on the Poor

Crack mothers are poor, they are frequently enrolled in benefit programs from public assistance and subsidized housing to Aid to Families with Dependent Children. They are not, however, seen as "deserving poor" to whom some compassion might be extended. They are rather perceived as indolent—able-bodied persons who apart from a refusal to work might contribute to the economy as low-waged, seasonal or part-time workers. Dishonesty is a persistent theme in attacks on the poor. In this respect crack mothers fall into the category of welfare cheats who use welfare to subsidize their drug use, who have babies to increase the size of their monthly check, or who engage more systematically in fraud. The crack mother activates the same resentments as more timeworn symbols, including the welfare queen or pregnant teenagers. What is new, is that the crack mother is also a source of resentment about the "bio-underclass."

Crack-using pregnant women were thought as noted above to give birth to permanently impaired babies. The nature of cocaine-induced impairment was perceived as neurological and thought to take form as physical tremors, irritability, and an inability to relate to others. These early symptoms, experts thought, portended later disruptive, asocial, and criminal behaviors. What was once thought of as a cultural problem, the transmission of welfare dependency from mother to daughter, became at once a biological matter. Poor women were giving birth to children who were biologically ordained to swell the ranks of the irredeemably poor. One wondered at the consequences for medical, education, social service, and criminal justice institutions when wave after wave of crack babies matured and entered institutional life.

Racial Fears

In addition to mobilizing resentment toward the poor, the image of the crack mother activated white antipathy toward race/ethnic minorities. Crack mothers were portrayed by the print and electronic media as Black or Hispanic. Often posed in groups of recovery addicts, the women pictured were reported to have entered treatment in order to regain custody of their crack babies. But the power of the visual image—that crack mothers belonged to minorities, took precedence over the printed or spoken word. The message was not that these women might be able to reorganize their lives. Rather the image which endured was racial, and it activated existing white fears about racial minorities.

While the source of racial fears is open to debate, it is difficult to avoid the observation that stigmatizing labels like crack mothers weaken if not disqualify the claims of Blacks and Hispanics on shrinking resources. White Americans tend to believe that Black Americans have benefitted far more from Affirmative Action than has actually been the case (Kluegel and Smith, 1982). On the other hand, many white Americans believe that whatever success they or their families have attained is attributable to hard work, talent, or other earned competitive advantage (Kluegel and Smith, 1982). As a result, white Americans tend to view opportunity as rightfully theirs and to see quotas as reserving opportunities that upwardly minorities no longer need or that stigmatized minorities (crack mothers) do not deserve (Kluegel and Smith, 1982).

Attack on Women

Finally, the stereotypes of crack mothers activate resentment toward feminism and reproductive freedoms. The New Right perceives feminism as an organized attack on male prerogatives, a conscious attempt to downgrade the traditional authority of the male in the family. Citing biblical sources to the effect that the husband is head of the family as Christ was head of the Church, right-wing evangelicals and New Right conservatives hold feminists responsible for the rise of materialism over moral values among the affluent. If women have careers, their children suffer and their families will be destroyed. Among welfare mothers, the New Right also attributes the decline of the traditional family to feminism (Faludi, 1991:230–33).

The political agenda of the New and the Religious Right has been to reverse the gains of women. It has called for a ban on abortion, censorship of birth control information until after marriage, a chastity bill, revocation of the Equal Pay Act, and defeat of the Equal Rights Amendment. The agenda, according to Faludi (1991:231,402), had it roots among downwardly mobile white males, was conceived by television evangelical ministers, and voiced by intellectuals housed in conservative think tanks. Its appeal has been to the males who felt passed over, whose declining economic prospects and family roles contrasted sharply to the perceived progress of women in professional circles and family decision making (Faludi, 1991:402). This is the group from which the anti-abortion movement arose, demanding among other restrictions the father's right to veto his partner's decision to terminate a pregnancy.

Crack mothers, the symbol that castigates women who use crack during pregnancy, is also a symbol that places fetal rights above the rights of the woman. The major imagery of the anti-abortion movement is the child-fetus; its construction as a miniature person undergirds claims that the law ought to play a role in protecting it from the exercise of reproductive freedoms. Likewise, the fetuses involved in crack pregnancies are thought by many to be in need of protection from "drug-crazed" women. This belief is so pervasive that administrative regulations, civil commitment, and criminal sanctions have been introduced as the vehicles for forcing errant women to abstain from drugs, seek prenatal care, and follow medical advice.

Conclusion

Throughout this essay, the phrase "crack mothers" has been used as a set of claims about the magnitude of the crack problem and the nature of its harmful consequences for mothering, pregnancy, and child rearing. Many of these claims come closer to myth than reality, but the ideas expressed by crack mothers are not isolated curiosities. Instead they have played an extremely important political role in launching the second War on Drugs, and by mobilizing support for prosecuting pregnant crack users; these ideas helped divert attention from that War's shortcomings. The political role played by crack mothers reflects deeper realities. The particular combination of class, race, and gender images that constitute crack mothers stirred up a simmering pot of resentments which had already been set to boil by New and Religious Right in its regressive attack on the poor, ethnic/racial minorities, and women.

NOTES

1. In focusing on crack mothers, i.e., its content, usage, and social roots, the paper overlooks other aspects of crack use among women of childbearing age, including the shift in social reaction from a prosecutorial model to social service model, the growing importance of treatment (its redesign for women with families and expansion of facilities), the persistence of discrimination in identifying maternal drug use, and the civil liberties issues raised by removing infants and other children from the custody of women who test positive for crack/cocaine (for an overview, see Humphries et al., 1991).

2. For a review of the evidence on the deterrence question, see Humphries, 1991.

REFERENCES

Akers, Ronald L. 1991. *Drugs, Alcohol, and Society: Social Process and Policy.* Belmont, CA: Wadsworth Publishing.

Brooke, James. 1991. "Cali, the 'Quiet' Cocaine Cartel, Profits Through Accommodation." *The New York Times* July 14 at p. 1 (National edition).

Chasnoff, Ira J. 1990. "The Prevalence of Illicit Drug or Alcohol Use During Pregnancy and Discrepancies in Mandatory Reporting in Pinellas County Florida." *New England Journal of Medicine* April: 1202–8.

———. 1988. "Newborn Infants with Drug Withdrawal Symptoms." *Pediatrics in Review* March (9): 273–277.

———. 1987. "Perinatal Effects of Cocaine." *Contemporary OB/GYN* May: 163–176.

———, Kayreen Burns, William J. Burns, Sidney H. Schnoll. 1986. "Prenatal Drug Exposure: Effects on Neonatal and Infant Growth and Development." *Neurobehavioral Toxicology and Teratology* 8: 357–362.

Chasnoff, Ira J., D.R. Griffith, C. Freier, and J. Murray. 1992. "Cocaine/Polydrug Use in Pregnancy: Two-Year Follow-up." *Pediatrics* 89(2):337–9.

Churchville, Victoria. 1988. "D.C. Judge Jails Women as Protection for Fetus." *Washington Post* July 23, pp. A1, A8.

Cimons, Marlene. 1989. "Illegal Drug Use Drops But Crack Addiction Soars." *Los Angeles Times* August 1 at p. 1.

Curridan, Mark. 1990. "Holding Mom Accountable." *American Bar Association Journal* March: 50–53.

Egan, Timothy. 1990. "Chief Judge Says Crack May Overwhelm Courts." *The New York Times.* December 3 at p. B3.

Faludi, Susan. 1991. *Backlash: The Undeclared War Against American Women.* New York: Crown Publishers.

Gieringer, Dale. 1990. "How Many Crack Babies?" *The Drug Policy Letter* March/April, p.4.

Hinds, Michael Decourcy. 1990. "Use of Crack Is Said to Stifle The Instincts of Parenthood." *The New York Times* March 17 at p A8.

Hofstadter, Richard. 1965. *The Paranoid Style in American Politics.* New York: Alfred A. Knopf.

Humphries, Drew. 1991. "Criminalization of Pregnancy: The Question of General Deterrence." Paper presented at the American Society of Criminology, November, San Francisco.

Humphries, Drew, John Dawson, Valerie Cronin, Phyliss Keating and Chris Winiewski. 1992a. "Mothers and Children, Drugs and Crack: Reactions to Maternal Drug Dependence." *Women and Criminal Justice* Fall (3): 81–89.

Humphries, Drew, Helen Polak, Kelly Behrens, John Weiner, and Vikki Schulter. 1992b. "Crack/Cocaine and Pregnancy: Issues in Treatment and Evaluation. Paper presented at the Eastern Sociological Society, April.

Inciardi, James A. 1992. *The War on Drugs II.* Mountain View, CA: Mayfield Press.

Isikoff, Michael and Eugene Robinson. 1989. "Columbia's Drug Kings Becoming Entrenched; Cocaine Profits Penetrating Economy." *The Washington Post* January 8, p. A1.

Isikoff, Michael and Tracey Thompson. 1990. " Getting Too Tough on Drugs: Draconian Sentences Hurt Small Offenders More Than Kingpins." *The Washington Post* November 4, p. C1.

Kluegel, James R. and Eliot R. Smith. 1982. "Whites' Beliefs About Blacks' Opportunities." *American Sociological Review* 42 (August):518–532.

Koren, Gideon, Karen Graham, Heather Shear, and Tom Einarson. 1989. "Bias Against the Null Hypothesis: The Reproductive Hazards of Cocaine." *The Lancet* December: 1440–42.

Kotlowitz, Alex. 1991. "Hidden Casualties: Drug War's Emphasis on Law Enforcement Takes a Toll on Police." *The Wall Street Journal* January 11 at p. A1.

Kusserow, Richard P. 1990. *Crack Babies.* U.S. Department of Health and Human Services. Office of the Inspector General. OEI-03–89–01540, June.

Lipset, Seymour Martin and Earl Raab (eds.). 1970. *The Politics of Unreason.* New York: Harper and Row.

Manning, Peter and K. and Lawrence John Redlinger. 1983. "Invitational Edges." Pp. 354–369 in Karl B. Klockars (ed). *Thinking About the Police: Contemporary Readings.* New York: McGraw-Hill.

Murphy, Sheigla and Marsha Rosenbaum. 1990. "Women Who Use Cocaine Too Much: Case Studies of Smoking Crack vs. Snorting Cocaine." Paper presented at the American Society of Criminology, Baltimore, November.

Murphy, Sheigla, Margaret H. Kearney, and Marsha Rosenbaum. 1992. Running Between the Rooms: Mothering on Crack. Paper presented at the American Society of Criminology, San Francisco, November.

NIDA. 1991a. *National Household Survey on Drug Abuse: Main Findings 1990.* Rockville, MD.: U.S. Department of Health and Human Services.

———. 1991b. *National Household Survey on Drug Abuse: Population Estimates.* Rockville, MD: U.S. Department of Health and Human Services.

———. 1989a. *Drug Use, Drinking, and Smoking: National Survey Results from High School, College, and Young Adult Population: 1975–1988.* Rockville, MD: U.S. Department of Health and Human Services.

———. 1989b. *Drug Use, Drinking, and Smoking: National Survey Results from High School, College, and Young Adult Population: 1975–1988:*

Population Estimates. Rockville, MD: U.S. Department of Health and Human Services.

New York Times. 1989. "U.S. Inmate Count Doubled Since 1980, Congress is Told." December 4 at p. A21.

Pitt, David E. 1989. "Top New York Judge Urges Makeshift Jail Courtrooms." *The New York Times* April 18 at p. A24 (National edition).

Pollit, Katha. 1990. "Fetal Rights: A New Assault on Feminism." *The Nation* March 16: 409–18.

Rosenbaum, Marsha. 1981. *Women on Heroin.* New Brunswick, NJ: Rutgers University Press.

Sherman, Roris. 1989. "Keeping Babies Free From Drugs." *The National Law Journal* October, pp. 1,28.

Somerville, Janice. 1989. "Heavy Cocaine Use Registers Steep Rise." *American Medical News* August 11, p.4.

Walker, Samuel. 1985. *Sense and Nonsense about Crime: A Policy Guide.* Belmont, CA: Brooks/Cole Publications.

KIMBERLY J. COOK

Pro-Death Politics:
Debunking the "Pro-Life" Agenda

This chapter examines the current right-wing political efforts to restrict abortion access in the 50 states of the United States. The conservative political agenda promotes the "right to life" of the fetus since they argue that life is sacred and should be protected from the moment of conception. In addition, this political agenda blames the women's movement for the "breakdown" of the family and advocates that women resume such primary roles as housewife and mother to regain the traditional social order (Klatch, 1987). Attempting to restrict access to abortion is one of the vehicles through which the conservative agenda has been launched. Are these attempts to restrict abortion access simply about the "right to life" of the fetus or do they entail a punitive element? The research described here suggests that restriction of reproductive freedom is significantly related to punishment, containing such goals as "making women pay" for their actions. Specifically, the variables of capital punishment, corporal punishment and incarceration, together are significant in predicting anti-choice[1] legislation at the state level. Also, the level of social disorganization is significant in predicting anti-choice legislation, suggesting that legislative restrictions on access to abortion may be an attempt to recapture the traditional status quo. The focus of this chapter is to empirically examine the punitive elements of anti-choice legislation.

Sociology has a tradition of exposing the myths in society, the debunking motif (Berger, 1963:38):

> [The] sociological frame of reference, with its built-in procedure of looking for levels of reality other than those given in the official interpretations of society, carries with it a logical imperative *to unmask the pretensions and propaganda* by which men [sic] cloak their actions with each other. This unmasking imperative is one of the characteristics of sociology particularly at home in the temper of the modern era (emphasis added).

Within this heritage of sociological debunking, it is possible to unmask the "pro-life" agenda and analyze it as an attempt at punitively controlling those members of society who do not follow traditionally prescribed roles, specifically women who control their fertility through induced abortion and thereby, according to the "pro-life" agenda, depreciate the role of motherhood in their lives (Luker, 1984).

Opposition to Abortion

Existing research on abortion covers diverse aspects of the abortion issue in contemporary society. Davis (1985, 1986) offers a comprehensive analysis of the sociohistorical legal process of abortion policy from criminalization of abortion to the liberalization of abortion laws. She argues that despite *Roe v. Wade* (reprinted in Walbert and Butler, 1973), the right to privacy in the abortion decision is not absolute (abortion can be regulated by the state in the second trimester and prohibited in the third trimester of pregnancy when the state's interest in the protection of fetal life outweighs the woman's right to privacy). Other scholars have examined the abortion issue as a power struggle between those who favor constitutional freedom for individuals and those who favor the right of Congress and state legislatures to regulate abortion (Keynes and Miller 1989; Pym, 1973). In contemporary debates on abortion, advocates of the right to privacy argue for a constitutionally guaranteed right (*Roe v. Wade* and *Griswold v. Connecticut*: 381 U.S. 479, 484–485; 1965) while advocates of limiting abortion policy argue for the right of state legislatures and Congress to regulate access to abortion.

Although women are not equal participants in policy making at the state and federal levels, they are involved in the abortion debate primarily at the grassroots level and on all sides of the issue (Luker 1984; Ginsburg, 1989; Gordon, 1976). According to Luker (1984:193) women become active in shaping abortion legislation based on their world views and the value of motherhood in their lives. She concludes that the abortion debate is a "referendum on the place and meaning of motherhood" in society. People who value motherhood as the primary role for women support restrictive abortion legislation and those who feel that motherhood ought to be voluntary and not necessarily the primary role of women support more liberal abortion legislation. The arguments about abortion are complicated and include emotional and religious beliefs about the value of fetal life. Opponents of access to abortion argue that life begins at conception and that fetuses have the same right to life as all citizens. Many define abortion as murder, and argue that it is illegal to willfully take the life of an *innocent* human being. Likewise, some anti-choice advocates assert that the primary roles of women are housewives and mothers and to deviate from that role, rejecting the traditional (and in their view "proper") social order, may necessitate punitive sanctions.

When reviewing research on support for anti-choice and capital punishment, it becomes apparent that there is significant overlap among the proponents of these punitive policies (Johnson and Tamney, 1988). Such research indicates that the political right-wing in the American legislative process is the home for these punitive sentiments. For example, President Bush argued for expansion of the death penalty and limitations on appeals for death row inmates, and announced his support, via telephone hookups to the annual Right To Life gatherings in Washington, D.C. Further examples of political officials espousing this punitive right-wing perspective are abundant: former Attorneys General Edwin Meese and Richard Thornburg, Louisiana State Representative David Duke, Vice President J. Danforth Quayle, to mention only a few of the more well known.

Ginsburg (1989) argues that at the grassroots level, punitiveness is so pronounced that supporters of restrictive abortion laws have advocated and used violent tactics to make their case and/or to prevent women from obtaining abortions by modifying the language of the Civil Rights movement. She quotes Joseph Scheidler, a leading "pro-life" activist who advocates violence as a response to abortion and justifies bombings and other terrorist acts:

> [W]hen the law is so twisted, it is obvious that one has to fight it, and when the law sanctions the killing of innocent people, maybe you have to break the law to save lives (Ginsburg, 1989:51).

This perspective venerates the violent terrorism of many pro-life activists as doing that which will promote the value and meaning of fetal life and of motherhood (enforced or voluntary). So, "pro-life" terrorism then becomes a route by which people (legitimately, in their view) try to make changes in the current paradigm. The Reagan Administration offered support to these groups "claiming that attacks on abortion clinics did not constitute 'terrorism' because they were not being carried out by an 'organized group' that claims responsibility for them" (Ginsburg, 1989:53).

In Springfield, Missouri, two abortion clinic workers were shot and hospitalized with serious injuries by a gunman who walked into a clinic (Keyes and Clark, 1991). While violent attacks on abortion clinics, their workers and clients increased, the Reagan and Bush administrations officially sanctioned this terrorism where people died and doctors stopped performing this procedure due to the fear of "pro-life" reprisals. These legislative and interest group activities have culminated in greater legislative and logistical restrictions on women's constitutional rights to reproductive freedoms.

In contemporary American society debate and activism over abortion rages. Judges are mandated by state legislatures to determine if a teenage girl should or should not terminate a pregnancy when she has expressed a desire to do so and cannot turn to her parents. An extreme example (and one where racism is apparent) is that of a Michigan judge who said that he would never allow a teenage girl to have an abortion unless she were pregnant as the result of incest, or were white and had been raped by a black man (Wilkerson, 1991). These parental consent laws can result in death for teenage girls, as with the tragic death of Becky Bell who did not want to distress her parents with the news of her pregnancy (*Washington Post*, 1990). Becky Bell's parents have since become vocal opponents of parental consent laws, claiming that if their daughter had had the freedom to choose she would have obtained a safer legal abortion and lived. Instead, Mr. Bell says "These laws are punitive, they're restrictive—they're deadly" (*Washington Post*, 1990).

In some states women are forced to wait a period of time before they can obtain an abortion, or must seek permission from their husbands. Waiting 24 hours for an abortion could mean further expense in obtaining a procedure that is constitutionally guaranteed. Women in rural areas may have to travel several hundreds of miles to locate an abortion provider, only to be told they must wait another 24 or 48 hours, adding expenses for overnight accomodations and meals. Since most married women who seek abortion discuss the choice with their husbands, the spousal consent law is especially dangerous for those women with abusive husbands. To "get permission" from them might be more perilous than an illegal abortion!

As a result of the Hyde Amendment in 1976, few states will allow Medicaid funding to finance abortions for low-income women. Poor women are therefore further penalized and controlled because they cannot afford to travel the hundreds of miles to an abortion clinic in addition to paying the cost of the procedure itself. In terms of fiscal cost-effectiveness, it would be less costly for a poor woman to obtain an abortion if she so chooses than to mandate that she continue the pregnancy and struggle to support the child and herself. This holds true at the legislative level as well. Cutright and Jaffe (1977) present some compelling statistics regarding the number of births averted due to Family Planning funding, including abortion prior to the Hyde Amendment. They estimate that Family Planning funding averted 1,097,596 births between 1970–75 for low- and marginal-income women. With a 1975

AFDC benefit level for one parent and one child at about $145 per month, and assuming that all the averted births were first children for single women (for simplicity), the Family Planning funding saved the state and federal governments $159,151,420.00 for one month of support. Furthermore, with the average time of eligibility for AFDC benefits being approximately 36 months, the three year savings would be approximately $5,729,451,120.00. Knowing that not all of these averted births are due to abortion—the majority are due to better contraceptive practices—these numbers may be generous estimates. However they are impressive, especially in view of the fact that many anti-choice advocates also oppose contraceptive use (Luker, 1984).

Many states are attempting to restrict abortion under various circumstances or to legislatively redefine abortion as first-degree murder. In another extreme example, Rep. Poirer of Massachusetts introduced a bill in January 1989 which recommended that:

> The termination of a pregnancy at any stage of the pregnancy, from the moment of conception through the time of birth, is prohibited. . . . Involvement in any abortion shall be murder in the first degree, punishable by a mandatory sentence of death in the electric chair (NARAL 1989:45).

Several states have established Declarations of Legislative Intent, which puts them in the position of being ready to prohibit abortion in the event that *Roe v. Wade* is overturned. In this hostile socio-political climate, women who seek abortion are confronted with picketers displaying photos of developing or aborted fetuses[2] and assaulted with verbal aspersions and occasional physical assaults—all while trying to exercise their constitutionally guaranteed (but not absolute) right to privacy.

To some it may seem that women are being punished for being nontraditional in terms of reproductive decisions and social change. There is a conservative backlash against women and the women's movement, despite the relatively progressive strides made prior to the 1980s with respect to race and class. Throughout the 1980s support for the death penalty rose to 80 percent (Fox, Radelet and

Bonsteel, 1990), social service spending was reduced substantially by the Reagan administration, infant mortality rose among the poor and ethnic minorities, and prison populations grew to overflowing (Tunnell, 1992). Attempts to restrict (or prohibit) abortion access have been successful because they are part of a growing conservative agenda that promotes punishment for difference and nonconformity. These legislative restrictions do not occur in a vacuum of abortion-only politics. Restrictions are passed by the same bodies that reinstate the death penalty, that allow corporal punishment in public schools, and that disapprove of social service spending.

Support for the Death Penalty

When pursuing justifications for supporting the death penalty in public opinion research[3], respondents claim that capital punishment deters capital murder, that capital punishment is necessary to wipe out crime, that it is cost-effective, that murderers deserve the death penalty, and that it is morally correct for society to seek revenge. This set of justifications for supporting the death penalty can be examined from two levels of analysis; utilitarian and symbolic. The first level of analysis, the utilitarian, includes beliefs in the deterrent value of the death penalty, the instrumental use of violence as a response to criminal activity, and the cost effectiveness of death vs. life without parole. It is this level of understanding where researchers find that opinions are expressions of seemingly rational thought and deliberate consideration of a situation.

The second level of analysis, the symbolic, includes retributive justifications, and the moral correctness of being "tough on crime" and criminals. Although the second level of support is most relevant for this chapter, a brief summary of both levels of death penalty support is warranted. As opinions are expressions of thought, attitudes are expressions of emotional commitment toward a particular situation. It can be argued that those who support restrictive abortion laws and support the death penalty share an attitudinal predisposition toward the social environment, and this becomes manifest in the conservative political agenda of the right.

Utilitarian Explanations

The utility of the death penalty has been linked to the belief that a potential murderer's fear of capital punishment will deter him or her from committing capital crimes. In fact, the belief in the deterrent effect of the death penalty is the most commonly offered justification by those who support capital punishment (Ellsworth and Ross, 1983, Thomas and Foster, 1975). However, a Gallup Poll (1986:11) claims that even though most people refer to deterrence as a primary reason for supporting capital punishment, "the principle of deterrence plays a relatively minor role in shaping basic attitudes." In addition, Thomas and Foster (1975) claim that the belief in deterrence is based on simplistic folk wisdom that the harsher the punishment the less likely people will commit the offensive behavior. The belief in deterrence is simplistic because it assumes that people who engage in criminal activity are making logical and rational choices. Katz (1989) makes a compelling argument that criminal activity is not necessarily a rational choice, but rather a reflection of seductive forces in the broader culture such as being challenged or defending "the Eternal Good." Nonetheless, harsh punishment is viewed as an effective route for solving the problems, including the use of capital punishment as a deterrent.

Ellsworth and Ross (1983:151) found that over 84 percent of death penalty proponents agreed that "society benefits more if the murderer is executed than if he [sic] is sentenced to life imprisonment." Also, 83.7 percent of the proponents disagreed that "executions set a violent example which may encourage violence and killing" (1983:153). Scholars claim that supporters of capital punishment see it as an instrumental solution to the problem of crime in the United States (Ellsworth and Ross, 1983, Thomas and Foster, 1975).

Research (Tyler and Weber, 1982:40) shows that conservative political and social beliefs are the precursors of death penalty support:

> In fact, the results of this study suggest that the findings associated with the instrumental perspective can best be explained as a result of beliefs in the value of the death penalty, beliefs which are closely associated with political-social attitudes.

So, whether support for capital punishment in the United States is largely an instrumental response to crime, it appears to be justified by political predispositions regarding social issues.

Finally, Ellsworth and Ross (1982) report that over 80 percent of the proponents of capital punishment believe that life without parole is more expensive than capital punishment. While this idea may initially appeal to common sense, research shows that this belief is erroneous (Nakell, 1982; Garey, 1985; Spangenberg and Walsh, 1989). In fact the average death penalty costs about $3.2 million whereas the average life without parole costs about $600,000 (Radelet, 1988).

After examining this utilitarian level of support, we see that most Americans claim to support capital punishment based on their rational and instrumental beliefs in the deterrent effect, social utility and cost-effectiveness of sentencing criminals to death. However, Ellsworth and Ross (1982:149) argue that attitudes precede reasoning.

> People believe that they know the facts about deterrence and that the facts support their opinions; however, it is clear that factual evidence is extraneous to their opinions, since they also say that if the facts were different, their opinions would be the same. This is particularly interesting in regard to evidence about deterrence, since this is usually the first evidence that people (especially Retentionists) spontaneously present in support of their opinions. It may be that the belief in deterrence is seen as more "scientific" or more socially desirable than other reasons; people mention it first because its importance is obvious, not because its importance is real.

Thus, these opinions which support capital punishment express what the respondents believe to be true based on their attitudes toward the situation. It is necessary to examine the symbolic explanations of death penalty support which may be at the root of this attitudinal predisposition, and contain an element similar to that of abortion opposition.

Symbolic Explanations

Retribution has been identified as one of the more salient justifications for supporting capital punishment. Since its goal is "doing justice" rather than deterring crimes, it makes no instrumental claims. Warr and Stafford (1984) report that retribution is the most commonly stated primary goal of punishment (42 percent of respondents). Normative validation (defined as "maintaining moral standard on our society . . . the maintenance or intensification of norms resulting from punishment" p. 98) is a primary goal of punishment, and is achieved through retribution. That is, the socio-political meaning of punishment is to reaffirm the moral standards of propriety and acceptable behavior. Therefore, supporters of capital punishment view it as a powerful means of maintaining the traditional social order (Warr and Stafford, 1984).

Through socialization and acceptance of culturally defined justifications for punishment, people come to believe in the cultural propriety of executing criminals. Vidmar and Miller (1980) assert that retributive attitudes are a consequence of the socialization process which instills deep beliefs that deviant behavior is an assault on the social system and that punishment is just and proper. In addition, this public knowledge and the expressions of approval serve to marginalize those who do *not* support the use of the specific punishment and crystalize the membership of those who do. Essentially, "the offender is merely an object through which group solidarity and consensus are achieved" (Vidmar and Miller, 1980:582). Thus, support for the death penalty can be viewed as an appeal to the popular sovereignty of retributive justice.

Retributive attitudes are an expression of the punitive ideology of American culture. As indicated previously, most people offer rational-instrumental justifications for supporting the death penalty. However, research shows that more than 40 percent of respondents would continue supporting capital punishment if it were demonstrated to their satisfaction that there were no rational-instrumental effects of the death penalty (Fox, Radelet, and Bonsteel, 1991). Ellsworth and Ross (1983:151) report that 44.9 percent of proponents agreed that "society has a right to get revenge when a very serious crime like murder has been committed." For those whose opinions are staunchly supportive of capital punishment, retributive justice is the basis of this support (Vidmar and Miller, 1980) and the socio-political legacy of punitive justice provides ample avenues by which people can justify these sentiments and other sentiments, such as opposition to abortion.

The growing public support for capital punishment since 1966 has been attributed to the growing "law and order" political agendas of recent elections (Rankin, 1979). Supporters of the death penalty are generally more politically conservative, punitive, and authoritarian than opponents of the death penalty (Rankin, 1979). This "law and order" syndrome is heavily influenced by the popular focus on a conservative political agenda from Nixon in the 1970s to Reagan and Bush in the 1980s and 1990s who all claim to be "tough on crime." During the 1988 presidential campaign Bush successfully appealed to these sentiments through the "Willie Horton" advertisement, which portrayed his opponent as "soft on crime" because he did not support capital punishment. In addition, this law and order syndrome advocates harsher penal policies, including capital punishment, which are supported by many political leaders in state and federal offices.

Tyler and Weber (1982) argue that predispositions in political and social attitudes have a significant impact on support for the death penalty as well as other punitive penal policies. As a result, the law and order syndrome and support for punitive policies are a reflection of the dominant cultural and political ideology, which in turn generate wide support for capital punishment based on the "morality" of killing criminals (*lex talionis*). In this respect, support for capital punishment can be viewed as an indicator of support for the law and order political agendas of recent years.

The relationship of support for capital punishment and opposition to abortion stem from the same right-wing political agenda of punitively controlling those who do not conform to the traditional social order. Both entail the potential for loss of human life; illegal abortions have been fatal for women and the death penalty takes life with judicial deliberation.

Methods

The United States Supreme Court ruling in *Casey v. Planned Parenthood of Pennsylvania* has declared legislative restrictions on access to abortion services as constitutional, provided these restrictions do not place an "undue burden" on women seeking abortions. Prior to this ruling several states had passed restrictive abortion statutes and many more are positioned to follow suit. Since restrictive abortion legislation is currently being debated in many state legislatures, this research uses the 50 states and the District of Columbia as the units of analysis. Earlier research suggests that "states are the theoretically appropriate unit for issues which involve many aspects of government, politics, taxes, schools, economics, administration and legal issues" (Straus, 1985:322). The data for this study are from the State and Regional Indicators Archives (Straus, 1985; Baron and Straus, 1990). The Archives contain thousands of variables relevant to broad areas of state level[4] social research (Baron and Straus, 1990).

The hypothesis being tested in this study is that states which are more punitive with respect to capital punishment, corporal punishment of children, and incarceration are also those with greater anti-choice legislations. The dependent variable is a composite of various aspects of abortion restrictions following the coding scheme of Johnson and Bond (1980). The anti-choice variable in these data were compiled by coding six elements of abortion legislation (NARAL, 1991) and measured on a scale of zero to three, with three being the most restrictive. The six elements of the legislation include the post-*Roe* restrictions, abortion restriction bills passed by the states post-*Webster* (in the 1990 sessions), spousal consent, parental consent, restrictions on public funding for abortions, and finally the states' declaration of legislative intent (for anti-choice). The coding scheme is:

0 = no law, or no restrictions
1 = lenient version of restriction
2 = regular version of restriction
3 = completely restricted

Thus, the highest score that any one state can have would be 18, and minimum would be zero. Any state could score 18 if it completely prohibited abortion (scored a 3 on all six elements) and had a declaration of legislative intent to completely prohibit abortion after *Roe* is overturned. The mean score is 4.176, with zero as the minimum (New York and Oregon[5]) and 9 as the maximum (Pennsylvania). (See Figure 1.)

The correlation matrix of the six elements of the anti-choice measure shows that the elements are fairly consistently correlated. The Declaration of Legislative Intent is strongly correlated to post-*Roe* restriction. In other words, the more restrictive the state's legislative intent the stricter its post-*Roe* restrictions. Likewise, parental consent is strongly correlated to the number of anti-choice bills passed in the state legislature; that is, if the state has a strict parental consent law, the greater is its likelihood of passing more anti-choice bills.

Figure 1. Scores of Abortion Restrictions by State

					Score					
	0	1	2	3	4	5	6	7	8	9
	NY	WI	KS	VA	MI	TN	FL	SC	MO	PA
S	OR	AK	OK	CA	RI	NV	GA	LA	KY	
t		WA	HI	MI	WV	OH	MA	AR	UT	
a		NJ	NH	DE	AL	ME		MN	ND	
t		VT	CT	ID		AZ		IL	SD	
e		IA	MD	NC				MT	IN	
s			CO	WY				NE		
			DC	NM						
			TX							
Totals: 2	6	9	8	4	5	3	7	6	1	51

Mean = 4.176

Table 1. Correlation Matrix of Anti-Choice Variables

(obs=51)

	postroe	bills	spscon	parcon	funds	legis
postroe	1.0000					
bills	0.1420	1.0000				
spscon	0.1798	0.1867	1.0000			
parcon	0.1853	0.2910	-0.0129	1.0000		
funds	0.2326	-0.0124	-0.1117	0.2890	1.0000	
legis	0.4473	-0.0024	0.2421	0.2583	0.2471	1.0000

Parental consent is also strongly correlated with abortion funding for low-income women. Usually, the more restrictive a state is with respect to parental consent for minors the more restrictive it will be regarding Medicaid funding for abortions (Table 1). Using factor analysis with the six anti-choice elements to construct an anti-choice factor, the Eigenvalues revealed only one factor worth retaining and the loadings of the six elements on the factor are displayed in Figure 2.

Figure 2. Diagram of Anti-Choice Factor

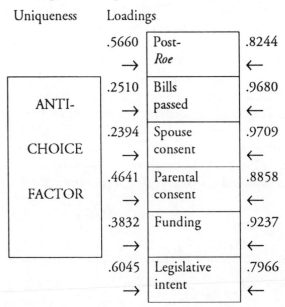

Uniqueness	Loadings		
	.5660 →	Post-*Roe*	.8244 ←
ANTI-	.2510 →	Bills passed	.9680 ←
CHOICE	.2394 →	Spouse consent	.9709 ←
FACTOR	.4641 →	Parental consent	.8858 ←
	.3832 →	Funding	.9237 ←
	.6045 →	Legislative intent	.7966 ←

The independent variables in this study include the percentage of the population in metropolitan areas, ethnicity, a six item social disorganization index, use of corporal punishment in public schools, incarceration rates, and use of capital punishment (number of executions per 100 homicides).

Capital punishment, corporal punishment in public schools and incarceration rates measure the punitive characteristics of the 50 states. Urbanicity has been suggested as a cause of higher crime rates (Stark, 1987), generating higher levels of punitive sanctions. In other words, the conventional wisdom is that the higher the urbanization, the higher the crime rate and therefore the higher the incarceration rates. Likewise, the majority of abortions are performed in larger metropolitan areas where women have greater access to abortion services (NARAL, 1990) and perhaps where their privacy can be protected. Therefore, to test for spuriousness, including the percent of the population in metropolitan areas is a valid parameter. African-Americans are disproportionately arrested and incarcerated in the United States (Reiman, 1990; Tunnell, 1992), therefore the percent of the population that is African-American is also a valid variable in this analysis.

The six item social disorganization index, created by Baron and Straus (1990:129) uses principal components factoring. This measure[6] of social disorganization includes "geographical mobility, lack of religious affiliation, households headed by males with no females present, female-headed households with children, and the ratio of tourists to residents in each state."

The correlation matrix (Table 2) shows that anti-choice is not directly related to the punitive elements. However, it does reveal interesting relationships with regard to punitive factors; capital

Table 2. Correlation Matrix

	Y	X_1	X_2	X_3	X_4	X_5	X_6
Y	1.00						
X_1	−.0267	1.00					
X_2	.0851	.3008*	1.00				
X_3	−.0466	.2321	.6905***	1.00			
X_4	−.1215	.1003	.0497	.2697	1.00		
X_5	.0726	.0784	.5605***	.4813*	.1881*	1.00	
X_6	−.3422**	·2944*	.1664	.3476**	−.0855	−.3180*	1.00

Significance Levels:
.05 = *
.01 = **
.001 = ***

Y = Anti-Choice Legislation
X_1 = Corporal Punishment Index (xvcp1)*
X_2 = Executions (z270r2)
X_3 = Incarceration: % in correctional institutions (v717r)
X_4 = % Population in urban areas (met80)
X_5 = % Population African American (blk80)
X_6 = Six item Social Disorganization Index (rapx18zp)

*(SRIA variable name)

punishment and anti-choice legislation have a weak positive correlation (.0851), corporal punishment has a strong positive correlation (.3008) with capital punishment and incarceration rate (.2321); capital punishment is very strongly correlated with incarceration rate (.6905) and the percentage of African-Americans in the population (.5605); incarceration is strongly correlated with urbanicity (.2697) and the percentage of African-Americans (.4813) as well as the level of social disorganization (.3476). Because there are strong positive correlations among corporal punishment, incarceration and capital punishment (Table 2a) factor scores were computed and a factor created.

The key punitive variables in the correlation matrix were scored using principal factor analysis (Hamilton, 1991). The Eigenvalues reveal that one factor is worth retaining. The scores reveal strong positive loadings on the factor labeled the Punitive factor (Figure 3). The OLS regression results (Table 3) show that the Punitive factor significantly predicts anti-choice legislation (b=.3423, prob>.037). Therefore, the more punitive each state is with regard to capital punishment, incarceration and corporal punishment, the more restrictive its anti-choice legislation is likely to be. The six

Table 2a. Correlation of Punitive Elements Only

	X_1	X_2	X_3
X_1	1.000		
X_2	.3008*	1.000	
X_3	.2321	.6905***	1.000

Significance Levels:
.05=*
.01=**
.001=***

X_1 = Corporal Punishment Index (xvcp1)*
X_2 = Executions (z270r2)
X_3 = Incarceration: % in correctional institutions (v717r)

Figure 3.
Principal Components Factor Loadings of Punitive Factor

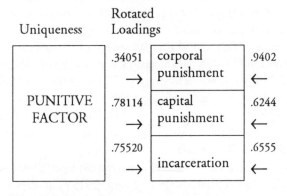

	Uniqueness	Rotated Loadings			
PUNITIVE FACTOR	.34051 →	corporal punishment		.9402	←
	.78114 →	capital punishment		.6244	←
	.75520 →	incarceration		.6555	←

item social disorganization index also significantly predicts anti-choice legislation (b=-.0222, prob>.001). Thus the greater the social disorganization (or nontraditional social organization) the less restrictive their anti-choice legislation is likely to be.

Discussion

These findings support the hypothesis that those states which are more punitive with respect to capital punishment, corporal punishment of children, and incarceration are also those with stricter anti-choice legislations. Furthermore, these findings suggest that anti-choice legislation has more to do with the punitive aspects of state-level phenomena, rather than with the humanitarian goals of the "pro-life" agenda. As such, anti-choice legislation may be an attempt to punish women who deviate from the traditional roles of mother and housewife in much the same way that states punish convicted murderers (capital punishment), other criminals (incarceration) and errant children (corporal punishment). These findings call into question the meaning of "pro-life" policies and debunk the "pro-life" façade of anti-choice policies.

Prior to the *Roe* decision in 1973 women died or suffered serious infections and sterilization as a result of turning to back-alley abortions (Boston Women's Health Book Collective, 1984).

Table 3. OLS Regression of Factors on Anti-Choice Factor

variable	coefficient	Std. Error	t	Prob>|t|
Punitive	.3423	.1870	1.830	.037
% Urban	-.0061	.0047	-1.318	.097
% Black	-.0232	.0170	-1.361	.090
Social Disorg.	-.0222	.0071	-3.140	.001
intercept	1.71	.5699	3.005	.002

N = 50
F = 2.81
Prob.>F = .03
R-square = .19
Adj. R^2 = .13

Further restrictions on abortion access would increase maternal mortality during advanced pregnancy (Legge, 1985) and perhaps be responsible for the deaths of women due to unsafe abortion procedures. Knowing that there exists a socio-political climate in which legislators can actively restrict access to abortion allows policy makers to curtail women's reproductive freedom even in light of the deadly consequences of recriminalized abortion. Thus, I see these relationships as indicative of pro-death rather than "pro-life" policies.

The social disorganization index offers some interesting insights into right wing anti-choice legislation as well. Given the strong negative relationship to anti-choice legislation, the greater the social disorganization states experience the fewer abortion restrictions there will be. Because abortion is a deviation from the traditional roles of mother and wife, it is not surprising that as the social order is redefined in a more nontraditional fashion access to abortion will be more liberalized. Therefore, in states that experience greater levels of social disorganization (or nontraditional social organization) there will be fewer legislative restrictions on access to abortion. Conversely, in states that experience a more traditional social organization, there may be greater attempts to restrict abortion to ensure the status quo. The populations will also be more likely to support such efforts and elect state legislators who reflect those positions. Consistent with the conservative "pro-death" agendas of the Reagan and Bush administrations, these punitive restrictions on abortion have not focused on reducing the need for abortion, but have made it more perilous and punishing to obtain abortions in the United States, despite the constitutional right to abortion.

These are preliminary findings and more research is needed into the relationship of anti-choice sentiments and punitive social control, particularly capital punishment. It would be particularly useful to examine public opinion data regarding these issues. Using the General Social Survey, Johnson and Tamney (1988) demonstrate that those who support abortion restrictions and those who support capital punishment are largely influenced by the Christian-Right Fundamentalist ideology. Public opinion on capital punishment reveals that most supporters of capital punishment believe in the utilitarian and symbolic use of violence for maintaining and reinforcing the social boundaries of appropriate behavior (Cook, 1991). Therefore, we can interpret these findings as a punitive attempt to control women's reproductive choices, in much the same way states sanction the control of those who do not conform to the traditional status quo.

Why Punishment?

The power to punish is one of the most influential social forces in human societies. In a national survey, 90 percent of American parents agreed that physical punishment of children was "normal, necessary and good" (Straus, Gelles, and Steinmetz, 1980). One of the primary motivations of incarceration is to punish those who breach the social and moral contract (Foucault, 1977; Garland, 1985 & 1990; Ignatieff, 1978). Of course, the major incentive to promote capital punishment is that of punitive vengeance (Ellsworth and Ross, 1983). Garland writes that punishment "rests, at least in part, upon a shared emotional reaction caused by the criminal's desecration of the sacred things" (1990:30). He goes on to argue that despite the veneer of utilitarian motivations of punishment there exists an underlying "vengeful, motivating passion which guides punishment and supplies its force" (1990:31). Therefore, to look at punishment as a simplistic social interaction between those with the power to punish and those who receive the punishment is inadequate. What is needed is a closer and more deliberate examination of the social forces giving rise to the social institution of punishment. Additionally, just examining those who are punished *as a class* and those who endorse such punishment misses the larger cultural context of punishment.

Nietzsche argued that viewing punishment brought pleasure to people, that it reaffirmed their sense of justice, "but to cause another to suffer affords even greater pleasure; [t]his severe statement expresses an old, powerful, human, all too human sentiment," (1958:198). An act of punishment is an appeal to the popular sovereignty of the society, it establishes the status of one person over another (or one group over another), keeps the punished subjugated, and finds its justification and motivation in the legal and moral authority of society. This then serves to reinforce the group solidarity and definition of propriety. According to Mead (1918), the punitive sentiments gain energy and emotional strength through the exemplary use and threat of punishment.

These punitive sentiments become formalized into laws designed to regulate social behavior. This serves to legitimate the "moral outrage" upon which punishment is based. In this Durkheimian analysis, the legislation is enacted with deliberation to establish the social boundaries and serves to crystalize the legitimate authority of the powers that be. However, the analysis must be taken a step further to examine the process by which punishment reinforces the traditional status quo (Garland, 1990). Garland offers an understanding of punishment based on two levels of analysis, those of mentalities and sensibilities. In this framework mentalities refer to the scientific and rationalistic objectivity in the use and understanding of punishment, while sensibilities refer to the emotional forces that appeal to the visceral nature of human interaction. In this sense, the evolving standards of civilized punishment is dependent on the overall cultural sensibilities of propriety and impropriety.

With regard to punishing women for not conforming to the traditional definition of femininity and reproductive purposes, these changing sensibilities are apparent. During the 18th and 19th centuries women were incarcerated and otherwise punished for giving birth to bastard children (Ignatieff, 1978). The punishment of women (not men) in this situation was based on the cultural shame of inappropriate pregnancy which was defined as pregnancy outside the marital union, and was seen as a threat to the moral authority of paternity and patriarchal society.

Women are still punished within the traditional cultural framework of femininity and "cultural understandings of what women are like, and how they ought to behave, operate to define the appropriate response to their misconduct and to structure the punishment of women" (Garland, 1990:202). Garland makes a similar argument with respect to ethnic minorities and charges that evidence of the deep-seated nature of these cultural forces is found in the slow pace of reform, even after discrimination is officially eradicated.

Abortion is not the only issue where this conservative political agenda is invoked. Page and Clelland (1978) describe this political element in the control over textbook use in public schools. The concerned group attempted to prevent the local school board from allowing the use of texts that "denounce traditional institutions" (Page and Clelland, 1978:268). Their demonstrations took the form of rallies and protests where violence escalated and bombings and shootings occured. These scholars argue that the protests were an attempt to preserve a lifestyle based on traditional morality and social order. Similarly, the anti-choice legislation is an attempt to politically preserve and ensure a particular lifestyle through punitive means, if necessary. This "cultural fundamentalism" is the result of the political right in the United States where vested interests in maintaining the traditional status quo is of paramount concern, not concern for the lives of people.

With respect to abortion, there is a significant punitive element to the restrictive legislation passed in recent years. Women have been targets of punitive control by the traditional patriarchal social order for hundreds of years. Cultural shifts toward redefining what is and what is not worthy of punishment have transpired. During the Victorian and Elizabethan eras women were not punished for having abortions early in their pregnancies, but rather were officially punished for bastardy. In contemporary American society it is not unusual to see single mothers without the "benefit of marriage" and most women can determine their child-bearing by practicing birth control (including abortion). At the same time, we see a punitive element in the anti-choice restrictions on access to abortion as an attempt to restore the traditional social order.

NOTES

An earlier draft of this article was presented at the National Council on Family Relations annual conference, November 19, 1991, Denver, Colorado. The current research is part of the State and Regional Indicators Archive and research program of the Family Research Laboratory, University of New Hampshire, Durham, NH 03824. A program description and publications list is available upon request.

I am grateful for the helpful comments and moral support of several people; Murray A. Straus, and other members of the Family Research Laboratory at the University of New Hampshire, editor of this book Kenneth D. Tunnell whose comments have been invaluable, William J. Bowers, Karen Smith Conway, Per Kjellson, Victoria Tepe Nasman, Michael L. Radelet, Sally K. Ward and Clifford J. Wirth. And especially to my son, Greg, for asking that all-important question, "Why do men think they can make women's choices for them?" and for always making me laugh when I needed it most!

1. I use the term "anti-choice" because the measure of abortion restrictions developed for this research is a measure of the state-level limitations of abortion choice. By imposing limitations on access to abortion, women's choice is being restricted. Some scholars argue for referring to "anti-choice" efforts by the name they call themselves—"pro-life" (Luker, 1984). However, the purpose of this research was to examine

the extent to which these policies are related to other "pro-life" governmental activities, and the findings debunk the motivations as those consistently respecting human life.

2. An unscientific observation of these posters reveals that all of the developing or aborted fetuses depicted are European-American. I have yet to see one of these "pro-life" posters depict the aborted African-American fetus.

3. Given that the literature on attitudes about abortion and the death penalty rely on different methods of research, I am forced to examine these issues based on the research available. Ideally, it would be best to examine the grassroots of death penalty organizing, but the literature on death penalty support does not contain such information (perhaps because it is not a widely threatened practice!). I must rely on public opinion research to examine this issue.

4. There are both conceptual and methodological problems associated with using state level data. First, Robinson (1950) warns researchers against the dangers of the "ecological fallacy" when using aggregate level data to make inferences about individual-level phenomena. Since this research is concerned with examining the socio-political characteristics of the 50 American states as distinct units of analysis and does not attempt to make inferences to individual behavior, the ecological fallacy is not committed. Second, since the maximum sample size of any given statistical model is 51, caution is required for examining multivariate regression analysis. As a rule of thumb, a regression should have at least ten times more cases than parameters (Hamilton, 1991). Therefore, multivariate regression analysis should not include more than five variables, or one dependent variable and four independent variables. (For an extensive and carefully articulated discussion regarding the use of state-level data see Baron and Straus, 1990:17–25.)

5. Oregon recently passed restrictions in the 1991 legislative session. These data cover the 1990 session.

6. For a detailed description of the construction of this index see Baron and Straus (1990:129).

REFERENCES

Baron, Larry and Murray A. Straus. 1990. *Four Theories of Rape in American Society: A State Level Analysis*. New Haven: Yale University Press.

Berger, Peter L. 1963. *Invitation to Sociology: A Humanistic Perspective*. Garden City, NY: Anchor Books.

Boston Women's Health Book Collective. 1984. *The New Our Bodies, Ourselves*. New York: Simon and Schuster.

Browne, Angela. 1987. *When Battered Women Kill*. New York: The Free Press.

Browne, Angela and Kirk R. Williams. 1989. "Exploring The Effect of Resource Availability and The Likelihood of Female-Perpetrated Homicides." *Law and Society Review*. 23:75–94.

Cook, Kimberly J. 1991. "Public Support for the Death Penalty: A Cultural Analysis." Paper Presented at the American Society of Criminology annual conference. San Francisco: Nov. 20.

Cutright, Phillips and Frederick S. Jaffe. 1977. *Impact of Family Planning Programs on Fertility: The U.S. Experience*. New York, Praeger.

Davis, Nanette J. 1985. *From Crime to Choice: The Transformation of Abortion in America*. Westport: Greenwood Press.

———. 1986. "Abortion and Legal Policy" *Contemporary Crises*. 10:373–397

Davis, Susan E. 1988. *Women Under Attack: Victories, Backlash and The Fight for Reproductive Freedom*, by the Committee for Abortion Rights and Against Sterilization Abuse. Boston: South End Press.

Ellsworth, Phoebe C. and Lee Ross. 1983. "Public Opinion and Capital Punishment: A Close Examination of the Views of Abolitionists and Retentionists." *Crime and Delinquency*. 29:116–169.

Field, Marilyn J. 1979. "Determinants of Abortion Policy in the Developed Nations." *Policy Studies Journal*. 7:771–781.

Foucault, Michel. 1977. *Discipline and Punish: The Birth of the Prison*. New York: Vintage Books.

Fox, James A., Michael L. Radelet, and Julie L. Bonsteel. 1990. "Death Penalty Opinion in the Post-Furman Years." *New York University Review of Law and Social Change*. 18:499–528.

Francome, Colin. 1984. *Abortion Freedom: A Worldwide Movement.* London: George Allen & Unwin.

Gallup, George. 1986. "The Death Penalty: 7 in 10 Favor Death Penalty for Murder." *Gallup Report.* 244 and 245, Jan./Feb. 10–16.

Garey, Margot. 1985. "The Cost of Taking a Life: Dollars and Sense of the Death Penalty." *University of California-Davis Law Review.* 18:1221–73.

Garland, David. 1985. *Punishment and Welfare: A History of Penal Strategies.* Brookfield, VT: Gower Publishing, Co.

————. 1990. *Punishment and Modern Society: A Study in Social Theory.* Chicago: University of Chicago Press.

Ginsburg, Faye D. 1989. *Contested Lives: The Abortion Debate in an American Community.* Berkeley: University of California Press.

Gordon, Linda. 1976. *Woman's Body, Woman's Right: Birth Control in America.* New York: Penguin Books.

Gould, Ketayun H. 1979. "Family Planning and Abortion Policy in the United States." *Social Service Review.* 53:452–463.

Hamilton, Lawrence C. 1989. *Modern Data Analysis.* New York: Brooks Cole.

————. 1991. *Regression With Graphics.* New York: Brooks Cole.

Hartnagel, Timothy F., James J. Creechan and Robert A. Silverman. 1985. "Public Opinion and the Legalization of Abortion." *Canadian Review of Sociology and Anthropology.* 22:411–430.

Johnson, Charles A. and Jon R. Bond. 1980. "Coercive and Noncoercive Abortion Deterrence Policies: A Comparative State Analysis." *Law and Policy Quarterly.* 2:106–128.

Johnson, Stephen D. and Joseph B. Tamney. 1988. "Factors Related to Inconsistent Life-Views." *Review of Religious Research.* 30:40–46.

Katz, Jack. 1989. *The Seductions of Crime.* New York: Basic Books.

Katzer, Jeffrey, Kenneth H. Cook and Wayne W. Crouch. 1982. *Evaluating Information: A Guide for Users of Social Science Research.* Second Edition. New York: Random House.

Keyes, Robert and Christopher Clark. 1991. "Two Wounded in Abortion Clinic Shooting." *The News Leader.* Springfield, MO. December 29.

Keynes, Edward with Randall K. Miller. 1989. *The Court vs. Congress: Prayer, Busing and Abortion.* Durham, NC: Duke University Press.

Klatch, Rebecca E. 1987. *Women of the New Right.* Philadelphia: Temple University Press.

Legge, Jerome S., Jr. 1985. *Abortion Policy: An Evaluation of the Consequences for Maternal and Infant Health.* Albany: State University of New York Press.

Lennertz, James E. 1986. "Human Rights and Institutional Process: Abortion Policy in Six Nations." *Policy Studies Journal.* 15:147–157.

Luker, Kristin. 1984. *Abortion and the Politics of Motherhood.* Berkeley: University of California Press.

Mathisen, Gerald S. and James A. Mathisen. 1988. "The New Fundamentalism: A Sociohistorical Approach to Understanding Theological Change." *Review of Religious Research.* 30:18–32.

Mead, George Herbert. 1918. "The Psychology of Punitive Justice." *American Journal of Sociology.* 23:577–602.

Nakell, Barry. 1982. "The Cost of The Death Penalty." In Hugo Adam Bedau (ed.) *The Death Penalty in America.* Third Edition. New York: Oxford University Press.

National Abortion Rights Action League. 1989. *Who Decides? A State by State Review of Abortion Rights in America.* Washington, DC: NARAL Foundation.

———. 1991. *Who Decides? A State by State Review of Abortion Rights.* Washington, DC: NARAL Foundation.

Page, Ann L. and Donald A. Clelland. 1978. "The Kanawha County Textbook Controversy: A Study of the Politics of Lifestyle Concern." *Social Forces.* 57:265–281.

Pfeiffer, Raymond S. 1985. "Abortion Policy and the Argument from Uncertainty." *Social Theory and Practice.* II:371–386.

Pym, Bridget. 1973. "The Making of a Successful Pressure Group." *British Journal of Sociology.* 24:448–461.

Radelet, Michael L. 1988. *Facing the Death Penalty: Essays on a Cruel and Unusual Punishment.* Philadelphia: Temple University Press.

Rankin, Joseph. 1979. "Changing Attitudes Toward Capital Punishment." *Social Forces.* 58:194–211.

Robinson, W. S. 1950. "Ecological Correlations and the Behavior of Individuals." *American Sociological Review.* 15:351–357.

Rothman, Barbara Katz. 1989. *Recreating Motherhood: Ideology and Technology in a Patriarchal Society.* New York: W. W. Norton and Co.

Sachdev, Paul, editor. 1985. *Perspectives on Abortion.* Metuchen, NJ: The Scarecrow Press.

Sarvis, Betty and Hyman Rodman. 1973. *The Abortion Controversy.* New York: Columbia University Press.

Stark, Rodney. 1987. "Decent Places: A Theory of the Ecology of Crime." *Criminology.* 25:893–909.

Straus, Murray A. 1985. "Social Stress in American States and Regions: An example of research using the State and Regional Indicators Archives." In Robert F. Allen (ed.). *Data Bases in the Humanities and Social Science.* Osprey, FL: Paradigm Press.

Straus, Murray A., Richard J. Gelles and Suzanne K. Steinmetz. 1980. *Behind Closed Doors.* New York: Doubleday Books.

Spangenberg, Robert L. and Elizabeth R. Walsh. 1989. "Capital Punishment or Life Imprisonment? Some Cost Considerations." *Loyola of Los Angeles Law Review.* 23:45–58.

Sumner, L. W. 1981. *Abortion and Moral Theory.* Princeton, NJ: Princeton University Press.

Tatalovich, Raymond and Byron W. Daynes. 1981. *The Politics of Abortion: A Study of Community Conflict in Public Policy Making.* New York: Praeger.

Thomas, Charles W. and Samuel C. Foster. 1975. "A Sociological Perspective on Public Support for Capital Punishment." *American Journal of Orthopsychiatry.* 45:641–657.

Tunnell, Kenneth D. 1992. *Choosing Crime: The Criminal Calculus of Property Offenders.* Chicago: Nelson Hall.

Tyler, Tom R. and Renee Weber. 1982. "Support for the Death Penalty; Instrumental Response to Crime, or Symbolic Attitude?" *Law and Society Review.* 17:21–45.

Vidmar, Neil and Dale T. Miller. 1980. "Social Psychological Processes Underlying Attitudes Toward Legal Punishment." *Law and Society Review.* 14:565–602.

Walbert, David F. and J. Douglas Butler, editors. 1973. *Abortion, Society, and the Law.* Cleveland: The Press of Case Western Reserve University.

Warr, Mark and Mark Stafford. 1984. "Public Goals of Punishment and Support for the Death Penalty." *Journal of Research on Crime and Delinquency.* 21:95–111.

Washington Post. 1990. "After Daughter's Death, Parents Campaign Against Abortion Consent Laws." August 8, p. C3.

Wilcox, Clyde. 1988. "Seeing the Connection: Religion and Politics in the Ohio Moral Majority." *Review of Religious Research.* 30:47–58.

Wilkerson, Isabel. 1991. "Michigan Judges' Views of Abortion are Berated." *New York Times.* May 3, p. A19

Personal AND Political: Violence Against Women and the Role of the State

> It is organized violence at the top which creates individual violence at the bottom.
>
> Emma Goldman

Many will find it surprising to discover a chapter defining violence against women as political crime. Historically, scholars have viewed violence against women as just one small part of the traditional "crime" problem, and a very insignificant part at that. Indeed, some harms were actually considered to be less "criminal" if women were victimized rather than men, despite the fact that women bruise and bleed just as easily as men do (Roberts Chapman, 1990; Stanko, 1985).[1] The popular conception of battering, rape, sexual harassment, and other forms of violence against women, is that they are "personal" problems, best resolved within the private sphere of home and family. As Koss (1990:374) states, "although most intimate violence qualifies as crime, a historical tradition that has condoned violence within the family has created strong forces toward secrecy that oppose disclosure of such incidents into the public record."

The central argument presented in this chapter is that the privatization and trivialization of violence against women is a highly political act, unrelated to the nature or seriousness of the harm. We argue that much violence against women can be characterized as political crime because of the critical and significant role the state plays in perpetuating the violence. More specifically, we argue that the state engages in political crime when it fails to define widespread and systematic harm against women as illegal, when it neglects to enforce laws that do provide some measure of protection to women, and when it provides structural support for institutional practices that clearly harm women.

Violence Against Women as Political Crime

Although early work on political crime reserved the term for action taken by dissenters against the state (Turk, 1982), our contention that violence against women is a form of political crime fits squarely within a growing literature that argues that political crime refers not only to crimes committed *against* the state, but also to crimes committed *by* the state (Barak, 1991; Michalowski, 1985). Central to this broader understanding of political crime is a recognition that individuals within the state, or the state itself, may commit socially injurious actions in order "to enhance or preserve political institutions and economic organizations" within society (Michalowski, 1985:379). It is our contention that the state's participation in perpetuating violence against women reflects the pivotal position that patriarchy plays in organizing social, economic, and political life in the United States.

There are two ways that the state fosters violence against women. First, the state, at times, engages in *crimes of commission*, in which the state or representatives of the state directly participate in violence against women, in violation of the law. Violence against women committed by individuals while performing their official state functions would fall into this category. This includes, for example, sexual assaults committed by police officers or correctional officials while women are in state custody, as well as rapes of indigenous women during state-supported wars and conflicts.

However, within the United States much violence against women is a result of state *crimes of omission*; a large proportion of such violence is directly related to the state's active choice not to intervene or limit serious harms if they are directed primarily toward women. This includes the failure to create law to address known harms, as well as the differential application of existing laws to harms committed against women. In addition, we consider it a crime of omission for the state to permit a culture of violence to permeate society with disproportionately adverse consequences for certain segments of the population. Such a climate is particularly dangerous when it is coupled with the structural vulnerability to violence that occurs when people live under conditions of poverty. We argue that many of the structural and institutional relations that constitute the state perpetuate a climate and ideology that condones violence: violence against nations (see, e.g., Chomsky, 1988), violence against subcultures (see, e.g., Caulfield, 1991), and, importantly, violence against women.

In order to present our argument, we divide the chapter into three parts. First, we present an overview of harms against women, emphasizing the public and political implications of violence against women. Second, we explore the structural dynamics of harms against women, placing emphasis on the role of the state in perpetuating violence against women. Lastly, we discuss the critical importance of identifying the state's failure to protect women as "political crime."

Violence Against Women: Personal AND Political

The experience of violence is very personal. Violence affects our emotions, our families, our work, our bodies—it affects our lives. The privatization of women's lives, and women's relative lack of influence in the public sphere, heightens women's perceptions that violence directed toward them is a personal problem. In this section we argue that violence against women is not simply a personal problem, but is instead a social problem of staggering proportions. More importantly, we argue that it is a political problem that reflects the power of patriarchy within our society.

Daly (1973) and Caputi (1989) both use the term "gynocide" to refer to the range and extensiveness of systematic violence against women by men. Throughout history, violence against women has taken many forms, including rape, bride-burning, female circumcision, inheritance systems, forced prostitution, sexual slavery, homicide, sexual harassment, unequal pay, lack of access to work, and sexual violence, which occurs both inside and outside of the family structure (Omvedt, 1986; Roberts Chapman, 1990). However, much violence against women is not, strictly speaking, "crime" since an act is not a crime unless there is a law specifically forbidding the behavior (Cole, 1989; Michalowski, 1985). Yet, to analyze only those harms that have been legislated against is to overlook the political nature of the process by which some behaviors are defined as crime while other serious harms are not.

We recognize that law is not a mere reflection of the interests of the entire society; law is a reflection of the struggle among various groups, and some groups fare much better in the struggle to have their interests reflected in the law than do others (Chambliss and Seidman, 1982). Thus, our strategy will be to first analyze the nature of harm against women, and then use that information to investigate the extent to which law responds (or fails to respond) to the harm. In order to highlight the value of this approach for understanding violence against women, we offer a brief critique of official definitions of violence against women. We then describe the range of harms that women experience within our society.

In the United States, our understanding of violence against women is largely shaped by official definitions of the problem and by statistics generated by the state. But, as others have pointed out (Koss, 1990), the procedures for both defining harms and gathering information about them are inherently biased. Although women make up over 50 percent of the adult population in the United States, their representation within legislative and judicial bodies is marginal. Women constitute only 6 percent of the United States Congress (Welch et al., 1992), 8 percent of all federal judges, and only 4 percent of all state trial judges (Feinman, 1986). As Price and Sokoloff (1982:12) point out:

Women, racial/ethnic minorities, the poor, and working-class
people rarely benefit from the law. A brief look at which groups
of people make laws will demonstrate the truth of this
unfortunate reality. On the surface, the facts are clear: rich white
men are most influential in creating laws.

Although it is not clear that women's entry into politics would
guarantee the end of patriarchy, it is fair to assume that some laws
might better represent women's interests.

Even more important in understanding the biases against
women within the law is the fact that law developed explicitly to
protect privilege and power in society (Michalowski, 1985; Price
and Sokoloff, 1982). Little wonder, then, that laws do not reflect
the harms women are most likely to experience, or that agencies of
the state feel such little compulsion to enforce the laws that do exist
for protecting women.

Bias also exists within the official data-gathering process. The
primary data source on criminal behavior, the Federal Bureau of
Investigation's Uniform Crime Reports, is unable to provide us
with a complete picture of the harms that women experience.
According to Koss (1990:374): "Unfortunately, these data are of
limited value to assess the scope of violence against women because
the crimes that were reported to police were likely to have differed
in important ways from the crimes that were hidden." Even the
National Crime Survey, which is supposed to render a truer picture
of crime, falls short when it comes to measuring the extent of
violence against women. "The wording of the crime-screening
questions operationalized street violence rather than the situations
that would be typical of intimate violence. No questions whatsoever
were included to identify child abuse, child sexual abuse, domestic
violence, or elder abuse" (Koss, 1990:375). Thus, the state protects
patriarchy, and itself, from criticism by failing to gather data that
would reveal the true extent of the problem.

Given the weaknesses of official definitions and statistics on
violence against women, how, then, are we to assess the nature and
extent of the problem? We believe that several indicators can be
combined with official data to inform us about the harms that

women experience. First, we can follow the advice given to us by those who work with survivors of violence and pay more attention to what women say about their experiences, rather than rely upon imposed conceptions of harm. To understand violence against women, "we need to know how oppression occurs where it occurs: in the context of our differing everyday experiences" (Stanley and Wise, 1983:173). Many people still contend that no violence has occurred if victims aren't bleeding (witness former heavyweight champion and convicted rapist Mike Tyson's recent comments that he didn't hurt anybody since there were no broken bones and no black eyes). However, what feminists, and many other women have learned, is that violence is not measured by the number of broken bones and lost teeth. The manifestations of violence in our society are endless, and open to interpretation, and women's conception of what constitutes violence may be quite different than men's.

It is true that the personal nature of violence is highlighted by the individual stories that women tell about the harm that they have suffered. However, the political nature of violence is not revealed until we aggregate those stories into a single narrative that eloquently describes the terror that women in our society live with, and reveals the statistics that lend support to women's fears.

Some scholars have commented on the fact that women have a much greater fear of violence than do men (Sheley, 1985; Stanko, 1985). We believe that understanding this fear reveals much about the pervasiveness of violence against women in our society. It is our contention that women's disproportionate fear of violence stems from two primary sources. The first is the reality that the violence women face is most likely to occur at home and at the hands of someone they know intimately. In other words, women's risk of violence is much more closely linked to their private, everyday lives. Current statistics on violence against women (which are likely to be quite conservative since they are drawn from the official sources described previously) indicate that a "majority of female assault victims knew their assailants" (Senna and Seigel, 1990:60). Similarly, most rapes are committed by acquaintances, rather than by strangers (Herman 1989; Russell, 1984).

The pervasiveness of violence also leads to widespread fear. Recent research indicates that "a woman is probably less safe from rape in this country than she is in any developed nation. The United States has one of the highest rape rates in the world" (Herman, 1989:23). Official statistics indicated that the U.S. had 35.7 rapes per 100,000 people; victimization surveys suggest that as many as 44 percent of all women report at least one completed or attempted rape (Russell, 1984). Some studies have specifically mentioned women's fear of rape as the primary source of women's disproportionate fear of crime (Caringella-MacDonald and Humphries, 1991; Hindelang, 1978). In addition, as Sheffield (1989:10) points out, "estimates that 50 percent of American wives are battered are not uncommon in the literature." Looked at from another angle, evidence suggests that one woman is battered approximately every 18 seconds in this country (Gillespie, 1989). Even more striking is the research that suggests that approximately one-fifth to one-third of all women have been victimized by incest (Stanko, 1985). Because incest happens before girls leave home to enter the public world, they learn early on to privatize their experiences, and to associate them with "normal" human relationships. However, the sheer magnitude of these harms offers persuasive evidence that violence against women is systemic, and it suggests that violence is integrally related to the political fabric of our society.

A second source of women's fear about crime is their perception of the fact that women are not protected from violence by the state. Although we will explore this point in greater detail below, it is important to note that many women seem to be as fearful of the criminal justice system and other state agencies as they are of their assailant. We believe that women's fear of "secondary victimization" at the hands of the system is one indicator that state responses to violence are highly politicized.

Although our focus here is primarily on interpersonal violence against women, we would be remiss if we did not note the tremendous harm perpetuated against women by state-sanctioned institutional violence in the United States. It is clear that the state's fiscal priorities are male-centered and biased toward those who already have privilege. The recent literature on the "feminization of poverty" (Gimenez, 1990) makes it clear that institutional violence—the violence that results from poverty, hunger and malnutrition, inadequate housing, and lack of health care—is more harmful than any of the harm committed in interpersonal altercations. In addition, because of women's relationship to the means of production, poverty affects them to a greater extent than it effects men (Gimenez, 1990). In particular, it makes women more vulnerable to violence because of their "lower social, economic, and legal status" (Roberts Chapman, 1990:57).

Perhaps the best example of the avoidable institutional violence that results from the privileging of male aspirations over female needs is the tremendous imbalance in the federal budget between social programs and the military. As Enloe (1983:207) tells us, "there are those people, largely women, who are most hurt when social programs . . . are cut back in order to satisfy the alleged needs of the military and its industrial supplies." Although militarization is touted as a necessary evil that protects us all, the cost of militarization is borne on the backs of women and children. As Virginia Woolf noted in 1938:

> If you insist upon fighting to protect me, or "our" country, let it be understood, soberly and rationally between us, that you are fighting to procure benefits which I have not shared and probably will not share; but not to gratify my instincts, or to protect either myself or my country. In fact, as a woman, I have no country. As a woman, I want no country. As a woman, my country is the whole world.

The choice to finance military hardware rather than daycare centers, shelters, and poverty reduction programs, is a political decision with personal and disproportionate consequences for the lives of women.

In sum, in order to ask the question, "How much violence is there in women's lives?" we must go beyond state-constructed definitions of violence. Instead, we argue that scholars must first explore the nature of the harm, in all of its manifestations, outside of the confines of patriarchal law (see the "Prologue" in this edition). Our brief investigation here suggests that violence against women encompasses a broad range of behaviors, behaviors that do not necessarily fit into state-constructed definitions of victimization. Indeed, in our analysis, the state itself is often a perpetrator of violence against women. Explaining why and how this is so is the substance of the next section.

Structural Dynamics: The Role of the State

To effectively argue that violence against women constitutes political crime, we must establish two conditions. First, we must explain motive: *why* the state fails to protect women. Second, we must explain method: *how* the state itself is responsible for harms against women. We will begin by explaining the motivation for state-supported violence against women.

Violence against women, as we know, is not simply a function of individual pathology. In its myriad forms, violence against women is rooted in the social structure. Violence against women is a manifestation of patriarchy. As Kate Millett noted, all avenues to power in the United States are in the hands of males. "Our society . . . is a patriarchy. The fact is evident at once if we recall that the military, industry, technology, universities, science, political offices, finances—in short, every avenue of power within the society, including the coercive force of the police, is in male hands" (Millett, 1970:25). Importantly, patriarchy has moved beyond any notion of kinship ties so that "men now use the state— its bureaucracies, its laws—to exert male superiority and female inferiority" (Elster, 1981:14).

The protection of male privilege and power within society takes many forms, but perhaps the most common is the use of "sexual terrorism" to keep women in their place (Sheffield, 1984). As Sheffield (1984:3) writes, "violence and the threat of violence against females represent the need of patriarchy to deny that woman's body is her own property and that no one should have access to it without her consent. Violence and its corollary, fear, serve to terrorize females and to maintain the patriarchal definition of a woman's place."

Contrary to popular perceptions that violence against women is "personal," the pervasiveness of the problem reveals the systemic and political character of the violence. This point has already been noted by several scholars. As Caputi notes, when you have sexually motivated murders, you have murders "rooted in a system of male supremacy in the same way that lynching is based in white supremacy. Such murder is, in short, a form of patriarchal terrorism" (1989:438). Caputi (1989:439) goes on to add that, "rape [too] is a direct expression of sexual politics, a ritual enactment of male domination, a form of terror that functions to maintain the status quo" (on this latter issue, see also Brownmiller, 1975; Griffin, 1971; and Russell, 1975). In a similar vein, Caputi and Russell (1990:34) discuss "femicide," what they refer to as "the murders of women by men motivated by hatred, contempt, pleasure, or a sense of ownership of women." As they aptly point out, "Most people understand that lynchings and pogroms are motivated by political objectives: preserving white and gentile supremacy. Similarly, the aim of violence against women— conscious or not—is to preserve male supremacy" (Caputi and Russell, 1990:34).

As Messerschmidt (1986:34) notes, "Patriarchal rule is maintained not only by the family and the economic system, but also by the state and ideological institutions of the 'superstructure.' Since males control the state, behaviors that tend to call into question patriarchy are repressed." Implicitly, Messerschmidt suggests that the state itself acts to promote patriarchy and to limit challenges to it posed by "uppity" women. "Society is outraged when a woman challenges . . . these assumptions, refuses to take the blame, refuses to be a helpless victim but instead picks up a weapon and defends herself" (Gillespie, 1989:12).

The state has at its disposal myriad ways to support and engage in violence against women. It is not our claim that the state supports patriarchy in a purely instrumentalist way (though in particular circumstances that may occur), but rather that there is a structural relationship between the state and patriarchy that limits the state's willingness to act in ways that might threaten the power of men in society or strengthen the power of women. Here, we describe two methods that the state uses to support violence against women. We believe that these actions constitute "political crime."

First, the state engages in political crime when it fails to extend the protections of law and the criminal justice system to individuals on the basis of their sex. As Hanmer (1990:445) writes: "While a rapist is an individual man, the state is composed largely of men, particularly at the top, operating a criminal justice system that does not protect women."

The state's failure to protect women begins with its failure to create laws that are sensitive to women's experience of violence and take women's experiences as seriously as men's. Writing about women who have killed their abusive partners in self-defense, Gillespie (1989:49) traces the history of law regarding self-defense. She notes that:

> As the American law developed, the only two situations in which a self-defense plea was felt to be appropriate (by male judges and male legislators) were still the ancient ones in which men most frequently found themselves: the sudden attack by a stranger and the fight between equals that gets out of hand. The law of self-defense may have been becoming increasingly stricter and more 'civilized,' but it was not in any way becoming more responsive to the circumstances faced by women who needed to defend themselves against violent husbands or lovers.

Another example of the failure of law to guarantee the safety of women is the fact that "the state definition of rape does not include *all* rapes that occur through the threat or actual use of physical violence" (Messerschmidt, 1986:131). Instead, historically, and in many states today, spousal rape is excluded from the law. Thus, a married woman's relationship to a man defines her ability to be legally raped, rather than the nature of the harm or its frequency. Yet, research indicates that "marital rape may be the most common form of sexual assault: more than two times as many of the women interviewed (in one study) had been raped by husbands as had been raped by strangers" (Herman, 1989:27). Research also suggests that marital rape "frequently involves *more* serious physical injury and psychological trauma than do stranger rapes" (Herman, 1989:27).

Although there are many more examples that could be cited to illustrate the failure of the state to extend the protection of law to women, one of the most grievous is the failure of the United States to support international efforts to halt violence against women. Although women are covered under the Universal Declaration of Human Rights, which the United States has signed, there are no specific provisions that address violence against women. In response to the failure of the Declaration to outline and protect abuses that are gender-based, the Convention on the Elimination of All Forms of Discrimination Against Women was drafted. The Convention "forbids discrimination in a number of specified areas, including political and public life, employment, education, health, marriage, and family. Although it does not include a specific provision on violence, several provisions in effect provide sanctions for violence directed at women" (Roberts Chapman, 1990:58). Roberts Chapman (1990:58) further states, "one hundred and one countries have ratified this U.N. convention; the United States is not among them." We believe that the failure of the U.S. to support efforts to protect the safety of all peoples—including women—is a form of political crime.

Of course, "just having 'good' laws on the books does not, in and of itself, guarantee a solution. Laws must be properly enforced throughout the criminal justice and judicial systems" (Roberts Chapman, 1990:59) Individual women often perceive the handling of their case by the police or court officials to be problematic, but many scholars have concluded that the inattention given to women who have been victimized by violence is so extensive that we need to consider it the ordinary state response to female victimization (Roberts Chapman, 1990; Wheeler, 1985). Wheeler (1985) notes that when formal structures, such as those designed to protect women, are routinely breached, it amounts to an informal institutionalization of the practices—practices such as rape, battering, and sexual harassment. As Browne (1987) mentions, even though there have been a number of improvements in the criminal justice system, especially regarding battering, "Police officers still routinely classify assaults between partners as misdemeanors, rather than as criminal offenses, and there is some evidence that they do not respond to the calls of a female victim as readily as calls made by a third party" (Browne, 1987:168–169). In addition, police may express their expectation that the case will not be prosecuted, thus dissuading the victim from initiating charges (Browne, 1987). This despite the fact that a large percentage of women request that their abuser be arrested, and few women refuse to go forward with a formal complaint once it has been filed (Stanko, 1985).

Historically, and currently, in many jurisdictions, police practices have stressed nonintervention in "family problems," thus legitimating violence against women in their homes. Yet, as we have already noted, the data suggest that for women, the family is a violent institution. However, since the state, especially state agencies and institutions, maintain that the American family is sacred, there is what Gelles termed a "perceptual blackout of the violence that goes on in 'normal' families" (Koss, 1990:375). The state's failure to protect women from violence may actually multiply the injuries that women experience by suggesting to men that they have a license to harm women. "Repeated violent victimizations render women less skilled at self-protection, less sure of their own worth and personal boundaries, and more apt to accept victimization as a part of being female" (Koss, 1990:376). It is our contention that the state's failure to enforce laws that could protect women from violence is a crime of omission and a form of political crime.

The second form of political crime engaged in by the state is the state's support of a culture of violence toward women. This culture of violence operates at both an institutional and an ideological level. The state supports violence against women by failing to regulate industries that market violence against women as a commodity and by providing support to various institutions that foster ideologies that justify the victimization of women in our society.

The state's failure to effectively regulate pornography promotes a culture of violence in society.[2] As Dworkin (1981:15, 16, 25) writes: ". . . power is the capacity to terrorize . . . the acts of terror run the gamut from rape to battery to sexual abuse of children to war . . . there is the legend of terror, and this legend is cultivated by men with sublime attention . . . the degradation of the female is the means of achieving this power" (as cited in Wheeler, 1985). Much pornography reflects a sexist ideology that contributes to violence against women by making the degradation and injury of women seem less reprehensible to people. Ideologically, much pornography also encourages acts of sexual hostility toward women. As Malamuth (1985) notes, antisocial effects are shown to result from nonsexual portrayals of violence in the mass media. It is likely that sexual depiction of aggression will have a similar effect, if not an even more dangerous effect on women. As Malamuth (1985:395) states: "To the extent that the media presents images of women as responding favorably to male aggression, such images may easily come to people's minds and affect their beliefs, attitudes, and behavior." Importantly, some activists seek to have violent pornography viewed not in terms of a First Amendment issue, but as a violation of the civil rights of women. The state's failure to respond to the evidence that links violent pornography with violence against women is an omission that jeopardizes the lives of women.

As we have already seen, state responses (or failures to respond) to violence, profoundly shape the safety that women experience in our society. They also promote "ideologies which assume that most rapes are really seduction, that marital rape cannot happen, or that the power held by a male employer is not a relevant part of a situation in which he may be sexually suggestive to his female employee" (Wheeler, 1985:375).

Such ideologies are also fostered when the state provides support for institutions in society that perpetuate such myths, and which promote a culture of violence that mobilizes and empowers men to victimize women. Several institutional spheres are of particular concern. First is the central place of the military within U.S. society. In order to foster citizen preparedness for armed conflict, the state tacitly supports violence and a war mentality in schools and in popular culture. Unfortunately, the processes and ideologies that justify violence during war also tend to justify violence in interpersonal relationships. As Burk (1991:4) writes:

> There are two reasons why the United States went to war in the Persian Gulf. They are the same two reasons why women are battered and raped: men in our culture are socialized to violence, and they are also in control of society and its institutions. Both conditions insure that men will continue to wage war, and also insure that men will continue to do violence against women.

The war mentality distorts the relationship between violence and humanity. As Burk implies, the message from war is that you can "kick ass" and still maintain a civilized existence. So, externally, you can be civilized, a good worker, a good provider, and so on, while at home (and elsewhere) you beat your wife or molest your children. Mead (as cited in Gioseffi, 1988) stresses that the need for men to "prove themselves" through organized killing is a function of how our society defines manliness.

Another sphere of state support for violence against women is the media. The state's failure to regulate violence in the media is unparalleled relative to other Western countries, and creates a climate of tolerance for violence generally, and violence against women, specifically (Miedzian, 1990). Indeed, "no country comes near us with respect to TV violence" (Miedzian, 1990:209), and, importantly, according to a report by the National Institute of Mental Health, "sex is commonly linked with violence. Just those stereotypes that tend to increase male violence are perpetuated. Males are often powerful, dominant, and violent" (Miedzian, 1990:213–214).

Several authors have examined U.S. culture in terms of children's television (war cartoons), Nintendo video games (where 80 percent of the games are violent), and films (Burk, 1991;

Miedzian, 1991).[3] Television violence is so pervasive, that many adults and children do not even recognize its existence. Although many adults try to limit children's viewing to children's programming, recent research indicates that "on all three networks children's weekend programs have long been and continue to be three to six times more violent than evening prime-time programs" (Miedzian, 1991). Slasher films are perhaps the most gruesome depictions of violence against women, and some commentators have noted that youth appear to be the primary audience attending such films. One media watch group, the National Coalition on Television Violence, reports in its newsletter that "it is now a standard part of American culture to view numerous extremely graphic and brutal horror films before the age of 12" (Miedzian, 1990:241). We avidly regulate the ability of youth to see pornographic films, but do little to prevent them from watching graphic depictions of violence in the media.

Burk maintains that the media, and other forces in society, foster the notion that female characteristics and traits are signs of weakness, and teach boys to systematically devalue women. As she notes, "their macho fantasy and need for self-validation through force is played out against those who are physically and politically weaker, usually women" (1991:4). One recent study of sixth-through ninth-grade children put the consequences of this socialization for violence in sharp relief. It indicated that:

> Most of the students surveyed accepted sexually assaultive behavior as normal . . . sixty-five percent of the boys and 57 percent of the girls in junior high schools said it is acceptable for a man to force a woman to have sex if they have been dating for more than six months. Eighty-seven percent of the boys and 79 percent of the girls approved of rape if the couple were married (Herman, 1989).

Although some would argue that state regulation of the media violates First Amendment privileges, Meidzian (1990:283–284) makes the important point that "if there exists a *real* threat to our First Amendment rights, I suspect it lies in the concentration of the means of communication in powerful and wealthy hands, not in the regulation of the mass media in order to protect our children from being exposed to antisocial, violent messages from the earliest age." We concur with this conclusion, and argue that the state's failure to regulate or exercise effective oversight over the media is a crime of omission that leads to the further victimization of women in our society.

Conclusion

One would think that since violence against women is such a daily part of life in the United States, it would be a subject of great discussion. However, as Griffin noted in 1971, "though rape and the fear of rape are a daily part of every woman's consciousness, the subject is so rarely discussed by that unofficial staff of male intellectuals . . . that one begins to suspect a conspiracy of silence" (1971:27). We have argued in this chapter that there *is* a conspiracy of silence around violence against women, and the silence benefits the state in fundamental ways.

The failure of the state to adequately protect women against violence is unrelated to the nature of the harm. We have provided overwhelming evidence that the harms women suffer are severe, and that the violence against them is widespread; so widespread, that the official wisdom is often to tolerate violence as "the rightful consequences of being female" (Roberts Chapman, 1990:54).

Instead, we have argued that the state fails to protect women from violence because the state benefits from the subjugation of women. Patriarchy serves the interests of those in power, and keeping women "in their place" through sexual terrorism limits the challenges that can be posed to that power. We have argued that the state engages in political crime when it fails to protect women through the state mechanisms of law and the criminal justice system. We have also argued that the state engages in political crime when it provides structural support, and/or fails to regulate institutions that perpetuate a culture of violence that legitimates harms perpetrated against women. Although there are other institutions that we might have targeted, we have specifically focused on the pornography industry, the military, and the media as violence-producing institutions that the state directly supports, and whose actions the state sanctions.

Why call violence against women "political crime?" Because it accurately reflects both the character of the state's behavior and the political situation of women in this country. The state engages in crimes of commission, and more commonly, crimes of omission, both of which regularly endanger the lives of women. As Barak (1991:4) points out:

> Often, crimes by the state are either ignored totally or defended totally. Either way, the political situation for state-crime victims is significantly more precarious than the political situation for victims of traditional street or suite crime. Because the victims of state criminality typically lack any means of judicial redress, they usually have very little, if any, political recourse against the perpetrators of their abuse.

To name violence against women a form of political crime is to highlight the relations of power between the state and women, and to begin to understand the tremendous pressure that exists for women to privatize their harm and see it only as a "personal problem."

Identifying violence against women as a form of political crime also suggests different strategies for reducing violence. First, strategies must be directed at the elimination of patriarchy, in all of its forms, but especially within the state. Second, we must work to reduce or eliminate structural and institutional inducements to violence, particularly those that are state-sponsored or state-supported. Third, we must continue to make every effort to provide individuals with the skills and resources necessary to reduce interpersonal violence in their daily lives. And, finally, we must find ways of doing all of these things simultaneously. Tifft and Markham (1991:139) said this quite eloquently when they wrote that:

If we wish to stop violence, we will have to explore more fully the similarities and linkages, both between and within spheres of violent actions. We will have to become more willing to believe that parents inflict atrocities on their children; that intimates inflict atrocities on their partners; and that elite decision-makers inflict atrocities on their constituents and subjects. We will have to reject the cultural assumption which pairs wisdom, just action, and benevolence with parental, interpersonal, organizational, corporate, and state power.

In writing this chapter, we wish to encourage scholars, practitioners, and victims to recognize that violence against women is both personal AND political, and to stimulate the development of solutions that take into account both of these realities.

NOTES

1. A classic example is provided by Stanko in her discussion of murder. Men who kill women are frequently able to receive leniency because "unfaithful or nagging women provoke men's emotions or some women are just in the way of the husband's stress and frustration" (Stanko, 1985:88). This same defense, and the subsequent leniency it yields, is almost unheard of for women.

2. When we use the term "pornography," we wish to excude erotica. Evidence suggests that mutual, consensual, and loving images do not perpetuate sexism and violence in our society (Gubar and Hoff, 1989).

3. For additional insight on television, see Pfohl (1990), especially his discussion of the depiction of a woman being raped in the form of "information."

REFERENCES

Barak, Gregg (ed.). 1991. *Crimes by the Capitalist State: An Introduction to State Criminality.* Albany: State University of New York Press.

Browne, Angela. 1987. *When Battered Women Kill.* New York: The Free Press.

Brownmiller, Susan. 1975. *Against Our Will: Men, Women, and Rape.* New York: Simon and Schuster.

Burk, Martha. 1991. "Common Patriarchy: War and Violence Against Women." *National NOW Times*, *23*(3): 4.

Caputi, Jane. 1989. The Sexual Politics of Murder. *Gender & Society*, *3*(4): 437–456.

Caputi, Jane and Diana E. H. Russell. 1990. "'Femicide:' Speaking the Unspeakable." *Ms.*, *1*(September/October): 34–37.

Caringella-MacDonald, Susan and Drew Humphries. 1991. "Sexual Assault, Women, and the Community: Organizing to Prevent Sexual Violence." Pp. 98–113 in Harold E. Pepinsky and Richard Quinney (eds.) *Criminology as Peacemaking.* Bloomington: Indiana University Press.

Caulfield, Susan L. 1991. "The Perpetuation of Violence through Criminological Theory: The Ideological Role of Subculture Theory." Pp. 228–238 in Pepinsky, Harold E. and Richard Quinney (eds.) *Criminology as Peacemaking.* Bloomington: Indiana University Press.

Chambliss, William and Robert Seidman. 1982. *Law, Order and Power.* Reading, Mass.: Addison-Wesley.

Chomsky, Noam. 1988. *The Culture of Terrorism.* Boston: South End Press.

Cole, George F. 1989. *The American System of Criminal Justice.* (Fifth edition.) Pacific Grove, Calif.: Brooks/Cole.

Daly, Mary. 1973. *Beyond God the Father: Toward a Philosophy of Women's Liberation.* Boston: Beacon Press.

Elster, Ellen. 1981. "Patriarchy." In Chapkis, Wendy (ed.) *Loaded Questions: Women in the Military.* Amsterdam: Transnational Institute.

Enloe, Cynthia. 1983. *Does Khaki Become You? The Militarization of Women's Lives.* Boston: South End Press.

Feinman, Clarice. 1986. *Women in the Criminal Justice System.* New York: Praeger.

Gillespie, Cynthia K. 1989. *Justifiable Homicide: Battered Women, Self-defense, and the Law.* Columbus: Ohio State University Press.

Gimenez, Martha E. 1990. "The Feminization of Poverty: Myth or Reality?" *Social Justice*, *17*(3):43–69.

Gioseffi, Daniela (ed.). 1988. *Women on War: Essential Voices for the Nuclear Age.* New York: Touchstone Books.

Griffin, Susan. 1971. "Rape: The All-American Crime." *Ramparts,* 26–35.

Gubar, Susan and Joan Hoff. 1989. "Mitigating the Effects of Violent Pornography." Pp. 218–239 in Gubar, Susan and Joan Hoff (eds.) *For Adult Users Only: The Dilemma of Violent Pornography.* Bloomington: Indiana University Press.

Hanmer, Jalna. 1990. "Men, Power, and the Exploitation of Women." *Women's Studies International Forum, 13*(5): 443–456.

Herman, Dianne F. 1989. "The Rape Culture." Pp. 20–44 in Jo Freeman (ed.), *Women.* Mountain View, Calif.: Mayfield Publishing.

Hindelang, Michael, Michael Gottfredson, and James Garafalo. 1978. *Victims of Personal Crime: An Empirical Foundation for a Theory of Personal Victimization.* Cambridge, Mass.: Ballinger.

Koss, Mary P. 1990. "The Women's Mental Health Research Agenda: Violence against Women." *American Psychologist, 45*(3): 374–380.

Malamuth, Neil M. 1985 "The Mass Media and Aggression against Women: Research Findings and Prevention." In Burgess, A.W. (ed.) *Rape and Sexual Assault: A Research Handbook.* New York: Garland Publishing.

Messerschmidt, James. 1986. *Capitalism, Patriarchy, and Crime: Toward a Socialist Feminist Criminology.* Totowa, N.J.: Rowman and Littlefield.

Michalowski, Raymond J. 1985. *Order, Law, and Crime: An Introduction to Criminology.* New York: Random House.

Miedzian, Myriam. 1991. *Boys Will Be Boys: Breaking the Link between Masculinity and Violence.* New York: Doubleday.

Millett, Kate. 1970. *Sexual Politics.* New York: Doubleday.

Omvedt, Gail. 1986. "'Patriarchy:' The Analysis of Women's Oppression." *The Insurgent Sociologist, 13*(3): 30–50.

Pfohl, Stephen. 1990. "Welcome to the PARASITE CAFE: Postmodernity as a Social Problem." *Social Problems, 37*(4):421–442.

Price, Barbara R. and Natalie J. Sokoloff (eds.). 1982. *The Criminal Justice System and Women: Women Offenders, Victims, Workers.* New York: Clark Boardman.

Roberts Chapman, Jane. 1990. "Violence against Women as a Violation of Human Rights." *Social Justice 17*(2):54–70.

Russell, Diane E. H. 1984. *Sexual Exploitation.* Beverly Hills: Sage.

———. 1975. *The Politics of Rape: The Victim's Perspective.* New York: Stein and Day.

Senna, Joseph J. and Larry J. Siegel 1990. *Introduction to Criminal Justice.* New York: West Publishing.

Sheffield, Carole J. 1989. "Sexual Terrorism." Pp. 3–19 in Jo Freeman (ed.) *Women.* Mountain View, Calif.: Mayfield Publishing.

Sheley, Joseph F. 1985. *America's Crime Problem: An Introduction to Criminology.* Belmont, Calif.: Wadsworth Publishing.

Stanko, Elizabeth. 1985. *Intimate Intrusions: Women's Experience of Male Violence.* Boston: Unwin Hyman.

Stanley, Liz and Sue Wise. 1983. *Breaking Out: Feminist Consciousness and Feminist Research.* London: Routledge and Kegan Paul.

Tifft, Larry and Lyn Markham. 1991. "Battering Women and Battering Central Americans: A Peacemaking Synthesis." Pp. 114–153 in Pepinsky, Harold E., and Richard Quinney (eds.) *Criminology as Peacemaking.* Bloomington: Indiana University Press.

Turk, Austin T. 1982. *Political Criminality: The Defiance and Defense of Authority.* Beverly Hills: Sage.

Welch, Susan, John Gruhl, Michael Steinman, and John Comer. 1992. *American Government.* New York: West Publishing.

Wheeler, Hollis. 1985. "Pornography and Rape: A Feminist Perspective." In Burgess, A.W. (ed.) *Rape and Sexual Assault: A Research Handbook.* New York: Garland Publishing.

Woolf, Virginia. 1938. *Three Guineas.* New York: Harcourt, Brace and Company.

JEFFREY IAN ROSS

Research on Contemporary Oppositional Political Terrorism in the United States: Merits, Drawbacks and Suggestions for Improvement

Introduction

Espionage, rebellion, sedition, treason, and terrorism are traditionally recognized as the more common political crimes against the state. By far the greatest number of documented incidents of political crime in the United States fall under the rubric of oppositional political terrorism.[1] Terrorism has existed throughout the history of the United States, being most prominent during the 1960s and 1970s. The emergence of this phenomenon gave rise to a rapid production of literature until the late 1980s. The incidence of oppositional terrorism has waned since then, and so has the amount of research on this subject.[2]

Whether the current lull in both its incidence and research activities is transitory or long-standing, oppositional terrorism will remain an important policy concern for federal, state and local law enforcement, and for national security agencies. As a social phenomenon it will continue to interest the media as well. Depending on domestic and international circumstances, which may not only be unpredictable, but also poorly monitored, terrorism can increase in intensity, scope, and frequency. In a proactive fashion, the literature produced on contemporary terrorism in America is analyzed in terms of its merits and drawbacks so as to suggest possible methods to guide future research.

In general, and following from Schmid's conceptualization (1983), terrorism is defined as a method of combat in which random or symbolic victims are targets of violence. Through previous use of violence or the credible threat of violence, other members of that group or class are put in a state of chronic fear. The victimization of the target is considered extranormal by most observers, which, in turn, creates an audience beyond the target of terror. The purpose of terrorism is either to immobilize the target of terror in order to produce disorientation and/or compliance, or to mobilize secondary targets of demands (e.g., government) or targets of attention (e.g., public opinion) (p. 100).

This definition has some advantages: it includes acts of terrorism by governments; by oppositions; and by international movements, and it helps to distinguish the action of one individual from that of the group in whose name it is carried out. That is, a person who commits a terrorist action is considered a terrorist but people like him/her who are from the same group (race, class, nation, etc.) are not perceived to be terrorists unless they engage in terrorist tactics.

With four qualifications, this conceptualization of terrorism suits present purposes. First, not all the five elements of the definition (i.e., method of combat, etc.) must exist for an action or campaign to be labeled terrorism.[3] Second, while terrorism sometimes appears random in its targeting, it may be actually selective (e.g., against particular races, classes, religious groups, etc.).[4] Third, violent attacks on symbolic nonhuman targets (e.g., statues, buildings, etc.) which meet the definitional criteria are also considered acts of terrorism.[5] And, fourth, only acts that have a declared political motive can justifiably be included.[6] Conversely, those events that are mainly "criminal" in nature (e.g., extortion) or committed by psychologically "abnormal" people and are not caused by political motives should be rejected. While definitions vary this one should suffice for our needs.

Literature Review

Introduction

Information on terrorism occurring in the United States is located in daily newspapers, popular magazines, private security trade journals, mercenary/soldier-of-fortune magazines, academic journals, private consultant reports, government documents and publications, chapters in edited books on terrorism, chapters in introductory texts on terrorism for the criminology/criminal justice and political science market, and books on American-based organizations that have engaged in terrorism. These sources vary in type and depth of coverage, and quality of analysis. Upon examining the academic literature, in particular, one is struck by the number of gains as well as the drawbacks of certain avenues of investigation in this area of research.

In general, the literature on oppositional terrorism in the United States seems copious and equally balanced among the different ideological bases of terrorism; scholars have examined both left-wing and right-wing groups and organizations with relatively equal interest. This may reflect the historical pattern of this type of activity; the majority of oppositional terrorism events emanated from the left during the 1960s and lasted until the mid-1970s. Since then until now, however, right-wing organizations have dominated the scene. This merit aside, upon closer examination, the literature is also riddled with many problems.[7]

Review of Drawbacks

The literature on terrorism occurring in the United States suffers from a series of difficulties, many of which can be categorized under definitional and conceptual, ideological, theoretical, and methodological problems. As the reader can appreciate, some of these drawbacks have been fundamental stepping-stones in research. They are now drawbacks because in many respects we have not transcended them.

Definitional and Conceptual Problems

The literature on terrorism in the United States is plagued with the problems of lack of consistent definition, overinclusivity, and neglect of state-sponsored incidents. Initially, the literature suffers from lack of a consistent definition. According to White (1991:163),

> no definition or approach to American terrorism is generally accepted. The lack of a social or legal definition creates problems. . . . American police and security agencies literally do not know what terrorism is. . . . Agencies charged with countering domestic terrorism often have no idea what they are looking for.

Additionally, there is a tendency for overinclusivity of both groups labeled terrorist in nature and actions which are interpreted as terrorism. Initially, the same culprits of terrorism are repeatedly mentioned by most scholars and commentators. Some of these groups (e.g., Industrial Workers of the World, Skinheads, Jewish Defense League, Black Panther Party, etc.) are not necessarily terrorist organizations, but political, racist, nationalist, and/or religious groups with a minority of their members, often without leadership and/or group approval, who engaged in terrorist actions. Similarly, other analysts (e.g., Vetter and Perlstein, 1991:52) use vague, thus overinclusive labels to classify actions as terrorism and encourage the reader to infer from their analysis that some groups such as pro-choice, gay rights, feminist, and American nationalists could very well have been terrorists. These authors' suggestion is problematic in view of the lack of evidence that actions of such groups meet the definitional criteria previously mentioned.

Moreover, many authors (e.g., Johnpoll, 1978; Gurr, 1989) tend to lump all acts of vigilantism, including such diverse events, personalities and groups which pursued alleged and actual criminals from the 1760s up to the activities of New York City subway patron Bernard Goetz, with terrorism. Many of the actions that these individuals and organizations committed were distasteful yet permissable under the existing laws of the day.

On the other hand, the academic literature often neglects to mention incidents of state-sponsored terrorism such as the 1980 attempted assassination of an anti-Qaddafi Libyan student in Fort Collins, Colorado, by the Libyan government (Monroe, 1982:147); the 1984 murder of journalist Henry Liu by the Taiwanese government (Downie and Milman, 1985); and the 1976 killing of Chilean ambassador by DINA (Dinges and Landau, 1980). While these can be seen as isolated events, much of this material is sequestered away in newspaper and magazine articles and rarely assembled by academics for analysis.[8]

Moreover, sensationalistic and emotional language often undermines the objectivity of some research and literature reviews. Take for example the statement, "Take a cool hard look at the problem of terrorism" and at its "serious consequences" (Monroe, 1982:142). Writing like this can produce unnecessary and misdirected fears.

Furthermore, there is an overemphasis of research which describes counterterrorism measures against international terrorism and a neglect of responses to domestic terrorism (e.g., Clawson, 1989). The fact that the number of international acts of terrorism is greater than the number of domestic ones is simply a case of heightened publicity, particularly since the media treats events of antiterrorism as incidents of international terrorism.

Finally, there is an overpreoccupation with classification of the types of terrorist groups with little consensus among the different typologies. For example, Homer (1983) suggests a classification of nationalist, international, and intimidating groups. Harris (1987) proposes white leftists, Puerto Rican leftists, black militants, right-wing extremists, and Jewish extremists. Gurr (1988) advocates vigilante, insurgent, transnational, and state divisions. Finally, White (1991) outlines foreign, revolutionary nationalists, ideological left, ideological right, and criminal groups using terrorist tactics (p. 167). The utility of these typologies is not explained by the authors and focuses too much on their differentiating characteristics among groups, even trivial ones. The utility of any of these typologies becomes questionable when one recognizes that many of the terrorist groups can and do belong to more than one category. Lack of mutually exclusive categorization of terrorists is not addressed by these authors. Moreover, many analysts neglect to mention that group membership or claim for an action may very well be posturing on the part of the alleged culprits. As well, individuals unconnected with terrorist groups may conduct a terrorist event, simply borrow the name of one in existence, and manage to convince the authorities, provide news for the media, and probably threaten the public that that particular terrorist group is larger, more sophisticated or better organized than they truly are. Most importantly, the majority of this work is not related to theory building, which generally is the most common reason for typology construction.

There should be a conscious attempt to minimize over- and underinclusivity and rehashing of information that is broadly agreed upon. Settlement of a widely agreed upon consensus definition would be part of the solution. It would have to be amenable to both academics and criminal justice practitioners, and national security agencies would help in the accurate identification of acts of terrorism and those who engage in this sort of behavior. So too would an effort by researchers to do proper literature searches and reviews. Publication of information which is already disseminated does not further the development of a subdiscipline such as terrorism. A purposive attempt should be made in the terrorism research community to understand that typology building is not an end in itself, but should act as a beginning.

Ideological Biases

Some of the literature in the field suffers from a liberal or pro-state bias towards terrorism, and a neglect of state or corporate complicity in acts of terrorism. First, while trying to appear balanced, liberal-minded authors, in fact, misrepresent the actions of certain groups. For example, Vetter and Perlstein (1991:63) outline "Pro-Life and Pro-Choice Activists" in one of their terrorist categories, but only describe the former's bombing activities and neglect any actions by the latter. Moreover, to date, there has been no evidence of pro-choice activists engaging in terrorist acts as defined here.

Second, most current research reflects a narrow pro-state bias. In many instances the research is done by people who work for government organizations and have their work published in either academic journals (e.g., Monroe, 1982; Tierney, 1977); accepted for inclusion as part of a larger compendium on terrorism (Stohl, 1990); or produced in private consulting firms working on contract for government agencies who publish their work. This type of research serves a variety of purposes ranging from public education, to public relations, to propaganda. For example, in October 1987 the FBI's entire *Law Enforcement Bulletin* was devoted to terrorism. Much of the content justified their policy decisions and targeting practices. Citing the agency's success in thwarting terrorist actions is often self-serving, evident in the following statement:

> The FBI's record in both criminal and foreign counterintelligence cases demonstrates that we use these tools effectively while balancing individual rights of citizens. We use, and will continue to use properly, these tools to counter the danger that the armed terrorist poses to our society (Monroe, 1982: 144).

Third, much of the pro-state literature rarely mentions state or corporate complicity in facilitating acts of terrorism. For example, Anti-Castro Cubans were once trained by the CIA (Marchetti and Marks, 1974). Similarly, the activities of the FBI, the lead agency responsible for gathering data on and combating domestic terrorism, with assistance by the Chicago and Los Angeles police departments, helped the Black Panther Party and the American Indian Movement both financially and strategically in their violent attacks against other organizations and individuals. Moreover, the FBI contributed to Ku Klux Klan terrorist actions against the civil rights movement (Churchill and Vander Wall, 1990). And, the Molly Maguires were aided by Pinkerton agent provocateurs (Johnpoll, 1978: 31).

The author proposes the organization of a body of researchers and the establishment of an international center committed to the systematic and nonideological social-scientific study of terrorism in the United States. Such an institution would ideally bring together researchers from different academic disciplines who would have as their agenda the pooling of reference material; development of independent data sources that will be shared among them; and the appropriation of funds from nonsecurity sources to study terrorism in the United States.

Theoretical Problems

Research on terrorism in the United states does not rigorously deal with the problems of causes, decline, and control. Initially, causes of terrorism in the United States in general, or with respect to certain groups (e.g., Sprinzak, 1990), are marshaled but do not build upon the work done by other theorists (e.g., Crenshaw, 1981). Much like the work on typologies, this disconnected theorizing about the causes of terrorism creates the perception that research in this area is noncumulative and exists in a theoretical vacuum. Coterminously, much of the literature is divorced from the broader literature of political violence and crime research. This link would not only be half the battle in controlling the genesis of terrorism and encouraging its decline, but "robust and provocative theories will [also] draw the best and brightest to the field of terrorism research."[9]

Additionally, declines in the number of terrorist acts are mainly attributed to intelligence agency efforts and "special techniques" (e.g., Monroe, 1982) rather than to indigenous reasons of the terrorists themselves. Like the literature on the causes of terrorism, the work on decline is not tied to previous research on theories which explain why terrorism declines (e.g., Ross and Gurr, 1989; Crenshaw, 1987).

Moreover, and closely related to research on decline, there is a paucity of research on responses, effects and outcomes of terrorism in the United States.[10] Most research done on countering the terrorist threat deals with international terrorist acts which are beyond the borders of the United States and neglect domestic terrorism. Another type of response to terrorism concerns itself with policy-making (e.g., Celmer, 1987; Farrell, 1982). Again, analysis of policy-making issues is mainly concentrated on international and rarely on domestic terrorism. With the exceptions of Flynn (1978) and Zwerman (1988), few pieces address ways the "correctional system" responds to terrorists. White provides an excellent critique of the problems that the FBI counterterrorist establishment faces. He writes:

> The lack of a common approach is complemented by the lack of routinized counterterrorist policies. Although the FBI is officially the lead agency in responding to domestic terrorism, in reality a whole host of law enforcement, national defense, and civilian security bureaucracies have some responsibility. Although many of these agencies have exchanged official rules and procedures for joint operations, the line-level workers usually have no idea what the joint responsibilities are. The FBI has a solid internal management system, but counterterrorism demands multiagency management structures (White, p. 163).

Finally, and most important, many of the hypotheses advanced are based on questionable or insufficient evidence. Others have not been subjected to testing or secondary analysis, hence buttressing the noncumulative nature of this type of research. Consider, for example, Johnpoll's (1978: 42) six "lessons . . . drawn" from his review of the history of terrorism in the United States. He states that "confrontations of the Weathermen had little effect on the social order," and that "the Weathermen died in a Greenwich Village blast." He provides no evidence to support his claims nor does he explain the close-to-a-decade worth of activities carried on by this group under a different name.

Only when theories are developed and tested can the social-scientic understanding of terrorism in the United States be approached. One of the methods might start with the application of common theories and models of political action, political violence, and criminal violence to the process of terrorism.

Methodological Problems

Beyond theoretical problems we have a series of methodological shortcomings. The literature is primarily descriptive, there is an overreliance on secondary and state-produced source material, studies suffer from questionable rigor, and there is minimal use of statistical and comparative analyses.

First, the majority of the literature, regardless of the source, is descriptive, listing the various terrorist groups, and providing a brief history of the organizations (e.g., Bell and Gurr, 1979; Gurr, 1988; White, pp. 22–30), rather than analytical and explanatory. Similarly, some authors have published only the manifestos of these groups (e.g., Pearsall, 1974) and not provided any interpretation. The end result is that there is little systematic analysis of the internal dynamics of such organizations, their causes, and their effects upon their targets. Such investigation is necessary in order to place terrorism in its proper political, social, economic, and historical contexts as well as to institute better methods of response. Researchers need to go beyond the descriptive data currently assembled and engage in theory development and testing. When the research and policy-making community reaches a point where we discover that we do not have the available data, then, and only then, should we return to collect descriptive data.

Second, with the exception of a series of case studies, most of the research uses secondary source material (e.g., media accounts and government documents). Moreover, those pieces that do involve primary data are questionable in terms of their validity and representativeness. Presently the research and policy-making community does not have an abundance of "thick descriptive" primary source material, such as Bell's or Chaliand's work on terrorist organizations, which rely upon observation and interviews with terrorists. Additionally we have very few insider accounts of terrorist organizations.[11]

Third, there is a shortage of rigorously performed and publicly available case studies of individuals and organizations that have engaged in terrorist activities and incidents of terrorism.[12] By underutilizing the case study method, the research and policy-making community limits discussion of first-hand accounts of terrorists and instead relies on secondary sources such as externally derived observer perceptions. Many well-known groups such as the New World Liberation Front, May 19 Communist Organization, United Freedom Front/Unit, Armed Resistance Unit, Black Liberation Army, American Nazi Party, Animal Liberation Front, and Anti-Castro Cubans have been ignored for case study analysis, and even less work has been done on individual terrorists.[13] Although the external validity (e.g., population validity, experimenter bias) of case studies has often been criticized (most case studies have been done only on those terrorists who have been caught, hence biasing the representativeness of the sample), these shortcomings can be overcome by developing several case studies or by using "analytic induction" to deal with the problem of generalizability (Denzin, 1978).

Fourth, with the exception of organizations such as Risk's International and the Rand Corporation, most of the marshaled statistics are derived from the FBI's *Uniform Crime Reports Bomb Summary* or *FBI Analysis of Terrorist Incidents and Terrorist Related Activities in the United States* annual reports (started in 1977).[14] This problem exists despite the fact that in addition to individual big-city police departments which have an intelligence section, there are six primary agencies responsible for anti-terrorism in the United States: the FBI, Treasury Department (through the Secret Service and the Bureau of Alcohol, Tobacco, and Firearms), the Central Intelligence Agency (CIA), Customs, the Department of State, and the Defense Department. FBI statistics are problematic. In this vein, Stinson (1984) argues that

> local police agencies almost always constitute the first force responding to a terrorist incident. In addition, local police agencies often must confront criminals who are using terrorist tactics, even though these incidents are not classified as terrorism by the FBI. Despite the Bureau's mandate, confusion seems to exist about the roles of the various law enforcement agencies with regard to terrorism. Policy makers need to define the functions of

local, state, and federal agencies in responses to terrorism (as quoted in White, pp. 168–169).

Another problem is that the FBI's reports have "failed to account for many terrorist incidents because the classification system was skewed" (White, p. 170). This led, for example, to data on abortion clinic bombings, which occurred primarily during the 1980s and 1990s, being picked up by the Alcohol, Tobacco, and Firearms (ATF) division statistics rather than by the FBI.[15] Although in 1986, "the FBI formalized and limited its definition of terrorism" (White, p. 170), "local and state law enforcement agencies are not required to abide by that definition . . . [and] there are no clear criteria for categorizing criminal actions under the terrorist rubric. Even the FBI classifies some terrorist actions as common crimes" (White, p. 163).

Fifth, we lack a nonpartisan data base assembled from sources beyond state agencies (e.g., the media). While the Rand Corporation has established its own terrorism data base (e.g., Hoffman, 1987), little has progressed since Karber's observation that "we lack . . . the accepted statistical base . . . necessary for identification" (1971:521). He notes differences between the National Bomb Data Center's statistics, "and those compiled earlier by the Permanent Subcommittee on Investigations of the Senate Committee on Government Operations" and the ATF. The differences lie in "distinguishing explosive . . . from incendiaries [bombs] . . ." and the "means of data collection" (p. 522). According to Karber "[t]he development and refinement of consistent coding criteria would not only facilitate the study of terrorism in varying urban environments but would also permit cross-national comparison" (p. 533).[16]

Sixth, regardless of the data source, much of the research avoids statistical analysis of data. Those investigators who do cite statistics often do so with little interpretation (e.g., Monroe, 1982). Almost all authors who present data use descriptive rather than inferential statistics.[17] Thus theory testing is kept to a minimum.

Seventh, there is a lack of comparative (geographical and historical) approaches to the study of terrorism in the United States, whether this be at the national, regional, state, group or individual levels.[18] And most authors who conduct comparative studies with other U.S. groups or other countries do so only at the descriptive level. Intra- and inter-country comparisons of terrorist groups, if theory driven, would help us refine causal theories as well as contribute to effects-based theories.

Some of the techniques that could be used more frequently to mitigate some of these difficulties, which are already starting to make their way into the literature, are the development of rigorously collected snowball samples of terrorist or terrorist-prone groups, who are administered questionnaires, the results of which are tested to determine the relative explanatory potential of commonly held theories on terrorism and crime activity (e.g., Hamm, 1992). Another method would be the development of biographies of terrorists through newspaper accounts, autobiographies, and historical accounts of individuals supplemented by government agency data provided on request (e.g., Handler, 1990); and the assembly of data from nontraditional sources such as the National Abortion Foundation (e.g., Wilson and Lynxwiler, 1988). Only when a conscious attempt to analyze terrorism in the United States in a systematic social-scientific fashion is approached will the research and policy-making community better understand its process and encourage its decline.

Summary

Some of the pitfalls of the early literature on terrorism can be seen as inevitable since it was produced when few studies of this form of political violence and crime had been published. When authors began to be interested in the phenomenon of terrorism as an area of research there was little understanding of its nature, incidence, causes, method of study, or utility. Consequently, there was a certain confusion as to where terrorism belonged in the academic literature. These early studies reflected the embryonic state of the field. However, some of the problems prevalent in the early studies are still very much present in much of the literature of the 1970s and 1980s. To increase the coherence of the study of terrorism both as a field, and as a part of the broader disciplines of political violence, behavior, and crime, we need to deal systematically with the problems discussed in this chapter.

Conclusion

Terrorist attacks are disruptive to the normal functioning of people's daily lives. More definitionally and conceptually rigorous, nonideological, methodologically sophisticated, and theoretically appropriate approaches to understanding terrorism in the United States are needed in order to prevent needless destruction of human lives and property. Most doctors diagnosing a sick patient suggest that the coherent and clear communication of the problem is half the battle to amelioration. It is hoped that this chapter has provided a similar process and that the suggestions outlined in this paper will allow us to minimize the occurrence of terrorism and prevent researchers, policy-makers, and agents of social control from going down blind alleys or targeting as terrorists those individuals and groups which engage in legitimate protest, dissent, and advocacy.

NOTES

This chapter has benefited from the comments of Natasha J. Cabrera, Mark Hamm, and Kenneth Tunnell, and research assistance of Sam Matheson.

1. Oppositional political terrorism is conducted by anti-state and anti-corporate individuals and organizations. It contrasts with state terrorism, which is carried out by government agencies against real or suspected threats to the regime. Hereafter, the author will use terrorism to refer only to oppositional terrorism.

2. There are two types of oppositional terrorism, international and domestic. More events of domestic terrorism take place in the world than those of the international variety. By far the greatest type of oppositional terrorism occurring in the United States is domestic.

3. As Schmid's is a consensus definition of terrorism it includes most, but not all, processes identified. This point is similar to diagnoses of the *Diagnostic and Statistical Manual* of the American Psychology Association.

4. This recognizes that terrorists make cost-benefit calculations regarding targets and method. This process mitigates the perception or charge of randomness.

5. Types of targets are chosen for a variety of reasons. Often terrorism starts with nonhuman targets and progresses to human targets. Most data bases of terrorism include both human and nonhuman targets as well as threats and hoaxes.

6. See Hacker (1976) for a more detailed elaboration of this distinction.

7. For a similar conceptualization of the Canadian state of affairs see Ross (1988).

8. See Gurr (1989: 224) for an exception.

9. Personal communication with Mark Hamm, June 10, 1992.

10. See Evans (1983) for an exception to this state of affairs.

11. See Stern (1975) for an exception.

12. Brohle (1964) reviews the history of the Molly Maguires. Chalmers (1965) outlines the history of the Ku Klux Klan. McClelland (1977) and Fernandez (1987) are well-written exposés of the Machateros organization. Hincle and Turner (1981) and Jacobs (1970) are rather superficial treatments of the Symbionese Liberation Army. Coates (1987) and Flynn and Gerhart (1989) are relatively good journalistic accounts on the survivalist right. Francis (1982) presents a relatively well-researched analysis of the 1981 Brinks car robbery by members of various terrorist groups.

13. Knutson (1981) interviewed a Croatian terrorist incarcerated in an American jail.

14. Before this incident the only other chronology was Trick (1976).

15. For a review of abortion clinic bombings see Nice (1988); Wilson and Lynxwiler (1988).

16. While not a critique of the literature, but perhaps a problem with the antiterrorism process, White (1991) writes that, "Gaining an understanding of domestic terrorism is also hampered by the anti-intellectual atmosphere common to most American police agencies . . . many local police agencies view terrorism as a matter for their special weapons teams and negotiators. Most police administrators have

little time for 'exotic' crimes such as terrorism, and they usually see no difference between a terrorist and a barricaded suspect" (pp. 163–164).

17. See Gleason (1980) for an exception. He uses Rand data on international terrorism only.

18. Some exceptions include Mauer (1978); Mitchell (1985); and Rycus (1991).

REFERENCES

Bell, J. Bowyer and Ted Robert Gurr. 1979. "Terrorism and Revolution in America." In Hugh Graham and Ted Robert Gurr (eds.) *Violence in America: Historical and Comparative Perspectives* (revised ed.). Beverly Hills: Sage Publications, pp. 329–347.

Brohle, David. 1964. *The Molly Maguires.* London: Oxford University Press.

Celmer, Marc. 1987. *Terrorism, U.S. Strategy and Reagan Politics.* New York: Greenwood Press.

Chalmers, David M. 1965. *Hooded Americanism.* Chicago: Quadrangle Books.

Churchill, Ward and Jim Vander Wall. 1990. *Agents of Repression.* Boston: South End Press.

Clawson, Patrick. 1989. "Coping with Terrorism in the United States." *Orbis,* Summer, pp. 341–356.

Coates, James. 1987. *Armed and Dangerous: The Rise of the Survivalist Right.* New York: Hill and Wang.

Crenshaw, Martha. 1981. "The Causes of Terrorism." *Comparative Politics,* Vol. 13, No. 4, pp. 379–399.

———. 1987. "How Terrorism Ends." Paper presented at the annual meeting of the American Political Science Association, Chicago, September 4.

Denzin, N.K. 1978. *The Research Act: A Theoretical Introduction to Sociological Methods.* New York: McGraw-Hill.

Dinges, John and Saul Landau. 1980. *Assassination on Embassy Row.* New York: Pantheon Books.

Downie, Mark and Joel Milman. 1985. "A Brazen Act of Terrorism: The Killing of Henry Liu." *Mother Jones*, May, pp. 16–23.

Evans, Ernest. 1983. "The Use of Terrorism by American Social Movements." In Jo Freeman (ed.) *Social Movements in the Sixties and Seventies*. New York: Longman, pp. 252–261.

Farrell, William. 1982. *The U.S. Government Response to Terrorism*. Boulder, CO: Westview Press.

Fernandez, Ronald. 1987. *Los Macheteros: The Wells Fargo Robbery and The Violent Struggle for Puerto Rican Independence*. Englewood Cliffs, NJ: Prentice Hall.

Flynn, Edith. 1978. "Political Prisoners and Terrorists in American Correctional Institutions." In Ronald D. Crelinsten, Danielle Laberge-Altmejd, and Denis Szabo (eds.) *Terrorism and Criminal Justice*. Toronto: Lexington Books, pp. 87–92.

Flynn, Kevin and Gary Gerhart. 1989. *The Silent Brotherhood: Inside America's Racist Underground*. New York: Free Press.

Francis, Samuel T. 1992. "The Jackel Reborn: The Brinks Robbery and Terrorism in the United States." *International Security Review*, Vol. 7, No. 1, Spring, pp. 99–124.

Gleason, John M. 1980. "A Poisson Model of Incidents of International Terrorism in the United States." *Terrorism: An International Journal*. Vol. 4, pp. 259–265.

Gurr, Ted Robert. 1988. "Political Terrorism in the United States: Historical Antecedents and Contemporary Trends." In Michael Stohl (ed.) *The Politics of Terrorism*. (third ed.) New York: Marcel Dekker, pp. 549–578.

———. 1989. "Political Terrorism in the United States: Historical Antecedents and Contemporary Trends." In Ted Robert Gurr (ed.) *Violence in America*, Vol. 2. Newbury Park, CA: Sage Publications, pp. 201–230.

Hacker, Frederick J. 1976. *Crusaders, Criminals, Crazies: Terror and Terrorism in our Time*. New York: Bantam.

Hamm, Mark S. 1992. "Chaos in the Soul: Neo-Nazi Skinheads and the Morality of Domestic Terrorism." Paper presented at the annual meeting of the Academy of Criminal Justice Sciences, Pittsburgh, March.

Handler, Jeffrey. 1990. "Socioeconomic Profile of an American Terrorist: 1960s and 1970s." *Terrorism: An International Journal.* Vol. 13, pp. 195–213.

Harris, J.W. 1987. "Domestic Terrorism in the 1980s." *FBI Law Enforcement Bulletin.* Vol. 56, pp. 5–13.

Hincle, Warren and William Turner. 1981. *The Fish is Red.* New York: Harper and Row.

Hoffman, Bruce. 1987. "Terrorism in the United States in 1985." In Paul Wilkinson and A.M. Stewart (eds.) *Contemporary Research on Terrorism.* Aberdeen, U.K.: Aberdeen University Press, pp. 230–240.

Homer, Frederic D. 1983. "Terror in the United States: Three Perspectives." In Michael Stohl (ed.) *The Politics of Terrorism.* (second ed., revised and expanded.) New York: Marcel Dekker, pp. 145–177.

Jacobs, Harold (ed.). 1970. *Weathermen.* Berkeley, CA: Ramparts Press.

Johnpoll, Bernard K. 1976. "Perspectives on Political Terrorism in the United States." In Yonah Alexander (ed.) *International Terrorism: National, Regional, and Global Perspectives.* New York: Praeger, pp. 30–45.

Knutson, Jeanne N. 1981. "Social and Psychodynamic Pressures Toward a Negative Identity: The Case of an American Revolutionary Terrorist." In Yonah Alexander and John Gleason (eds.) *Behavioral and Quantitative Perspectives On Terrorism.* New York: Pergamon Press, pp. 105–153.

Marchetti, Victor and John D. Marks. 1974. *The CIA and the Cult of Intelligence.* New York: Dell Publishing.

Mauer, Marvin. 1978. "The Ku Klux Klan and the National Liberation Front: Terrorism Applied to Achieve Diverse Goals." In Marius H. Livingston (ed.) *International Terrorism in the Contemporary World.* Westport, CT: Greenwood Press, pp. 131–152.

McClelland, Vin. 1977. *The Voices of Guns.* New York: Putnam.

Mitchell, Thomas H. 1985. "Politically-Motivated Terrorism in North America: The Threat and the Response." Ph.D. Dissertation, Carleton University.

Monroe, Charles P. 1982. "Addressing Terrorism in the United States." *Annals, AAPSS.* Vol. 463, September, pp. 141–148.

Nice, David. 1988. "Abortion Clinic Bombings As Political Violence." *American Journal of Political Science*, Vol. 32, pp. 178–195.

Pearsall, Robert Brainard (ed.). 1974. *The Symbionese Liberation Army: Documents and Communications*. Amsterdam: Rodopi.

Ross, Jeffrey Ian. 1988. "An Events Data Base on Political Terrorism in Canada: Some Conceptual and Methodological Problems." *Conflict Quarterly*, Vol. VIII, No. 2, Spring, pp. 47–65.

Ross, Jeffrey Ian and Ted Robert Gurr. 1989. "Why Terrorism Subsides: A Comparative Study of Canada and The United States." *Comparative Politics*, Vol. 21, No. 4, July, pp. 405–426.

Rycus, Mitchell J. 1991. "Urban Terrorism: A Comparative Study." *The Journal of Architectural and Planning Research*, Vol. 8, No. 11, Spring, pp. 1–10.

Schmid, Alex. 1983. *Political Terrorism: A Research Guide to Concepts, Theories, Data Bases and Literature*. New Brunswick, NJ: Transaction Books.

Sprinzak, Ehud. 1990. "The Psychopolitical Formation of Extreme Left Terrorism in a Democracy: The Case of the Weathermen." In Walter Reich (ed.) *Origins of Terrorism*. Cambridge: Cambridge University Press, pp. 65–85.

Stern, Suzan. 1975. *With the Weathermen*. Garden City, NY: Doubleday.

Stohl, Michael (ed.) 1990. *The Politics of Terrorism* (third ed., revised and expanded). New York: Marcel Dekker.

Tierney, John J. 1977. "Terror at Home: the American Revolution and Irregular Warfare." *Stanford Journal of International Studies*, Vol. 12, pp. 1–19.

Trick, Marcia M. 1976. "Chronology of Incidents of Terroristic, Quasi-Terrorist, and Political Violence in the United States: January 1965 to March 1976." National Advisory Committee on Criminal Justice Standards and Goals. *Disorders and Terrorism: Report of the Task Force on Disorders and Terrorism*. Washington, D.C. Law Enforcement Assistance Administration, Department of Justice.

Vetter, Harold and Gary R. Perlstein. 1991. *Perspectives on Terrorism*. Pacific Grove, CA: Brooks/Cole.

Weinberg, Leonard and Paul B. Davis. 1989. *Introduction to Political Terrorism*. New York: McGraw-Hill.

White, Jonathen. 1991. *Terrorism: An Introduction.* Pacific Grove, CA: Brooks/Cole.

Wilson, Michele and John Lynxwiler. 1988. "Abortion Clinic Violence as Terrorism." *Terrorism: An International Journal,* Vol. 11, pp. 263–273.

Zwerman, Gilda. 1988. "Special Incapacitation: The Emergence of a New Correctional Facility For Women Political Prisoners." *Social Justice,* Vol. 15, No. 1, pp. 31–47.

Hate Crime and the Far Right: Unconventional Terrorism

Introduction

Terrorism in the United States, as in the rest of the world, is designed to alter and/or overthrow a political system. Terrorists work outside the legitimate political arena in an attempt to cause political change. Terrorists are dissatisfied with a current political system (or parts of that system) and believe the only way to change it is through violence. Some terrorists focus on a single issue and only want a specific set of laws changed. An example would be antiabortionists, who attack only abortion clinics, its workers, and patrons. Other terrorists advocate the complete overthrow of the government and the establishment of more radical forms of government (under their leadership, of course). For example, various organizations of the far right in America have openly called for the overthrow of the current political system and replacing it with their religious form of government. Terrorists attempting to effect political change use a variety of techniques, ranging from high-profile activities such as bombing and murder, to low-profile activities such as hate crime (e.g., beating of minorities, painting of swastikas on Jewish synagogues, etc.). High-profile activities are designed to attract mass-media attention and draw world-wide publicity to the cause of the terrorist, such as the bombing of the PanAm flight over Lockerbee, Scotland. Low-profile terrorism attempts to avoid media attention and wide-spread public recognition. For example, the majority of instances of vandalism and destruction of Jewish Synagogues are not usually known of outside the Jewish community. The news media does not report these activities and as a consequence, most Americans are not aware of the problem. The Jewish community, however, is very aware of these activities and are duly terrified. Most terrorists in the United States engage in low-profile activities.

United States citizens and law enforcement communities perceive terrorism as a problem only for other countries and not for the United States. (Mullins, 1988b). Why do law enforcement authorities and the public have this perception? Primarily because terrorism in the United States takes a very different form than elsewhere in the world. Terrorists outside the United States are primarily left wing and engage in high-profile activities. Conversely, terrorists in the United States tend to be right wing and base their political ideology on racial or religious supremacy. They desire a government of fascism and a government which will subjugate particular racial and/or religious groups of people.

Terrorists outside the United States usually engage in acts designed to draw widespread publicity to their cause, the far right in America practices a far more "covert" (not intended to draw media attention) form of terrorism. The far right terrorist in America engages in numerous forms and types of low-visibility terrorism—hate crime.

Most Americans would say that terrorists do not operate within the United States. The author has even been told by a high-ranking federal law enforcement official that the far right does not pose a serious threat, that their actions are limited to rhetoric, and that Americans are not in danger from them. The far right does in fact pose a serious threat to America and their use of public rhetoric is carefully designed to hide the true range and scope of their activities. Later in this chapter, data are presented showing just what a serious threat the far right poses to the general public.

Definitions

Most people would probably define terrorism as acts of violence intended to harm, maim, or kill for the purpose of overthrowing a government. This definition certainly defines what terrorist do, but does not define what terrorism is. Although there are numerous definitions of terrorism, many are too encompassing and include activities which would not be considered terroristic and/or include persons who would not be considered terrorists. One such example would be the definition of terrorism as "the threat or use of violence and fear to produce change." This definition would include many criminal acts which are not terroristic in purpose. Bank robbery would fit within this definition of terrorism. Other definitions of terrorism are too restrictive. The Federal Bureau of Investigation has defined terrorism as "the unlawful use of force or violence against persons or property to intimidate or coerce a government, civilian population, or any segment thereof, in furtherance of political or social objectives" (Pomerantz, 1987). This definition is somewhat restrictive in that it requires the actual use of some type of force for an act to be considered terroristic. Many terroristic acts and many right-wing activities in the United States do not involve the actual use of force. Threats against a particular group of people would be an example. If the threats produced a change in behavior in the threatened group, then that group has been victimized by terrorism. These threats do not fit within the framework of the FBI definition of terrorism.

Jenkins (1975, reprinted in Milbank, 1978, p. 54) defines terrorism as "the threat of violence, individual acts of violence, or a campaign of violence designed primarily to instill fear—to terrorize. Terrorism is violence for effect; not only, and sometimes not at all, for the effect on the actual victims of the terrorists. In fact, the victim may be totally unrelated to the terrorist's cause. Terrorism is violence aimed at the people watching. Fear is the intended effect, not the byproduct of terrorism." Jenkins' definition is fairly comprehensive, yet at the same time quite specific in the identification of terrorist activity. Terrorism does not have to be a physical act of violence. The painting of swastikas on a synagogue, racial epithets, and parades by the Ku Klux Klan are as much acts of terrorism as are cross-burnings, beatings of a minority, or bombs in a church. The true intent of terrorism is to produce fear to cause change (Fromkin, 1978). Cross-burnings or threatening letters are designed to make people (or a government) afraid enough to alter their behavior in some manner. Violence, when used, is not the end result of terrorism, rather only a tool to be used to achieve a goal (Stohl, 1985). Finally, the target audience of the terrorists are not victims of the terrorist activity, but others who learn of the activity. The shooting of a white male who has married a black female may certainly change the behavior of that particular male or female, but the intent of the act is to prevent other whites and/or blacks from marrying across races.

The Jenkins (1975) definition also recognizes the basic political nature of terrorism. The basic purpose of terrorism is to bring about political change. Terrorism, whatever its form, is political crime. The lynching or beating of a minority by the Ku Klux Klan, for example, can be a political act designed to bring about political change. Sometimes, the act is intended to change a law or group of laws and other times to change a political system. Also, many people have been misled by those terrorist organizations which practice rhetoric/violence under the guise of religious righteousness. To these organizations, their religiosity is a thinly disguised veil for political change.

For Jenkins (1975), terrorism is much more than an isolated act or series of acts; terrorism is a process with clearly defined goals and objectives. Several components of this process are important to fully understand its application to right-wing terrorism in the United States. First, terrorist acts are perpetrated with a clearly defined purpose and are consistent with the goals of the terrorist organization. For example, the lynching of a black person is not only an attack on a racial minority, but an attack against a government that allows for racial equality. Second, terrorists need only produce a perception that they are capable of violence to achieve their goals. For example, if the Ku Klux Klan's threats can force a racial group from a neighborhood, then one of the organization's goals has been achieved. Third, terrorist organizations must have the resources to achieve their goals. The far right often is not taken seriously because of a perception that it is small in number, fragmented, and has few resources. Fourth, terrorist organizations have predictable strategies which identify their goals. The Ku Klux Klan, for example, has become synonymous with cross-burnings. Fifth, terrorist activities are designed to produce a certain predictable reaction from the target audience (e.g., fear, panic, shock, and compliance). Finally, terroristic activities are designed to achieve certain goals. Terrorists do not conduct activities for the sake of good theater; rather they conduct activities to effect political change.

The concepts terrorism and hate crime are often used interchangeably. Hate crime as used here is more than criminal activity; it is a specific form of political terrorist activity used by the far right to achieve its goals. Using the definition of terrorism presented above, hate crime fits neatly into the right-wing terrorist typology. Just because hate crime tends to focus on the individual rather than the group as a whole does not remove it from the terrorist realm. Focusing on the individual personalizes terrorism more than conventional forms of terrorism, and in some cases may produce more fear than other forms of terrorism.

Right-wing Belief Structures

Although there is diversity across organizations, the far right has a basic belief structure rooted in racial superiority. The basis for this belief varies depending on the organization being discussed. Several authors have attempted to classify right-wing organizations based on the origins of the racial superiority belief. Coates (1987) identified six categories of right-wing extremism. These included: (1) true terrorist organizations such as The Order, whose sole purpose is to conduct campaigns of terrorism against minorities; (2) Identity Churches, which support racial supremacy and violence based upon Biblical scripture, such as the Covenant Sword and Arm of the Lord; (3) protest groups, such as the Posse Comitatus; (4) lone wolves fighting the system, like the American Resistance Movement; (5) survivalists, such as the Euro-American Alliance Inc.; and (6) compound dwellers, such as Elohim City. This classification scheme is somewhat cumbersome and redundant. Several organizations could be classified into two or more categories. For example, the Ku Klux Klan could be classified as a terrorist group, a protest group, survivalists, and in some instances, compound dwellers. Also, a separate designation of organizations as terrorist organizations is misleading, since all of the far-right extremist organizations are terrorist organizations.

Suall and Lowe (1987) argue that all far-right groups are hate groups and can be classified into four categories. The first category includes the Ku Klux Klan and its variants. These organizations are racist simply by the fact that members belong to a majority group. The second category includes the militant Christian Identity groups. These organizations base their belief of racial superiority on some type of perverted interpretation of Biblical scripture. The third category includes the neo-Nazis, organizations who follow the tenets of Hitler and the German Nazi party of World War II. The final category includes the hybrid organizations. The hybrid organizations are the least terrorist of all the hate groups, limiting their activities to political expression and freedom of speech and politics (White, 1990). As with the typology proposed by Coates (1987), the typology proposed by Suall and Lowe is too imprecise. There is too much overlap between categories and some organizations could be multi-classified.

Sapp's (1985, 1986c) parsimonious scheme classified the far right as being either (1) white supremist, (2) patriotic and survivalistic, or (3) Christian Conservative Identity. Although considerable overlap between categories exists, this classification provides advantages over earlier schemes (e.g., Coates, 1987; Suall and Lowe, 1987). First, organizations can be readily identified by their belief structure. Second, Sapp's typology simplifies the distinction between the various right-wing organizations. The distinction between right-wing organizations can be further simplified. Right-wing extremist groups can be classified as either (1) secular based or (2) Christian Identity based. Patriotism and survivalism are considered common to most organizations. The secular-based organizations include the neo-Nazis and Arizona Patriots. The Aryan Nations and the Mountain Church of Michigan are examples of Christian Identity organizations. Even with this simplified typology, there is still some overlap. The Ku Klux Klan, for example, historically is considered secular, although in recent years many Klan members have espoused the Christian Identity philosophy. At present, most secular-based far-right organizations have turned to Christian Identity philosophy, due to several factors. One, many Christian Identity leaders became involved in a secular-based far-right movement and have since converted to Christian Identity theology. Past associates still in the secular-based organizations have followed suit and have thus brought the Christian Identity beliefs into those secular organizations. Two, Christian Identity leaders tend to be more charismatic than the secular-based organization leaders (Mullins, 1988a). The Christian Identity organizations are able to grow and expand faster than the secular-based organizations (Mullins, 1988a). Three, Christian Identity religion provides a justification and rationale for supremist beliefs. Four, Christian Identity promises Aryan dominance and eternal life for Aryans.

All Christian Identity right-wing organizations and many of the secular-based organizations, believe in postmillenialism, a belief that Jesus cannot return to earth until God's law has been reestablished (Mullins, 1988a). The Second Coming cannot occur until the white race has established dominance and control over the world and has deposed Satan's forces (Holden, 1986a). The overthrow of government is especially important in the United States, for postmillenialists believe that Jesus will establish the Second Kingdom in the United States (Holden, 1987). The far right, in fact, refers to the United States government as ZOG—the Zionist Occupational Government.

The belief that Jews are agents of Satan is the cornerstone of the Christian Identity Movement and dates to the 1800s, when Richard Brothers first preached anti-Jewish doctrine as part of a philosophy of Anglo-Israelism (Benware, 1984) which argues that the Israelites described in the Old Testament are white people. God created Adam in His image, which was white, and gave Adam rule over all other, lesser races (Finch, 1983). Adam and Eve started the Israeli (or white) race. When the Roman Empire fell, the lost tribes of Israel fled to and conquered Europe. God gave the tribe of Mannasah the United Kingdom and charged that tribe with spreading the true gospel. When English colonists settled in America, those settlers were descendents of the original Mannasah tribe members. Thus, America is the land God promised Moses. Further, the Declaration of Independence and the United States Constitution are holy covenants between God and the white man, or Israelites. Shortly after World War II, the Reverend Wesley Swift added the tenets of racism and supremacy to the basic beliefs of Anglo-Israelism. Thomas Robb, chaplain and former Grand Dragon of the Ku Klux Klan summed up the Anglo-Israeli philosophy when he said, "The Jews are not the Chosen people of God. The Bible is an Israel book. It does not give the history of the negroes, or any other people or any other race. It gives the history of only one race" (WMAQ, 1985).

Since the Christian Identity Movement takes the Scripture very seriously, one must next ask how the far right can justify violence against Jews, minorities, and other religions. They believe, first that Jews and minorities are not human and therefore there is no conflict with the Bible and no moral dilemma since there is no violation of God's commandments. Second, God has decreed that the Jews cannot be stopped peaceably because they are Satan's agents, and thus it is the responsibility of true Christians to do them harm. Other minorities and religions have also been denounced by God as agents of Satan and are no better than Jews. Third, the far right practices eschatology, that is, they interpret the Book of Revelation literally and believe that Armageddon is at hand. Fourth, the Christian Identity Movement merely reinterprets the Bible to justify their violence (White, 1986). Jews are responsible (according to doctrine) for racial equality, racial mixing, drugs, crime, and society's other ills. To save society and the Christian way of life, Jews must be destroyed. Blacks, other minorities, and other religions are part of the Satanic/Jewish conspiracy to defeat God.

The far right further believes that the ZOG government has so perverted the Constitution and the Declaration of Independence that those two documents are no longer covenants between God and man. Thus, in 1982, in Hayden Lake, Idaho, members of the Christian Identity Movement, including the Aryan Nations, the British Columbia Ku Klux Klan, the Ku Klux Klan of the United States, the Mountain Church of Michigan, and the Texas Emergency Reserves drew up a document referred to as the Nehemiah Township Charter and Common Law Contract (Sapp, 1986b). This document is considered the new covenant between man and God and will be the Constitution under the new government. According to the Nehemiah Township Charter, Jesus Christ will be the Chief Executive Officer of the new government whose purpose "is to safeguard and protect the Christian faith" (Mullins, 1988a). According to the Nehemiah Township Charter, there would be no legislative body, no taxation, no governmental laws, and only freemen (i.e., whites) would have personal freedoms. Courts would decide cases according to Scripture for there would be no man-made laws. Freemen could carry any type of firearm they wished, including automatic and heavy weapons. The government could form a Posse Comitatus, and could fight war under the dictates of Scripture. The Nehemiah Township charter specifies that war will be waged according to Deuteronomy, Chapter 20, which reads in part:

> When you take the field against an enemy and are faced by horses and chariots and an army greater than yours, do not be afraid of them; for the Lord your God, who brought you out of Egypt, will be with you. . . . When you advance on a city to attack it, make an offer of peace. If the city accepts the offer and opens its gates to you, then all the people in it shall be put to

> forced labour and shall serve you. If it does not make peace with
> you but offers battle, you shall besiege it, and the Lord your God
> will deliver it into your hands. You shall put all its males to the
> sword, but may take the women, the dependants, and the cattle
> for yourselves, and plunder everything else in the city. You may
> enjoy the use of the spoil of your enemies which the Lord your
> God gives you (New English Bible).

This "order of battle" was interpreted as giving freemen the right to
kill all members of other races and religions in the United States.

In Christian Identity theology, law-enforcement officers
(considered ZOG agents) are just as susceptible to attacks by the far
right as minorities and other, non-Identity religions. Members of
the far right may provoke law-enforcement agents by refusing to
carry licenses and automobile registrations, refusing to produce
identification, refusing to sign citations, and/or carrying concealed
or illegal weapons (Melnichak, 1986). Several members of the law-
enforcement community have been killed by members of the far
right. The most infamous was the murder of two federal marshals
and an Arkansas sheriff by Gordon Kohl of the Posse Comitatus
(Bowers, 1987).

For the non-Christian far-right member, the white supremacy
philosophy is that of Adolf Hitler and the German Nazi party of
World War II. They believe the white race is physically and morally
superior to other races, that the civil rights movement, racial
equality, and other governmental controls are erosions of the
superiority of the white race, and feels obligated to restore the white
race to its true place of prominence. Hate crimes directed against
other races are overtly political, as these activities are the first step in
the overthrow of the United States government. These supremists
also see the Jewish "race" as holding the economic purse-strings and
leading the movement to destroy the white race. They believe that
Jews fabricated the Holocaust to gain world sympathy for their
plight and to turn people against Aryans. The white race, they
believe, is destined to rule the world.

Regardless of whether doctrine is Christian Identity or white
supremacy, the far right believes Armageddon is at hand and will

come from one or more of five sources. One, nuclear war will bring about Armageddon (Wiggins, 1987). Two, the end of the world could be caused by natural disasters. Floods, earthquakes, volcanic eruptions, drought, massive tidal waves, and other natural disasters will be brought by God to punish the Aryan race for allowing racial and religious equality, mixing, and proliferation. Three, Armageddon could be brought about by the spread of world communism. Even though Russia and eastern Europe have renounced communism, they believe China, the Middle-East and Central and South America must be contended with. In addition, the far right sees the major communist threat coming from within the United States. Communists, they assert, run the government, manage the banking system, control the media, control law enforcement, and conspire in various other ways against Aryans (Blumberg, 1986). Four, changing economics, societies, and technologies will hasten Armageddon (Besser, 1982). The Jews, who control the world's economy, will cause a collapse of the world's economic and agricultural markets (Gurr, 1988; Mitchell, 1983). When farms and agricultural markets collapse, society will collapse. For Aryans and other people, only those who are self-sufficient will be able to survive (Marty, 1983). Five, and what they define as most likely, race wars will hasten Armageddon (Stimson, 1986). It is the responsibility of the Aryan race to promote and spur these race wars in any way they can. Many of the hate crimes perpetrated by the far right are intended to turn blacks against whites and speed the coming race wars.

Since they belive that Armageddon is near, the far right is heavily involved in survivalism and paramilitary training. John B. Harrell, leader of the Christian Patriots Defense League, has identified a mid-America survival zone, from southern Nebraska to west Texas to north Alabama to south Pennsylvania, and is the only safe place for Aryans during Armageddon. This survival zone is isolated, relatively absent of minorities, and is home to numerous camps and safe havens for Aryans. Harrell further claims that Aryans' salvation will be Christian patriots who will resurrect and protect Aryan society and prepare the country for the Second

Coming and the new world leader—Jesus Christ. The far right sponsors numerous paramilitary and survivalist training centers and camps, and also regularly holds meetings and conclaves to share training and survivalist strategies. The training is very thorough and quite extensive and in fact is better than most law enforcement and military personnel training. Table 1 (from Mullins, 1988a) illustrates some of the training that members of the far right receive, including some foreign terrorists. For example, one of the Sikh terrorists involved in the killing of Indira Gandhi and suspected of sabotage in the crash of an Air India jet which killed 329 people was trained at Frank Camper's Reconnaissance Commando School near Birmingham, Alabama (World Press Review, 1983). There are even paramilitary/survivalist training centers for members' children (Sapp, 1985).

Major Groups of the Far Right

There are several problems with keeping track of the far right. One, new organizations spring up almost daily. New groups, churches, and demonstrations signal the formation of new organizations. In most cases, however, they disappear as fast as they arise. Two, members of the far right often belong to two or more organizations. Unlike the case in more classical forms of terrorism, it is not unusual to see a member of the far right hold joint membership in several organizations. This is true even for the leaders of the far right. Three, many far-right organizations do nothing more than engage in inflammatory oratory. Although it is not illegal to engage in free speech, when it crosses the line into action, law enforcement attempts some counteraction. Many organizations have not crossed this line, so law enforcement has had no reason to build active intelligence files on these organizations. Thus, many right-wing organizations remain semi-secret. Although many are semi-secret, in this section, I describe some of the largest and most active far-right organizations.

Table 1. Training Curricula for Three Right-Wing Organizations in the United States

The Covenant, the Sword, and the Arm of the Lord	Christian Patriots Defense League	Armed Resistance Movement
Attack formation	Archery	Actions against tanks/armored vehicles
Basic rifle and pistol	Brainwashing techniques	Ambushes
Christian martial arts	City escape	Assassinations
Christian military truths	Caombat medicine	Base camps
First aid	Crossbow	Booby traps
Hand signals	Unarmed defense	Camping and woodcraft
Military dress	Government control by the Jews	Code and cypher systems
Military equipment	Guns and reloading	Combat and reconnaissance patrols
Military fieldcraft	Intelligence gathering	Communications and security
Personal home defense	Knife making and use	Counter intelligence techniques
Searching landscapes	Legal use of lethal force	Escape and evasion techniques
Special weapons	Marksmanship and handgun use	Espionage
Urban warfare	Military fieldcraft	Explosives
Weapons proficiency	Organizing CEDS units	First aid
Wilderness survival	Personal and home defense	Guerrilla warfare
	Recruitment of new members	Hunt and kill groups
	Safe houses (patriots in flight)	Improvised weapons and techniques
	Security control	Infiltration and espionage
	Self-defense	Intelligence gathering
	Stick fighting	Interrogation techniques
		Personal combat
		Physical and psychological training
		Posting of sentries
		Principles of organization
		Psychological defense against communism
		Raids
		Recruiting new members
		Rifles
		Sabotage
		Scouting and patrolling
		Security
		Small arms
		Small unit combat
		Subversion
		Theory of resistance movements
		Unconventional weapons and warfare
		Underground warfare

(From Mullins, 1988a)

Aryan Nations
Headquarters: Hayden Lake, Idaho
Leader: Richard Butler

One of the largest of all right-wing organizations, founded in the late 1970s by Richard Butler, is the Aryan Nations whose philosophy is rooted in Christian Identity theology and is often referred to as the Church of Jesus Christ Christian. Butler is sometimes represented at functions by close assistants Harold Wheeler Hunt or William Fowler. Fowler was a former Grand Dragon in the California Ku Klux Klan.

Although Richard Butler vehemently denies that the Aryan Nations is violent or espouses a philosophy of violence, members have engaged in hate-crime activity. In fact, there is a formula whereby members can become Aryan Warriors, an exalted status based in part on Norse mythology. Members earn points for killing specified members of ZOG (Stinson, 1987). FBI agents and federal marshals are worth 1/10 of a point, journalists and local politicians 1/12 of a point, judges and the FBI director 1/16 of a point; members of Congress are worth 1/5 point, and the President of the United States is worth one full point. When a member has amassed one point, they are given Aryan Warrior status (Stinson, 1987). To date, no member has attained Warrior status.

The Aryan Nations has called for the establishment of a "white homeland" in the northwest corner of the United States. This white nation would include the states of Washington, Oregon, Idaho, Montana, and Wyoming. In addition, their activities have included the stockpiling of weapons, harassing minorities, defacing currency, tax protesting, calling for the overthrow of the federal government, training in guerilla warfare, and producing literature calling for action against ZOG (Broadbent, 1987). The Aryan Nations reportedly have contacted the Syrian government in an attempt to buy weapons and secure finances (Melnichak, 1986).

Every year, the Aryan Nations sponsors a far right convention in Hayden Lake, Idaho (Barker, 1985; Sapp, 1987; White, 1990), which is open to all leaders and members of the far right. Guest speakers have included Robert Miles of the Mountain Church of

Jesus Christ, Louis Ray Beam of the Ku Klux Klan, William Pierce who authored *The Turner Diaries*, and Manfred Roeder, a German neo-Nazi.

In the early 1980s, Butler began bringing prisoners into the Aryan Nations. The Aryan Brotherhood is now a white protective association for persons in penal institutions. They hope that prisoners who join the Aryan Brotherhood will join the Aryan Nations after their release. One credo of the Aryan Brotherhood is that prisoners will, upon release from prison, kill the law enforcement official who arrested them. The Aryan Brotherhood has spread to prisons nationwide, although the largest membership is in California and Texas.

In 1987, Richard Butler and twelve members of the far right, were charged with Sedition by the federal government. After a lengthy trial, all defendants were acquitted. For more on this trial, see the section in this chapter on The Order.

Christian Defense League
Headquarters: Baton Rouge, Louisiana
Leader: James K. Warner

In 1977, James Warner founded the Christian Defense League, an anti-Jewish organization which believes Jews are the offspring of Satan and whose sole purpose on earth is to eliminate the white race. The Christian Defense League operates a large mail-order book service called The Sons of Liberty and publishes the *Christian Vanguard*. In recent issues, the *Christian Vanguard* has published articles titled "Inequalities of the Negro Race," "New Research Into Jewish Ritual Murder," and "Sex Practices of the Jew" (ADL, 1983).

Christian Patriots Defense League (CPDL)
Headquarters: Louisville, Illinois
Leader: John R. Harrell

Founded in 1977, the CPDL is a Christian Identity movement which emphasizes patriotism and survival. Each year the CPDL holds a Freedom Festival for members of the far right where survivalist training, ideological indoctrination, and paramilitary training are emphasized. The CPDL owns land in Rolla, Missouri, and Smithville, West Virginia, where similar activities also occur. The CPDL is the umbrella organization for the Christian Conservative Churches of America, which preaches that the only way to defeat Zionism and communism is by fundamentalist Christianity and patriotism. There are two subgroups under the CPDL—the Paul Revere Club, which is charged with fundraising and the Citizens Emergency Defense System, which fancies itself as a private militia.

The Covenant, The Sword, and The Arm of The Lord (CSA)
Headquarters: Marion County, Arkansas
Leader: Jim Ellison

The CSA was formed in 1970 on a 224-acre compound in Marion County, Arkansas, called Zaraphath-Horeb. The CSA, a Christian Identity movement, believes that whites are God's chosen race, communists and Jews are the sons of Satan, and that Jews train blacks to kill whites (Mullins, 1988a). The CSA operated the Endtime Overcomer Survival Training School at their compound, where they trained far-right members in survival and paramilitary techniques. They published a training manual called the *CSA Journal and Basic Training Manual*, which, in addition to standard survival tactics, the *Manual* covered urban warfare, personal home defense, Christian martial arts, and Christian military truths. Members of the CSA performed security duties at the CPDL Freedom Festivals.

The CSA's leader, Jim Ellison, has been charged with various crimes. In 1980, he was indicted for burning his sister's house (arson for hire), in 1983 for burning a gay church, for arson of a Jewish community center, and for bombing a natural gas pipeline. In 1985, federal and state officials raided the Zarephath-Horeb compound, where they found Kruggerands, LAW (Light Anti-tank Weapon) rockets, 94 long rifles, hand guns, 35 automatic weapons, numerous shotguns, 2 land mines, 25 explosive devices, 40 hand grenades, 50 sticks of dynamite, 38 sticks of kinetic explosives, 3-

1/2 blocks of C-4 military explosive, 400 feet of detonation cord, smoke grenades, military trip flares, 320 blasting caps, safety fuse, black powder, and thousands of rounds of ammunition. In September, 1985, Jim Ellison and two other members of the CSA were charged and sentenced to prison under RICO statutes. In 1988, Jim Ellison testified at the Sedition trial of Richard Butler and others and was later placed in the witness protection program.

In 1984, just after attending a CPDL Freedom Festival, CSA member Richard Wayne Snell killed a Texarkana, Arkansas, pawn shop owner and Arkansas State Trooper Louis Bryant. Snell was convicted of killing Bryant and sentenced to life in prison.

Ku Klux Klan (KKK)
Headquarters: Numerous locations
Leader: Numerous persons

One of the largest and oldest of all right-wing organizations, the Ku Klux Klan has been a part of American history for over 100 years. The KKK originally was formed in Pulaski, Tennessee, in 1886, by Civil War general Nathan Bedford Forrest (Wiggins, 1985a). The original Klan was formed in response to the freedom of blacks and to drive the carpetbaggers from the reconstructive south. In 1869, the Klan disbanded.

In the 1920s, the Klan resurfaced as a southern political party and at its apex in the mid-1920s, claimed over a half-million members. Political scandal and disenfranchisement with the goals of the Klan led to its demise in the late 1930s.

In response to school desegregation (*Brown* vs. *Board of Education*), the Klan resurfaced in the 1950s with a philosophy of racial purity and white supremacy (Randel, 1965). The third resurrection of the Klan has been one of the most active and violent of all far-right organizations. The Klan has engaged in hundreds of acts of murder, assassination, execution, lynching, bombing, and harassment. One of the most identifiable activities of the Klan is the midnight cross burning.

Unlike other far-right organizations, the Klan is many organizations. One such faction is the Invisible Empire, Knights of the Ku Klux Klan which was headquartered in Denham Springs, Louisiana, and led by Bill Wilkenson. When Wilkenson stepped down in 1986, the Invisible Empire chose James Farrands as its leader (ADL, 1991c). The Invisible Empire is presently headquartered in North Carolina and has large chapters in Louisiana, Alabama, Connecticut, and Pennsylvania. The Invisible Empire operates several paramilitary/survivalist camps, one of the most notorious in Cullman, Alabama, called My Lai. This is a youth camp, were children are indoctrinated in Klan philosophy, given weapons training, and taught guerilla warfare tactics.

A second Klan faction is the Knights of the Ku Klux Klan (KKKK). The KKKK was originally formed by David Duke, who currently is involved heavily in Louisiana politics. When Duke stepped down as Grand Dragon of the KKKK, Don Black took over. In 1981, Black and nine other Klan members were arrested by federal agents for conspiracy to take over the island of Dominica for the purpose of establishing a white nation. Upon Black's arrest, the KKKK fragmented into two organizations. One faction was led by Stanley McCollum in Tuscumbia, Alabama. The other, headquartered in Metaire, Louisiana, has had numerous leaders (including at one time David Duke). Because of internal politics, many members of the KKKK transferred membership to other Klan factions. In the last couple of years, the KKKK has reunified under the leadership of Thomas Robb. Robb, based in Harrison, Arkansas, and minister of the Church of Jesus Christ, an Identity church, is working toward the active acceptance of Christian Identity as the major philosophy of the KKKK. One of Robb's major thrusts of hatred is directed toward Jews. He has written, "I hate Jews. I hate race-mixing Jews. We've let anti-Christ Jews into our country and we've been cursed with abortion, inflation, homosexuality, and the threat of war" (ADL, 1991c).

A third major faction of the Klan is the United Klans of America (UKA). Of all Klan factions, the UKA is the largest, the most secretive, and the most conservative (Wiggins, 1985b). Led by Robert Shelton, the UKA is headquartered in Tuscaloosa, Alabama, and is extremely active in Alabama, Florida, Indiana, Kentucky,

North Carolina, South Carolina, and Virginia. In 1987, UKA member Henry Hays was convicted of the lynching of Michael Donald in Mobile, Alabama. In the only case of its kind, Donald's mother sued the UKA in federal court for violation of civil rights and was awarded a $7 million judgment against the UKA (Kornbluth, 1987) causing the UKA to become almost defunct. Many members are "old-line Klan," having been involved since the 1950s and are presently assisting Robert Shelton in reorganizing and reestablishing the UKA.

Klan members have been encouraged to adopt a revisionist policy since having been bolstered by David Duke's success in Louisiana politics. As a result, they see their future as less violent and with less violent rhetoric. Leaders of the Klan argue that more can be accomplished by focusing the country on the dysfunctions of affirmative action, immigration policy, crimes, drugs, welfare, and AIDS. Still underlying the revisionist philosophy is the belief that minorities and Jews are responsible for these social ills.

In addition to these three major Klan factions, there are numerous others scattered across the United States. Table 2 lists some of the more active subfactions.

National Socialist Liberation Front (NSLF)
Headquarters: Metaire, Louisiana
Leader: Karl Hand Jr.

The NSLF was formed in 1969 and of all neo-Nazi parties within the United States, has been the most outspoken and one of the most violent. The NSLF actively recruits in prisons and among ex-felons, believing these people not only have the necessary level of hatred toward other minorities and religions, but the requisite skills necessary to successfully conduct campaigns of violence.

National Socialist Party of America/American Nazi Party (ANP)
Headquarters: Chicago, Illinois
Leader: Dennis Milam

The National Socialist Party of America was formed in 1970 by Frank Collins who, in 1980, was convicted and sent to prison for

Table 2. Ku Klux Klan Organizations in the United States

State	Organizations
California	Invincible Empire, Knights of the White Rose
	California Knights of the Ku Klux Klan
	White Heritage Knights of the Ku Klux Klan
Iowa	White Knights of the Ku Klux Klan
Florida	Church of the Christian Knights, KKKK
	Florida Biker Klan
	Fraternal White Knights
Georgia	Confederate White Knights
	Lookout Mountain Knights
	New Order Knights of the Ku Klux Klan
	Royal Confederate Knights
	Southern White Knights
	True Knights of the Aryan Nations
Michigan	White Ku Klux Klan
Mississippi	New Order Knights
	White Knights of the Ku Klux Klan
Missouri	Confederation of Independent Orders
	Knights of the Ku Klux Klan
	National Knights of the Ku Klux Klan
	New Order Ku Klux Klan
New Jersey	Flaming Sword Ku Klux Klan of the Confederate Knights of America
Nevada	Nevada Ku Klux Klan
North Carolina	Aryan Christian Knights
	Carolina Ku Klux Klan
	Confederate Knights of America
	Federated Knights of the Ku Klux Klan
	New Empire Ku Klux Klan
	White Knights of the Ku Klux Klan
Oklahoma	White Knights of the Heartland
Ohio	Belpre Dixie Knights
	Independent Invisible Knights
	Ohio Knights of the Ku Klux Klan
	U.S. Knights of the Ku Klux Klan
Pennsylvania	Ku Klux Klan White Unity Party
	United Empire Knights of the Ku Klux Klan
	White Knights of the Ku Klux Klan
South Carolina	Christian Knights of the Ku Klux Klan
	Confederate White Knights
Tennessee	Dixie Knights
	Justice Knights of the Ku Klux Klan
	Soddy Knights of the Ku Klux Klan
	Tennessee Knights
	United Empire Knights of the Ku Klux Klan
Texas	Knights of the White Camellia

sexual abuse of a child. Dennis Milan took control and renamed the organization the American Nazi Party. A favorite tactic of the ANP is to hold a demonstration, provoke onlookers with rhetoric until the onlookers take action, and then attack the onlookers when ANP members can claim self-defense. The most notorious activity of the ANP took place in 1977 and 1978 in Skokie, Illinois, when the ANP applied for a demonstration permit in Skokie, which has a large Polish community of former prisoners of World War II concentration camps.

The ANP perceives itself as a world-wide organization and actively recruits members from other countries, especially Canada and across Europe. John Hinkley, who attempted to assassinate President Reagan, claimed membership in the ANP. However, the ANP claimed to have dismissed him because he was too violent.

New Order/National Socialist White People's Party (NSWPP)
Headquarters: Arlington, Virginia/Milwaukee, Wisconsin
Leader: Matthias Koell

In 1958, George Lincoln Rockwell formed the first neo-Nazi party in the United States, the American Nazi Party, but soon changed its name to the New Order (Holden, 1985). The NSWPP practices racism as preached by Adolf Hitler and the German Nazi party and has a violent history of attacks on Jews, Catholics, and other minority members. When Koell took control of the New Order, he rapidly expanded the NSWPP into a national organization, forming chapters in Chicago, Cleveland, Milwaukee, Minneapolis, Los Angeles, San Francisco, and Orange County, California. The NSWPP's telephone recording, the White Power Message, daily gives an oratory on white rights and anti-Semitic propaganda.

In the past two years, the New Order has actively recruited on college campuses, trying to enlist members by preaching a philosophy of National Socialism. This doctrine is based on three principles:

1. Natural Order—The belief that the universe is governed by natural laws, and that humanity must follow those natural

laws. Today's society, they assert, is in opposition to those laws.

2. Racial Idealism—Placing one's race above all else and doing all one can to protect the race. They believe that races are not created equal, and it is Aryan's right to maintain its biological, cultural and political independence, and the right to control its own destiny.

3. Upward development of the white race—They encourage a high birthrate among whites that are the strongest and healthiest, and the elimination of hereditary weaknesses and defects.

One basic difference between the Christian Identity movement and the neo-Nazis in America is that the neo-Nazis do not normally unify with other neo-Nazis. In fact, it is not uncommon for neo-Nazis to commit acts of violence against other neo-Nazis. Each neo-Nazi organization believes it is the only true white supremist party and other organizations are pretenders to the throne. This has also been true of the NSWPP.

Some subgroups of the NSWPP include the National Socialist Youth Movement, the National Socialist Women's Organization, and the Storm Troopers.

The Order
Headquarters: Hayden Lake, Idaho
Leader: Unknown

Of all far-right organizations in the United States, the Order has been the most violent and best organized (Harris, 1987). Formed in 1984 by Robert Mathews, the Order consists of members of the Aryan Nations who believe in a more organized, widespread, and violent campaign to overthrow the federal government and establish a nation of white rule (Mullins, 1989). The Order has used several names, including Bruder Schweigen (Silent Brotherhood), the White American Bastion, the Aryan Resistance Movement, and the White American Army of National Liberation for the Aryan Nations (Sapp, 1986a; Wiggins, 1986a; Mullins, 1988a; White, 1990).

Members of the Order have been involved in numerous criminal and terroristic activities including the robbery of City Bank in Seattle (1983), robbery of a Continental Armed Transport in Seattle (1983), murder of Walter Earl West (1984), murder of a Missouri State Trooper (1984), murder of Alan Berg in Denver (1984), robbery of a Brinks Armed Truck in Ukiah, California (1984), several shootouts with the FBI, and the planned assassination of presidential candidate Jesse Jackson (1988). Mathews and Order members had prepared a hit list of federal judges, prosecutors, FBI agents, law enforcement officers, and civil rights leaders (Wiggins, 1986c). Also, the Order stockpiled weapons, made plans for blowing up the Boundry Bridge in Seattle, Washington, disrupting the shipping lanes in Puget Sound, Washington, with LAWs rockets, and poisoning various municipal water supplies (Mullins,1988a). Using information from a federal informant, the FBI built a case against Robert Mathews (Dubin, 1988). Rather than "surrender to ZOG," Mathews died in a shootout with the FBI on Whidbey Island, Washington, in 1984.

In 1985, a federal grand jury indicted 23 members of the Order for numerous crimes, including murder, counterfeiting, robbery, and weapons violations (Wiggins, 1986b). In 1987, a federal grand jury in Ft. Smith, Arkansas, charged leaders of the Order, along with various other leaders of the far-right movement, with sedition (Mullins, 1988a, 1991). Among those charged were (1) Richard Joseph Scutori, chief security officer for the Order; (2) Bruce Carroll Pierce, suspected trigger man in the Alan Berg killing; (3) Jean Margaret Craig, the only female "warrior" in the Order; (4), David E. Lane, also charged with the killing of Alan Berg; (5) Richard Butler; (6) Robert Miles, of the Mountain Church of Jesus Christ the Savior in Cohoctah, Michigan; (7) Louis Ray Beam, Jr.; (8) Ardie McBrearty, intelligence chief and legal advisor to the Order; (9) Robert N. Smalley, member of the CSA; (10) Richard Wayne Snell; (11) Andrew V. Barnhill, member of the CSA; (12) William Wade, member of the CSA, Posse Comitatus, and KKK; (13) David M. McGuire, son-in-law of Jim Ellison; and (14) Lambert Miller, member of the CSA.

Additionally, Wade, McGuire, and Miller were indicted for attempting to kill Chief U.S. District Judge Franklin Waters and FBI agent Jack Knox. All 14 defendants were acquitted of the charges (Mullins, 1988a).

For a short time following the death of Mathews, the Order disbanded, but in 1986, reformed as the Bruder Schweigen Strike Force #2 (Broadbent, 1987). To date, the BSSF #2 has not been as violent as its predecessor.

Posse Comitatus
Headquarters: Numerous locations
Leader: Numerous persons

The Posse Comitatus was formed in 1973, in Portland, Oregon, by Gordon Kohl. The Posse Comitatus is also referred to as the Sheriff's Posse Comitatus and the Citizen's Law Enforcement Research Committee. The Posse Comitatus has several tenets, among them (1) the elimination of all taxes, (2) the overthrow of the "Jewish federal government" and a return of America to Anglo-Saxon origins, (3) the elimination of all federal, state, and municipal law enforcement agencies, (4) the establishment of county government as the primary form of government in the United States, and (5) hate campaigns against Jews and other minorities.

The Posse Comitatus has been involved in numerous violent activities, including a shoot-out between Gordon Kohl and federal marshals and a local sheriff (Bowers, 1987), and a shoot-out with agents of the ATF in 1979. The Posse Comitatus has engaged in paramilitary/survivalist training, stockpiling of weapons, and the creation of armed compounds around the country.

The economic downturn in farm prices, crop failures, and farm foreclosures of the 1980s have provided the Posse Comitatus (as well as the entire far right) a host of opportunities and new members. Selling the concept of Jewish control of the government and a Jewish conspiracy to drive the American farmer out of business, the Posse Comitatus has greatly increased its membership. Many farmers have looked to the Posse Comitatus to assist them through the economic hard-times and help defeat government controls. In order to help clarify the doctrine of the Posse Comitatus, part of a death note left by Gordon W. Kohl is printed below:

> I realize that being an enemy of the Jewish-Communist-synagog of Satan—is not condusive [sic] to a long life, so I am writing this while I still can. I am saddened by the fact that my hand had to be the instrument which sent these men to their reward, however—they attacked me and fired first, so I feel I was right, and justified in defending myself, and all those who were placed in this extreme danger with me. Had I to do it over again, I would have to do the same (From a display in the *U.S. Marshal's America Star: U.S. Marshals 1789–1989* museum).

The Posse Comitatus is fragmented. At various locations, the local chapters identify themselves by different names. For example, the chapter in Dallas, Texas, uses the name Citizens For Constitutional Compliance; in San Diego, California, the Know Your Rights Groups; in Canton, Ohio, the Citizens For Constitutional Rights; and in Racin, Wisconsin, the Christian Posse.

Skinheads
Headquarters: Numerous locations
Leader: Numerous persons

In the late 1980s, a new movement, from Europe and England, and involving a combination of neo-fascism and Christian Identity, appealed to some American youth. The Skinhead movement, the fastest growing of all right-wing movements, first appeared in the U.S. in 1985, in Michigan. This group called itself the "Romantic Violence." Unlike the punk-rock movement which preceded the Skinhead movement, the Skinheads represent a way of life which combines appearance, lifestyle, music, and philosophy into an ethos of racial hatred. In 1988, there were only about 300 Skinheads nationwide; in 1991, over 5,000, with chapters in most major cities. Skinheads are not unified in a national organization. Rather, they are localized at the community level and are autonomous from other organizations. Table 3 illustrates the more active and larger Skinhead organizations in the United States.

Although there is no one leader of the Skinhead movement, Thomas Metzger and his son, John, of California, proclaim themselves leaders. Thomas Metzger hosted a satellite television show called *Race and Reason,* which he used to provide information, recruit, and attempt to unify the Skinheads.

The ADL (1990a) has indicated that of all the far-right movements, the Skinheads are the least organized. Skinhead organizations are generally unstable and heavily dependent on their leaders. If the leader resigns, moves, or is imprisoned, the organization generally disbands. Also, Skinhead members are mobile, moving from organization to organization.

In and of itself, the Skinhead movement would pose little danger. The far right, however, has embraced the Skinheads as the salvation of the country and has provided indoctrination, training, weapons, and other material necessary to incorporate them into the white supremist movement. The far right sees the youthful exuberance of the Skinheads as the next wave of racial and religious violence. Speaking of the contributions skinheads could make to the goals of the far right, Richard Butler has stated that the Skinheads are the result of a ". . . natural biological reaction of white teenagers banding together after they have been taught that non-white kids are great and that white kids are scum. Skinheads will clean up the streets after receiving proper guidance" (Mullins, 1991). Richard Butler has even used Skinheads for security at the annual conventions in Hayden Lake, Idaho. Joe Grego, head of the Oklahoma White Man's Association and allied with the Klan, has led several Skinhead Aryan Fests in Oklahoma (ADL, 1990). The Texas Knights Klan organization has assisted the Confederate Hammer Skinheads, a Dallas, Texas, based Skinhead organization. In 1990, a group of Skinheads and KKK members demonstrated in Houston at the Economic Summit meeting. Far right participants included Louis Ray Beam, Richard Butler, Charles Lee, Kirk Lyons, and Thomas Robb.

Table 3. Skinhead Organizations in the United States

State City	Organization
Alabama	
Birmingham	Birmingham Area Skinheads
Homewood	No Name
Huntsville	Alabama Confederate Hammer Skinheads
Arizona	
Phoenix	Arizona Hammer Skinheads
Tucson	No Name
Yuma	No Name
California	
Bakersfield	War Skins
Garden Grove	American White Separatists
Los Angeles	Western Hammer Skins
Modesto	American Front Vikings
Orange County	18 organizations
San Diego	American Front and War Skins
San Francisco	American Front
San Luis Obispo	Peni Skins
Santa Barbara	Santa Barbara Boot Boys
Simi Valley	SVH Skins
Ventura	Ventura Boot Boys and Skinhead Dogs
Colorado	
Denver	Aryan Alliance, Boot Boys/Boot Girls, Rocky Mountain Confederate Hammer Skinheads
Connecticut	
Various Cities	No Names
Florida	
Orlando	Florida Corps Skins, Old Glory Skins, Young Southern Nationals, Youth Corp 87
Tampa	Bros
Temple Terrace	No Name
Treasure Coast	American Front
West Palm Beach	American Front
Georgia	
Atlanta	American Front, SS Strike Team
Illinois	
Chicago	Blue Island Skinheads, Chicago Area Skinheads, Chicago White Vikings
Indiana	
Indianapolis	Pure American Freedom Party
Louisiana	
New Orleans	National White Resistance
Maryland	
Baltimore	American Resistance, Baltimore Area Skinheads, Maryland Knights
Prince Georges County	No Name
Southern Maryland	Southern Maryland Area Skinheads (SMASH)

Table 3. Skinhead Organizations in the United States (cont'd.)

State City	Organization
Massachusetts	
Quincy	North Quincy Skinheads, South Boston Skinheads
Michigan	
Clio	United White Youth of Clio
Detroit	Northern Hammer Skins
Grand Rapids	Pit Bull Boys
Minnesota	
Minneapolis/St. Paul	Northern Hammer Skins, Nordic Fist
Nevada	
Las Vegas	Aryan Long Hairs, Las Vegas Skinheads
New Jersey	
Atlantic County	Atlantic City Skinheads
Burlington	Whit Combat Skinheads, White Power Skinheads
Hudson County	Bayonne Bulldog Bootboys
Mercer County	Trenton Guards, Trenton Posse
Middlesex County	Brunswick Skins
Monmouth County	Aryan Resistance, New Third World, New Way, Throckmorton Boys
Ocean County	Brick Town Guards
New Mexico	
Albuquerque	No Name
New York	
Long Island	No Name
Rochester	Buffalo Rochester Areas Skinheads (BRASH)
Oklahoma	
Tulsa	Boot Boys
Oregon	
Portland	American White Aryan Resistance (AWAR), United White Front, National White Separatists
Pennsylvania	
Philadelphia	White Combat, White Justice
Pittsburgh	No Name
Tennessee	
Chattanooga	Chattanooga Area Confederate Hammer Skins
Memphis	Memphis Area Skins
Nashville	Nashville Area Skinheads (NASH)
Texas	
Austin	Creativity Skins, Teutonic Order of Skinhead Aryan Youth Movement, United Skins of Austin
Dallas	Confederate Hammer Skins, Confederate White Vikings
Houston	National Socialist Skinheads of Houston
San Antonio	San Antonio Metropolitan Area Skinheads (SMASH)
Washington	
Seattle	American Front, League of American Workers (LAW)
Wisconsin	
Milwaukee	Northern Hammer Skins
Wyoming	
Casper	Casper Area Skinheads (CASH)

In the past couple of years, numerous Skinheads have been arrested and successfully prosecuted for hate crime activity. For example, in 1990, in Dallas, Texas, five Confederate Hammer Skinheads were convicted in federal court of civil rights violations for assaults on blacks and Hispanics, and for acts of vandalism against Jewish institutions. Skinheads in California, Colorado, Florida, Nevada, Oregon, and Pennsylvania have been convicted of murder. Hundreds of other Skinheads throughout the country have been convicted of assault, arson, burglary, illegal possession of weapons, kidnapping, and vandalism. The most significant case against Skinheads took place in Portland, Oregon, when in 1989, the ADL and the Southern Poverty Law Center brought a wrongful death suit against Tom and John Metzger, Kenneth Mieske (aka Ken Death), Kyle Brewster, and the White Aryan Resistance organization for the wrongful death of Mulugeta Seraw (ADL, 1990b). In 1990, a Portland jury returned a $12.5 million verdict against the five defendants; $3 million against Tom Metzger, $4 million against John Metzger, $5 million against WAR, and $500,000 each against the two Skinheads, Mieske and Brewster.

In the past year, changes have occurred within the Skinhead movement (ADL, 1990a). For example, Skinheads are recruiting younger members, they are moving around more than ever, probably in response to law enforcement initiatives, they are changing their physical appearance by letting their hair grow, and they are increasingly recruited and indoctrinated by the far right.

The above listing of far-right organizations is by no means complete. There are numerous other right-wing organizations operating in the United States. Some are quite violent while others limit themselves to inflammatory rhetoric. Some have only two or three members while the membership of others number in the hundreds. Table 4 lists some of the more active right-wing organizations not discussed in this chapter.

Table 4. Far-Right Extremist Groups in the United States

America First Committee	National Socialist League
American Resistance Movement	National Socialist Liberation Front
American White Nationalist Party	National Socialist Movement
Arizona Patriots	National Socialist Vanguard
Arizona Rangers	Nationalist Movement
Barristers Inn	National States Rights Party
California Rangers	Oklahoma White Man's Society
Citizen Emergency Defense System	Oregon Militia
Citizen's Emergency Network	Pure American Freedom Party
Civilian Military Assistance	Security Services Action Group
Church of the Creator	Social Nationalist Aryan People's Party
Elohim City	Texas Emergency Reserves
Euro-American Alliance Inc.	Universal Order
Farmers Liberation Army	Western Front
Florida National Socialist Party	White American Resistance
Guardian Knights of Justice	White Knights of Liberty
Heritage Society	White Patriots Party
Iowa Society for Educated Citizens	White Supremist Party
National Agriculture Press Assoc.	Wyoming Rangers
National Alliance	Yahweh Church (Black Hebrews)

Summary of Hate Crime Incidents

Any attempt to provide a complete listing of hate crimes occuring during any one particular time is fraught with problems. For example, not all hate crimes are reported; incidents of vandalism, assaults, attempted shootings, etc., are very often handled informally and go unreported; and others, when reported to law enforcement, are not classified as hate crimes. Whites assaulting a black, for example, may be classified as a neighborhood dispute, an argument between individuals, a crime of circumstances, or some other type of criminal activity. Other reported crimes between races or religions may be falsely recorded as a hate crime when the motive was not racial. Reported hate crimes may also not go beyond the reporting officer, lost in the vast archive of some local police department. Until recently, there has been no repository for hate crimes and police have not been required to report hate crime-activity. Often ignored or missed by the police and news media when dealing with hate-crime incidents is the political intent of the act, which indicates terrorism. Hate crime is not simply a "crime against property" or "crime against persons." Hate crime is a form of political crime. With these, and many other data collection problems data are bound to be inaccurate and biased.

Newton and Newton's (1991) chronology of hate crimes covers American history from 1501–1989, and is one of the most complete listings available. Using this, an analysis of hate-crime activity in the United States was conducted. Beyond the constraints described above, there are several other limitations to the following data analysis. One, the chronology of incidents provided by Newton and Newton were content analyzed and any incident which was not clearly identified as a hate crime was not included in the analysis. Second, as a rule, police brutality against a minority was not included as a hate crime unless the police involved in the incident specifically indicated that the incident of brutality was a hate crime. Three, incidents which occurred in jails and prisons were not included in the data analysis. As with acts of police brutality, there are too many other variables or factors involved in these incidents to classify them with any degree of certainty as hate crimes. Four, minority sniper attacks on police officers or firefighters were not included, since they are crimes against authority rather than race. Five, some multiple incidents were classified as single incidents. If several bombs were planted in different locations on the same day, that was considered a single episode of hate crime. Likewise, if a riot lasted several days, it was considered a single episode. Six, where several activities happened at one location or to one person, the incident was classified according to the worst activity which occurred. For example, if a person was beaten and then shot, that incident was classified as a shooting.

The majority of hate-crime incidents reported by Newton and Newton (1991) were not committed by members of the far right. In fact, only about 10 percent can be directly attributed to them. This is entirely understandable since one of the goals of the far right is to serve as a catalyst for action and to provide the impetus for action by others.

Incidents provided by Newton and Newton (1991) were analyzed for the period 1951–1989. The early 1950s began the long struggle for equality and civil rights and was the first decade in which whites and minorities began interacting daily in all aspects of life. Minorities began opening and operating businesses on a wide scale. Schools and neighborhoods became desegregated. Minorities and whites began interacting socially, and interracial relationships became a reality. On the religious front, Catholics and Jews began openly professing their faith and demanding religious equality. In sum, truly for the first time in United States history, America had the appearance, at least, of a "melting pot."

Figures 1–4 give the number of hate-crime incidents per year.

In Figure 1, the significant rise in events in 1956 correspond to school desegregation. Many of the incidents in 1956 (19), 1957 (14), and 1958 (11), can be directly linked to school desegregation issues and others are likely indirectly attributed to school desegregation. In 1964, court ordered school desegregation came to Mississippi. In 1964 (Figure 2), of 169 incidents of hate crimes, 137 occurred in Mississippi. As also shown in Figure 2, in 1968, the country erupted in a series of riots and other hate crimes following the assassination of Martin Luther King in Memphis (April 4). By the early 1970s, most of the activity in response to King's assassination had died out. Overall, in the decades studied, whites committed over 90 percent of all hate crimes reported by Newton and Newton (1991). In the 1960s, almost 40 percent of hate crimes were committed by blacks and mostly during the years 1968, 1969, and 1970.

There apparently is little explanation for the rise in hate-crime activity in 1980, 1985, and 1986 (Figures 3 and 4). It is likely that in large part, the rise in hate-crime activity in 1985 and 1986 can be explained by public awareness of the far right. Right-wing meetings, criminal activities, and other activities were covered extensively by the media. The public became much more aware of the far right, and in some pockets it became "fashionable" to participate in hate-crime activities. Additionally, the mid-1980s saw America enter a recession. During periods of recession, it is

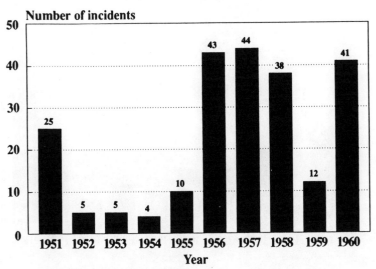

Figure 1. Sampling of hate crime
incidents from 1951 to 1960

NOTE 1: 1956 was the start of school desegregation.

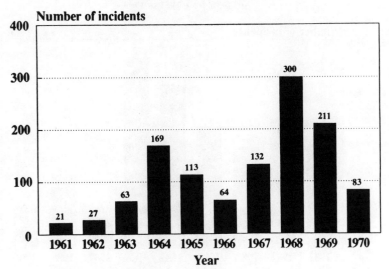

Figure 2. Sampling of hate crime
incidents from 1961 to 1970

NOTE 1: Martin Luther King was assassinated in April 1968.

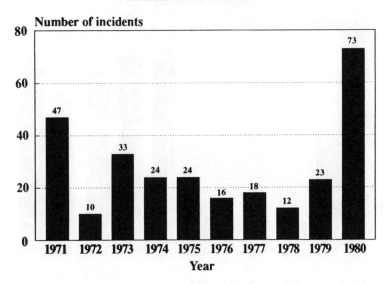

Figure 3. Sampling of hate crime incidents from 1971 to 1980

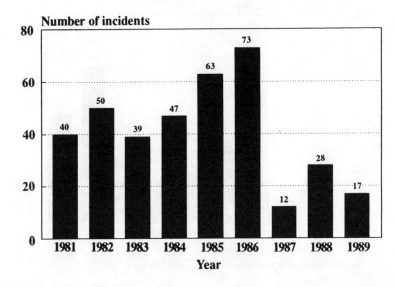

Figure 4. Sampling of hate crime incidents from 1981 to 1989

common for whites to blame economic woes on minorities (e.g., ZOG). In general, the mid-1980s provided an opportune political environment for the right-wing terrorist. The Republican administration virtually ignored the social, economic, and racial woes of America. Important issues concerning minorities such as jobs, housing, and education were ignored. Thus, the Reagan/Bush administration gave the implied signal that minorities were truly second-class citizens. In fact, President Reagan even considered disbanding the Equal Employment Opportunity Commission. It did not take long for the far right to pick up on the signals being sent by the Washington administration. Many other whites also interpreted the governmental "deaf ear" as approval of racism. An incident which occurred during the 1988 Presidential campaign serves to illustrate the Republican conservatism and the message being sent to the people. A Massachusetts prisoner, Willie Horton, a black inmate serving a prison sentence for murder, was paroled. While on parole, Horton raped a woman (both victims were white). The Republicans used the Horton incident to show that Democrats and their candidate, Massachusetts governor Dukakis, were soft on crime. On a much larger scale, the Horton incident served to fuel the already growing fires of racial hatred in white America. The Republican party did nothing to douse the flames. Thus, some increases in hate-crime activity can be attributed both to the recession and the conservative political climate in the country.

An examination of where hate crimes occur may help understand them better. Table 5 lists the frequency of hate crimes by state. Mississippi, for example, had a very low rate of hate crimes when school desegregation incidents of the 1960s were factored out (from 288 to 24 incidents). Discounting Mississippi's turbulent 1960s, the states with the highest incidents of hate crime are New York (181), Alabama (166), Georgia (149), California (117), and Illinois (110). States with the lowest incidents of hate crime include Maine and North Dakota (0), Hawaii and Wyoming (1), New Hampshire (2), Utah (2), Vermont (2), New Mexico (3), Nevada (4), West Virginia (5), Arizona (6), Colorado (6), Iowa, (7), and Minnesota (7). Many of these states, of course, have either

Table 5. Hate Crimes by State for Decades Since 1951

	1951–1960	1961–1970	1971–1980	1981–1989	Total
Alabama	50	85	23	8	166
Arizona	0	3	1	2	6
Arkansas	10	15	5	2	32
California	1	50	37	29	117
Colorado	0	2	1	3	6
Connecticut	0	22	3	6	31
Delaware	3	5	0	2	10
D.C.	0	10	1	0	11
Florida	19	62	14	12	107
Georgia	23	59	13	54	149
Hawaii	0	1	0	0	1
Idaho	0	0	0	10	10
Illinois	5	74	10	21	110
Indiana	0	11	8	9	28
Iowa	0	6	0	1	7
Kansas	0	8	1	1	10
Kentucky	4	10	1	6	21
Louisiana	7	46	5	6	64
Maryland	1	16	1	17	35
Massachusetts	0	11	18	14	43
Michigan	0	39	7	8	54
Minnesota	0	4	2	1	7
Mississippi	12	266	3	7	288
Missouri	2	11	2	5	20
Nebraska	0	4	3	1	8
Nevada	0	3	1	0	4
New Hampshire	0	0	0	2	2
New Jersey	0	58	16	4	78
New Mexico	0	1	1	1	3
New York	1	101	39	40	181
N. Carolina	18	40	10	29	97
Ohio	2	34	7	6	49
Oklahoma	1	0	2	0	3
Oregon	0	4	0	4	8
Pennsylvania	0	43	3	13	59
Rhode Island	0	8	0	2	10
S. Carolina	14	11	1	4	30
S. Dakota	0	0	24	0	24
Tennessee	30	19	5	6	60
Texas	12	11	7	20	50
Utah	0	0	1	1	2
Vermont	0	0	1	1	2
Virginia	9	10	1	2	22
Washington	0	7	0	3	10
West Virginia	3	1	0	1	5
Wisconsin	0	12	2	4	18
Wyoming	0	0	0	1	1

Note: Maine, Montana, and North Dakota reported no hate-crime incidents low populations or low minority populations, excluding New Hampshire, Vermont, and West Virginia.

Table 6 lists incidents of hate crime by geographical region.

Not surprisingly, most incidents of hate crime occurred in the Southeast (44%) and least in the Northwest (2%). In the last two decades, however, incidents of hate crime have been fairly well distributed across the Northeast, Southeast, and Midwest. Incidents of hate crime have been increasing in the Northeast and decreasing in the Southeast. These data tend to dispel the widespread belief that most hate crimes occur in the South. For example, data on anti-Semitic vandalism reported by the ADL (1991b) show that in 1990, 55 percent of all reported instances of vandalism occurred in the Northeast (see Table 6 for a list of states for each region), 9

Table 6. Hate Crime Incidents by Geographical Area for Decades since 1951

	1951–1960	1961–1970	1971–1980	1981–1989	Total
No. of Incidents % for Decade					Total number and % of Total
Northeast[1]	17	285	83	104	489
	.07	.24	.30	.28	.24
Southeast[2]	166	542	69	120	897
	.73	.46	.25	.33	.44
Midwest[3]	13	213	67	63	356
	.06	.18	.24	.17	.17
Midsouth[4]	30	72	19	28	149
	.13	.06	.07	.08	.07
Northwest[5]	0	13	2	22	37
	.00	.01	.00	.06	.02
Southwest[6]	1	58	40	32	131
	.00	.05	.14	.09	.06
Totals	227	1183	280	369	= 2059
(% of total)	(.11)	(.57)	(.14)	(.18)	

1. CT, DE, DC, ME, MD, MA, NH, NJ, NY, PA, RI, VT, VA, WV
2. AL, FL, GA, MS, NC, SC, TN
3. IL, IN, IA, KS, KY, MI, MN, MO, NE, OH, SD, WI
4. AR, AL, OK, TX
5. CO, ID, OR, UT, WA, WY
6. AZ, CA, HI, NV, NM

percent in the Southeast, 13 percent in the Midwest, 1% in the
Midsouth, 5 percent in the Northwest, and 17 percent in the
Southwest. According to ADL data, the Southwest is "catching up"
with the rest of the country in incidents of hate crime. This increase
in the Southwest is to be expected as the population there increases.

Another question of interest concerns the part of the year in
which hate crimes are most likely to occur. Table 7 provides data
on hate crimes by month. It is immediately apparent that there is
some validity to the notion of the "long hot summer," as hate
crimes occur in July and August more often than in any other
month. Again, April is inflated in the 1960s due to Martin Luther
King's assassination. The least number of hate crimes occur in
December. It may be that even racists are infected with the "peace
on earth, goodwill to men" spirit that Christmastime brings.

Table 7. Summary of Hate Crime Incidents by Month for Decades Since 1951

	1951–1960	1961–1970	1971–1981	1981–1989	Total
January	31	50	18	24	123
February	14	80	17	28	139
March	13	85	15	27	140
April	19	266	24	36	345
May	14	99	23	28	164
June	11	89	27	44	171
July	14	192	31	40	277
August	25	154	22	23	226
September	27	70	31	34	162
October	22	38	26	32	118
November	15	41	30	27	113
December	22	19	16	24	81
Totals	227	1183	280	369	2059

Table 8 gives a listing of types of incident by decade.

Table 8. Types of Hate Crime Incidents by Decade

	1951–1960	1961–1970	1971–1980	1981–1989	Total
Bombing	97	139	22	62	320
Burning/Arson	13	135	16	49	213
Mob/Riot	39	613	86	29	767
Assault	52	152	63	140	407
Shooting	21	129	89	58	297
Vandalism	5	15	4	31	55
Totals	227	1183	280	369	2059

The reader should be aware of some issues concerning the data. One, for multiple activities committed at one time, only the most serious activity is included. If a building were vandalized and bombed, the incident would be classified as a bombing. Two, if it was reported that an individual was killed (with no further explanation), that incident was classified as an assault. Three, all categories include attempts. If an explosive device was placed in a building but failed to detonate (for whatever reason), that incident was classified as a bombing. Four, the assault category covers many types of incidents including beatings, knifings, use of other weapons (clubs, chains, bottles, etc.), abduction, and threats of violence. Five, mobs or riots had to involve four or more people (otherwise the incident was classified as an assault) and had to involve multiple acts, such as beatings and vandalism. Also, takeovers of a building or office by four or more people were classified as mobs or riots.

The data show that hate crimes are well distributed across types of incident. Assaults are higher than other types of incidents because that category contains various types of incidents. Mobs/riots were somewhat elevated because of the 1960s. Vandalism is probably significantly underrepresented, since vandalism, more than any other type of hate crime, is probably not reported to authorities or to the media.

Table 9 gives the number of persons killed each year in instances of hate crime. Again, the race riots of the 1960s greatly elevated hate-crime figures. Although it appears that deaths due to hate crime have been decreasing in the past decade, the proportion of deaths to total number of yearly incidents have been increasing. Over the past decade, although instances of hate crime decreased slightly, violence against persons increased.

Table 10 lists acts of vandalism and assaults, threats, and harassments on minorities as collected by the ADL (1991b). These data illustrate that incidents of hate crime are significantly greater than reported by Newton and Newton (1991). In addition, the ADL reported that in 1990, there were 38 serious crimes of arson, bombings, and cemetery desecrations. One disturbing trend in particular reported by the ADL concerns hate crime on college and university campuses. The ADL reported 69 instances of hate crimes committed on 54 college and university campuses across the nation in 1989, and 95 instances of hate crimes committed on 57 college and university campuses in 1990. The very people who we surmise should be most resistant to the message of the far right are those who are becoming actively involved in spreading that message.

Although problematic, these data are the most acccurate available. Some incidents, specifically mob/riot incidents, are probably overrepresented and vandalism underrepresented.

The Future of Hate Crime in the United States

Hate crime in the United States undoubtedly will become a more serious problem in the coming decade. Issues now confronting our society more than likley will become more severe in the foreseeable future and result in increased numbers of people who turn to the far-right's messages to solve their problems. Drugs, crime, unemployment, AIDS, and homelessness have no easy solutions. With no identifiable solutions, many people will accept

Table 9. Deaths from Hate Crime Incidents by Year

Year	No.	Year	No.	Year	No.	Year	No.
1951	3	1961	1	1971	11–3	1981	1
1952	0	1962	4	1972	6	1982	18
1953	0	1963	11	1973	25 (b)	1983	4
1954	0	1964	9	1974	10 (b)	1984	4
1955	6	1965	9	1975	10	1985	14
1956	12	1966	7	1976	10	1986	9
1957	2	1967	84–81 (a)	1977	10 (c)	1987	4
1958	1	1968	75–61	1978	10 (c)	1988	3
1959	1	1969	15–9	1979	10 (c)	1989	5
1960	2	1970	23–9	1980	50–16		

Notes: (a) Whenever a second number appears, that number indicates the the number of deaths which occurred during mob/riot incidents for that year.

(b) Black Muslim splinter group Death Angels were responsible for a series of Zebra killings in California. In 1973, there were 10 Zebra killings, in 1974, there were 6.

(c) Racist serial killer Joseph Paul Franklin killed 3 people in 1977, 3 people in 1979, and 9 people in 1980.

Table 10.
ADL Summary of Vandalism and other
Hate Crime Incidents for the 1980s

	Number of Vandalisms	Number of Assaults, Threats, Harassment
1980	377	112
1981	974	350
1982	829	593
1983	670	350
1984	715	363
1985	638	306
1986	594	312
1987	694	324
1988	823	458
1989	845	587
Totals	7159	3755

the far-right's political messages that these social ills are caused by minorities and religious groups. The far right may intensify its efforts to recruit from the white population most affected by these social ills—the blue collar worker (Flynn & Gerhardt, 1989; Strentz, 1990). Persons with low employment opportunities, persons vulnerable to crime, persons whose families are faced with the issue of drug abuse, persons with changing demographic patterns around them, and persons affected by other assorted societal influences will be those recruited by the far right. To many, the solutions of violence and extermination will become solutions of reality and logic instead of solutions grounded in fantasy and insanity. By increasing hate-crime activity, the far right will continue to spread the messge that the current political system is ineffective and does not work. The far right will continue to use campaigns of hate to attempt to convince other citizens of the necessity for political change.

To prey on the vulnerabilities of a society seeking cures, the far right, in some instances, has toned down its violent rhetoric. The involvement of David Duke in Louisiana and national politics is a clear example of the "new" direction some members of the far right advocate. Claiming to have abandoned his racist ways, Duke successfully ran under the Republican banner for the Louisiana state legislature in 1989 and since has continued to engage in far-right activities. He appeared at a meeting of the right-wing Populist Party (where he shared the podium with Art Jones of the American Nazi Party), sold neo-Nazi books from his state-funded district constituent's office (including *Mein Kampf; Did Six Million Die? The Truth At Last*, a book claiming the Holocaust was a Jewish hoax), and allowed his organization, the National Association for the Advancement of White People, to publish an anti-Semitic newsletter which argues for the creation of ghettos for Jews (Cohler, 1989; Vetter & Perlstein, 1991). This newsletter has over 30,000 subscribers. As recent as January 1987, in Cummings, Georgia, Duke was arrested, along with 54 other whites, including many KKK members, at a March Against Fear rally (Newton & Newton, 1991). Other far-right members conceivably could enter politics.

In the next decade, the far right could become stronger and better unified, actively recruit youth into its movement, and provide training. The far right may increase its use of modern technology to unify, recruit, and spread its message of hate. The far right now makes use of computer bulletin boards to share information, and (Mullins, 1988a) satellite and cable television to reach white America. In addition to Metzger's *Race and Reason* television show, the far right has programs airing in 24 of the 100 largest television markets in the United States, including Los Angeles, San Diego, Minneapolis, Seattle, Chicago, Tampa, Pittsburgh, Phoenix, Atlanta, Boston, Denver, and Houston (ADL, 1991a). Shows are titled *The Other Israel, Airlink, Crusade for Christ and Country, Our Israelite Origin,* and *The Joe Goyim Show.*

On a more positive note, America is fighting back. One of the most significant responses in several years is the Hate Crime Statistics Act. Signed on April 23, 1991, by President Bush, this Act requires that the United States Attorney General acquire data on hate crimes and annually publish those findings. Hate crime statistics became a part of the FBI's Uniform Crime Reporting Program in 1992. Several states already require law enforcement personnel to provide information on hate crimes (viz., Connecticut, Florida, Idaho, Illinois, Maryland, Massachusetts, New Jersey, New York, Oklahoma, Oregon, Pennsylvania, and Virginia). In addition to federal statutes, many states have hate-crime laws, providing criminal punishments for acts ranging from vandalism to intimidation and harassment. Some states even have statutes assigning parental liability for juveniles who engage in hate crimes. Table 11 lists the states having hate-crime statutes. Several states (Illinois, Minnesota, Oregon, and Pennsylvania) require that law enforcement personnel receive training in identifying, responding to, and reporting hate crimes. Other states may follow suit in the coming years.

While the far right continues to use hate crime as a tool to change and/or overthrow the government, and will probably always continue to do so, many people are engaged in efforts to stop such movements. Americans need more education to understand that hate crime is political crime and to realize that hate crime affects all Americans, not just targeted minorities. Only then can this particular form of political terrorism be contained.

Table 11. Summary of State Hate Crime Laws

	Vandalism	Harassment Intimidation*	Parental Liability	Data Collection
Alabama	Yes	No	Yes	No
Alaska	No	No	Yes	No
Arizona	Yes	No	Yes	No
Arkansas	Yes	No	Yes	No
California	Yes	Yes	Yes	Yes
Colorado	Yes	Yes	Yes	Yes
Connecticut	Yes	Yes	Yes	Yes
Delaware	Yes	No	Yes	No
D.C.	Yes	Yes	Yes	Yes
Florida	Yes	Yes	Yes	Yes
Georgia	Yes	Yes	No	No
Hawaii	Yes	No	No	No
Idaho	No	Yes	Yes	Yes
Illinois	Yes	Yes	Yes	Yes
Indiana	Yes	No	Yes	No
Iowa	No	Yes	Yes	No
Kansas	Yes	No	Yes	No
Kentucky	Yes	No	No	No
Louisiana	Yes	No	No	No
Maine	Yes	No	Yes	No
Maryland	Yes	Yes	Yes	Yes
Massachusetts	Yes	Yes	Yes	Yes
Michigan	No	Yes	Yes	No
Minnesota	No	Yes	Yes	Yes
Mississippi	Yes	Yes	Yes	No
Missouri	Yes	Yes	No	No
Montana	No	Yes	Yes	No
Nebraska	No	No	Yes	No
Nevada	Yes	Yes	Yes	No
New Jersey	Yes	Yes	Yes	Yes
New Mexico	Yes	Yes	Yes	No
New York	No	Yes	Yes	No
N. Carolina	Yes	Yes	Yes	No
North Dakota	No	Yes	Yes	No
Ohio	Yes	Yes	Yes	No
Oklahoma	Yes	Yes	Yes	Yes
Oregon	Yes	Yes	Yes	Yes
Pennsylvania	Yes	Yes	Yes	Yes

Table 11. Summary of State Hate Crime Laws (cont'd.)

	Vandalism	Harassment Intimidation*	Parental Liability	Data Collection
Rhode Island	Yes	Yes	No	Yes
South Carolina	No	Yes	Yes	No
South Dakota	No	Yes	Yes	No
Tennessee	No	Yes	No	No
Texas	Yes	No	Yes	No
Utah	No	No	No	No
Vermont	Yes	Yes	Yes	No
Virginia	Yes	Yes	Yes	Yes
Washington	Yes	Yes	Yes	No
West Virginia	No	Yes	Yes	No
Wisconsin	Yes	Yes	Yes	No
Wyoming	No	No	Yes	No

*Category of harassment and intimidation includes cross burning and otherwise interfering with religious worship.

REFERENCES

Anti-Defamation League. 1983. *Extremism on the Right*. New York: Anti-Defamation League of B'nai B'rith.

———. 1990a. *Neo-Nazi Skinheads: A 1990 Status Report*. New York: Anti-Defamation League of B'nai B'rith.

———. 1990b. *Skinheads on Trial*. New York: Anti-Defamation League of B'nai B'rith.

———. 1991a. *Electronic Hate: Bigotry Comes to TV*. New York: Anti-Defamation League of B'nai B'rith.

———. 1991b. *1990 Audit of Anti-Semitic Incidents*. New York: Anti-Defamation League of B'nai B'rith.

———. 1991c. *The KKK Today: A 1991 Status Report*. New York: Anti-Defamation League of B'nai B'rith.

Barker, W. E. 1985. "Linkages and Co-participants in Right-wing Groups." Paper presented at the Academy of Criminal Justice Sciences, Las Vegas, Nevada (April).

Benware, P. N. 1984. *Ambassadors Of Armstrongism*. Fort Washington, Pa.: Christian Literature Crusade.

Besser, J. D. 1982. "The Doomsday Decade." *Progress*, 46–66.

Blumberg, M. 1986. "A Comparative Analysis of Violent Left- and Right-wing Extremist Groups in the United States." Paper at the American Society of Criminology, Atlanta, Ga. (Oct.).

Bowers, R. 1987. "White Radicals Charged with Sedition." *Arkansas Gazette,* April 25, 1, 11.

Broadbent, L. 1987. *Terrorism.* Law Enforcement Satellite Training Network. Kansas City: Kansas City Police Department.

Coates, J. 1987. *Armed And Dangerous: The Rise of the Survivalist Right.* New York: Hill and Wang.

Cohler, L. 1989. "Republican Racist: Dealing with the David Duke Problem." *The New Republic,* 201, 11–14.

Dubin, M. 1988. *Fugitive from Hate.* Philadelphia, Pa.: *Philadelphia Inquirer.*

Finch, P. 1983. *God, Guts, and Guns.* New York: Seaview Putnam.

Flynn, K. and T. G. Gerhard. 1989. *The Silent Brotherhood: Inside America's Racist Underground.* New York: Free Press.

Fromkin, D. 1978. "The Strategy of Terrorism." In Elliot, J.D. and L. K. Gibson (eds.). *Contemporary Terrorism: Selected Readings.* Gaithersburg, Md.: International Association of Chiefs of Police.

Gurr, T.R. 1988. "Political Terrorism in the United States: Historical Antecedents and Contemporary Trends." In Stohl, R. (ed.). *The Politics of Terrorism.* New York: Dekker.

Harris, J. W. 1987. "Domestic Terrorism in the 1980s." *FBI Law Enforcement Bulletin,* 56, 5–15.

Holden, R. N. 1985. "Historical and International Perspectives on Right-wing Militancy in the United States." Paper presented at the Academy of Criminal Justice Sciences, Las Vegas, Nev. (March).

———. 1986a. "Postmillennialism as a Justification for Right-wing Violence." Paper presented at the Academy of Criminal Justice Sciences, Orlando, Fla. (April).

———. 1986b. "Right-wing Ideology as Expressed in the Writings of William P. Gale." Paper at the Academy of Criminal Justice Sciences, Orlando, Fla. (March).

———. 1987. "Conservatism, Fundamentalism and Identity Theology: The Road to Religious Extremism." Paper presented at the Academy of Criminal Justice Sciences, St. Louis, Mo. (March).

Jenkins, B. M. 1975. *International Terrorism: A New Mode Of Conflict.* Research paper 48, California Seminar on Arms Control and Foreign Policy. Los Angeles: Crescent Publications.

Kornbluth, J. 1987. "Taking on the Klan." *San Antonio Light,* Nov. 8, 1, 3e.

Magnuson, E. 1989. An Ex-Klansman's Win Brings the G.O.P. Chickens Home to Roost. *Time,* Mar. 6, 29.

Marty, M.E. 1983. "Survivalism." *Christian Century,* 831, 14–21.

Melnichak, J. M. 1986. "Chronicle of Hate: A Brief History of the Radical Right." *The Police Marksman,* Sep./Oct., 42.

Milbank, D. L. 1978. "International and Transnational Terrorism: Diagnosis and Prognosis." In Elliot, J.D. and L. K. Gibson (eds.). *Contemporary Terrorism: Selected Readings.* Gaithersburg, Md.: International Association of Chiefs of Police.

Mitchell, J. G. 1983. "Waiting for Apocalypse." *Audobon,* Mar, 18–25.

Mullins, W. C. 1988a. *Terrorist Organizations In the United States: An Analysis of Issues, Organizations, Tactics and Responses.* Springfield, Ill.: Charles C. Thomas, Pub.

———. 1988b. "Stopping Terrorism: The Problems Posed by the Organizational Infrastructure of Terrorist Organizations." *Journal of Contemporary Criminal Justice,* 4, 214–228.

———. 1989. "Domestic Terrorism into the 1990s: The Aftermath of the Ft. Smith, Arkansas, Sedition Trial." Paper presented at Society of Police and Criminal Psychology, Savannah, Ga. (Oct.).

———. 1990. "Terrorism in the United States: Predictions for the 1990's." *Police Chief,* Sep., 44–46.

———. 1991. "The Awakening of the Far Right: The Bootsteps of Hate March Forward." Paper presented at the Academy of Criminal Justice Sciences, Nashville, Tenn. (March).

Nehemiah Township Charter and Common Law Contract. 1982. *Deed of Records,* County of Kootenai, Idaho, Vol. 120, 387.

New English Bible. 1970. Cambridge, England: Oxford University Press.

Newton, M. and J. A. Newton. 1991. *Racial And Religious Violence In America: A Chronology.* New York: Garland Publishing.

Pomerantz, S. L. 1987. "The FBI and Terrorism." *FBI Law Enforcement Bulletin*, 56, 15–23.

Randel, W. P. 1965. *The Ku Klux Klan: A Century of Infamy*. New York: Chilton Books.

Sapp, A. D. 1985. "Basic Ideologies of Right-wing Extremist Groups in America." Paper presented at the Academy of Criminal Justice Sciences, Las Vegas, Nev. (March).

———. 1986a. "Rationalization for Domestic Violence: An Analysis of the Secret Army . . . Wenn Alle Bruder Schweignen." Paper presented at the Academy of Criminal Justice Sciences, Orlando, Fla. (April).

———. 1986b. "The Nehemiah Township Charter: Applied Right-wing Ideology." Paper presented at the Academy of Criminal Justice Sciences, Orlando, Fla. (April).

———. 1986c. "A Philosophy of Terrorism as Expressed in the Turner Diaries." Paper presented at the American Society of Criminology, Atlanta, Ga. (October).

———. 1987. "Organizational Linkages of Right-wing Extremist Groups." Paper presented at the Academy of Criminal Justice Sciences, St. Louis, Mo. (April).

Stills, P. 1989. "Dark Contagion: Bigotry and Violence Online." *PC Computing*, Dec., 144–149.

Stimson, E. 1986. *Christianity Today*, Aug., 30–31.

Stinson, J. 1987. "Domestic Terrorism in the United States." *The Police Chief*, Sep., 62–69.

Stohl, M. 1985. "States, Terrorism, and State Terrorism: The Role of Superpowers." *Proceedings Of The Symposium On International Terrorism*. Washington, D. C.: Defense Intelligence Agency.

Strentz, T. 1990. "Radical Right vs. Radical Left: Terrorist Theory and Threat. "*Police Chief*, Aug., 70–75.

Suall, I. and D. Lowe 1987. Special Report—The Hate Movement Today: A Chronical of Violence and Disarray." *Terrorism*, 10, 345–364.

Vetter, H. J. and G. R. Perlstein. 1991. *Perspectives on Terrorism*. Pacific Grove, Calif.: Brooks/Cole Pub. Co.

White, J. R. 1986. *Holy War: Terrorism as a Theological Construct*. Gaithersburg, Md.: International Association of Chiefs of Police.

————. 1990. *Terrorism: An Introduction.* Pacific Grove, Calif.: Brooks/Cole.

Wiggins, M. E. 1985a. "Rationale and Justification for Right-wing Terrorism: A Politico-social Analysis of the Turner Diaries." Paper presented at the American Society of Criminology, Atlanta, Ga. (October).

————. 1985b. "The Relationship of Extreme Right Ideologies and Geographical Distribution of Selected Right Wing Groups." Paper at the Academy of Criminal Justice Sciences, Las Vegas, Nev. (March).

————. 1986a. "An Extremist Right-wing Group and Domestic Terrorism." Paper presented at the Academy of Criminal Justice Sciences, Orlando, Fla. (April).

————. 1986b. "The Turner Diaries: Blueprint for Right-wing Extremist Violence." Paper presented at the Academy of Criminal Justice Sciences, Orlando, Fla. (April).

————. 1986c. "A Descriptive Profile of Criminal Activities of a Right-wing Extremist Group." Paper presented at the Society of Police and Criminal Psychology, Little Rock, Ark. (October).

————. 1987. "Preparing for War: Right-wing Paramilitary Training." Paper presented at the Academy of Criminal Justice Sciences, St. Louis, Mo. (April).

WMAQ. 1985. *The Dragons of God.* News documentary (Feb.). Chicago, Ill.: WMAQ Television.

World Press Review. 1985. *"Born" in the U.S.: Terrorist training in the South,* Sep., 39–40.

JUDY ROOT AULETTE AND RAYMOND MICHALOWSKI

Fire in Hamlet: A Case Study of a State-Corporate Crime

Introduction

On September 3, 1991, an explosion and fire at the Imperial Food Products chicken processing plant in Hamlet, North Carolina, killed 25 workers and injured another 56 (Morell and Perlmutt, 1991:4). This human disaster, which devastated the small working-class community of Hamlet, immediately became the subject of both controversy and investigation. Shortly after the fire there was speculation that Imperial might face felony manslaughter charges in the deaths because fire doors that would have led the workers to safety were deliberately kept locked. According to a number of workers at the plant, fire doors were "routinely locked to keep employees from stealing chicken nuggets" (Drescher and Garfield, 1991:1). Subsequent inquiry indicated that not only did the company lock the fire doors, one of which displayed the bloody footprints of workers who tried to batter it open before they died, but also that an interwoven pattern of regulatory failure on the part of several state and federal agencies played a significant role in creating the conditions that led to the tragedy. This regulatory failure was facilitated by the State of North Carolina through its refusal to fund and support the state's Occupational Safety and Health Program even to the limits of *available* Federal monies. In 1990, a year before the Imperial plant fire, the State of North Carolina returned $453,000 in unspent OSHA money to the Federal government, even though its OSHA program was "underfunded and overwhelmed" and state safety inspections had fallen to their lowest level in 16 years (Parker and O'Brien, 1991:1). The fire at the Imperial Food Processing plant and the regulatory environment that made it possible underscore the importance of the interplay between corporations and government in the production of life-threatening criminal conduct by businesses. The *technical cause* of the Imperial plant fire was the rupture of a hydraulic line near a deep fryer. This resulted in an explosion and a fireball that not only destroyed, the plant and the lives of 25 workers, but also shattered the social make-up of an entire town. Those who died or were injured in the Hamlet fire, however, were the victims of much more than a simple mechanical breakdown. They were the victims of a series of *social decisions* made by a broad array of institutions. These include Imperial Food Products, the U.S. Occupational Safety and Health Administration, the U.S. Food and Drug Administration, the legislature and governor of the State of North Carolina, the North Carolina Occupational Safety and Health Administration, and, finally, local agencies responsible for building inspection and fire protection. These organizational units pursued a pattern of actions and relations that made it possible and routine that workers in the Imperial chicken processing plant would be denied adequate escape routes in case of fire. This pattern does not represent an aberrant moment in North Carolina labor history. Rather, we argue, it is only a current reflection of North Carolina's long-standing commitment to a development policy based on attracting industry by offering low taxation and, particularly relevant in the immediate case, a lax regulatory environment.

   In this chapter we will examine the ways in which the interplay of government and business interests in North Carolina culminated in the disastrous fire at the Imperial chicken processing plant. Specifically, we will argue that the deaths and injuries in Hamlet represent an example of what Kramer and Michalowski (1990) term *state-corporate crime*, and we will explore three nested contexts—the societal context, the organizational context, and the control context—that shaped the conditions which produced 25 new graves in Hamlet, North Carolina in the fall of 1991.

State-Corporate Crime in Context

In his 1939 Presidential Address to the American Sociological Association, Edwin Sutherland introduced the concept of *white-collar crime*, which later served as the basis for his pioneering book by the same title. Although Sutherland was primarily concerned with the social class positions of "white-collar" offenders as *individuals*, the data he actually analyzed consisted of violations charged against corporations and businesses as *organizations* (Sutherland, 1940). This contradiction in Sutherland's work ultimately led to the study of what has become known as "corporate crime." The study of corporate crime focuses on deviant organizational patterns rather than on the deviance of individuals (Clinard and Yeager, 1980; Braithwaite, 1985; Kramer, 1984). This approach has resulted in an important insight and an important oversight. The *insight* is that corporate crime is a form of organizational deviance (Hagan, 1988:3; Clinard and Yeager, 1980:17). Insofar as corporations are formal organizations, the study of corporate crime can and should incorporate the theoretical and substantive insights of organizational research (Vaughan, 1983). The *oversight* is the failure to recognize that since the modern corporation emerged as the basic unit of economic activity within private-production systems in the late 19th century, corporations and governments have been functionally interdependent. The modern corporation in the United States could not have developed, nor could it currently function, without the legal, economic, and political infrastructure provided by government (Sklar, 1988). Governments in private-production systems, in turn, depend upon corporations and other economic organization to supply necessary goods and services, to provide the economic base in the form of individual salaries and/or corporate profits upon which governments must depend for their revenues, and to make possible the fulfillment of government development policies (Offe and Ronge, 1982).

Despite its ubiquity, the relationship between corporations and governmental units has been peripheral to the study of corporate crime. Instead, two nearly independent bodies of research have developed. Theory and research in the area of corporate crime has concentrated primarily on organizational deviance *within* private business corporations. Parallelling corporate crime research, but seldom intersecting with it, others have examined crimes and malfeasance by governments, what Chambliss (1989) terms "state-organized crime." These latter are crimes or socially injurious actions that result as governmental organizations pursue goals that cannot be attained, or cannot be attained easily, within the boundaries of the government's own laws (Ermann and Lundman, 1987; Roebuck and Weber, 1978; Simon and Eitzen, 1990).

Our argument here is that many injurious events, such as the killing fire at the Imperial chicken processing factory, are generated at the interstices of corporations and governments. Kramer and Michalowski (1990) have defined these state-corporate crimes as follows:

> State-corporate crimes are illegal or socially injurious actions that occur when one or more institutions of political governance pursue a goal in direct cooperation with one or more institutions of economic production and distribution.

This definition appears to give particular weight to the ways in which governments utilize businesses in order to achieve *government* goals, and in their initial work on the subject Kramer and Michalowski offer the explosion of the space shuttle Challenger as their prototype for state-corporate crime. In another context Kauzlarich and Kramer (1993) utilize the concept of state-corporate crime as a device to examine the relationship between the U.S. government and weapons manufacturers in the production of a nuclear arsenal, again emphasizing the central role of the government in organizing a cooperative activity involving both government and business. The case at hand, however, suggests a different kind of relationship, one where government omissions permit private businesses to pursue illegal and potentially injurious courses of action which, *in a general way,* facilitate the fulfillment of certain state policies.

The relationship between the overarching government policies and the specific goals of business and industry is well illustrated by North Carolina's labor history. Since the late 19th century the political leadership of North Carolina has pursued a policy of industrial development through, among other things, limiting unionization and blocking the power of regulatory agencies. This pursuit of industrial development is a more general and less delimited goal than the specific pursuit of such things as a space program or nuclear weapons production. By contrast, the Imperial Food Processing company, like most industries, had a very specific goal of profit maximization through (among other things) worker discipline. This goal and the methods used to attain it, however, dovetailed nicely with the state's general concern with industrial development through (among other things) creating a climate within which businesses where not burdened with either unions or extensive safety regulation.

Like the state-corporate crimes examined by Kramer and Michalowski, and Kauzlarich and Kramer, the Imperial plant fire depended on the *interaction* between the pursuit of government and corporate goals. Thus, we think the general framework state-corporate crime is appropriate for the task at hand. We would, however, modify the definition of state corporate crime to read:

> State-corporate crimes are illegal or socially injurious actions that result from a mutually reinforcing interaction between (1) policies and/or practices in pursuit of the goals of one or more institutions of political governance and (2) policies and/or practices in pursuit of the goals of one or more institutions of economic production and distribution.

State-corporate crimes occur within a capitalist economy when two or more organizations, at least one of which is in the civil sector and one of which is in the state sector, pursue goals that intersect in such a way as to produce some form of social injury.

The following discussion of the Imperial plant fire as state-corporate crime is divided into three parts. First, we establish the *societal context* in which the Imperial fire occurred by examining the history of industrial regulation in North Carolina as it relates to the state's overall development policy. Second, we will construct the *institutional context* for the disaster by examining the specific pattern of industrial relations characteristic of the Imperial Food Processing company. And lastly, we will examine the *control context* within which the fire occurred by exploring the ways in which the activities of regulatory agencies intersected with the activities of Imperial in a way that resulted in the disastrous fire of September 3, 1991.

The Societal Context

Political-Economic History of North Carolina

The societal context within which the Hamlet fire occurred is characterized by a set of political economic arrangements that have historically centered around broad, state-supported latitude for investors, and extensive state-enforced or state-permitted controls over labor (Wood, 1986). The overall climate in North Carolina, since the end of the Civil War, has been one in which state policies toward both development and labor have been breathtakingly tilted in favor of capital accumulation and away from advancements in wages or work conditions for labor (Myerson, 1982). The result has been a history of economic growth without real economic development. As Tomaskovic-Devey (1991:2) observes:

> Economic growth is a process of economic change which leads to increased employment and production activity. Economic development, on the other hand, is a growth process which leads to increased standards of living for the people in a region.

North Carolina's recent economic history has certainly produced economic growth, but development, in the form of improved living standards for the mass of the state's industrial workers, has lagged behind substantially. Between 1976 and 1986 nonagricultural employment in the South overall grew by 44 percent, as compared to only 10 percent in the Northeast (SWEC, 1986:11), and North Carolina enjoyed a substantial share of this growth explosion in the so-called "Sunbelt." By 1987, the state was ranked first among all the states in the number of new manufacturing plants opened, and the North Carolina Department of Commerce boasted that businesses had invested nearly $5.4 billion dollars in new and expanded industrial facilities with the subsequent creation of 76,600 jobs. Yet, at the same time the state retained its long-standing position as last among the fifty states in average manufacturing wage, as well as attaining the highest infant mortality rate of any state in the United States, and being only 44th in median family income (Tomaskovic-Devey, 1991:27).

Since the emergence of the "New South" at the end of the 19th century, North Carolina's ability to attract capital investment in industry has been linked to the state's ability to offer what state officials like to refer to as an "attractive business environment." In practice this meant high rates of return due to lower production costs, preferential tax policies for industry, and most importantly, extremely low rates of unionization which, in turn meant, both a lower wage bill for investors, and a limited ability of workers to press for improvements in working conditions.

The pro-business/anti-labor characteristics of the North Carolina political economy are not the outcome of simple market forces. They are the fruits, first, of a war on progressive political organizations in the late 19th-century, and then, of a concerted battle against unionization throughout the 20th century (Key, 1950; Crow, 1984; Bloom, 1987; Luebke, 1990). Regarding the destruction of 19th century political movements that might have developed as a force for the protection of the industrial and agricultural labor force in North Carolina, Tomaskovic-Devey (1991:20) says:

The only effective challenge to capitalist elite rule occurred during the populist period in which black and white farmers created a populist party, the Farmers Alliance. The Populist and Republican parties created a fusion alliance in the 1890s, in 1894 won two-thirds of the seats in the General Assembly, and in 1896 elected a reformist Republican Governor [Crow, 1984]. The Democrats, the party of the planter-industrialist elites, countered with a violent white supremacy campaign, successfully institutionalizing Jim Crow legislation and disenfranchised blacks and many poor whites and led to nearly complete conservative pro-business, anti-labor Democratic control of the state for the entire twentieth century.

The destruction of populist parties, although setting the stage for North Carolina's 20th-century labor policy, was not the final struggle. Throughout the 20th-century business and political leaders in North Carolina struggled against unionization, an effort that was punctuated by a number of bitter and often bloody labor battles in which the police powers of the state, and the state-supported moral authority of dominant religious institutions, usually weighed in heavily on the side of capital, and against labor (Pope, 1942).

The consequences of this political history have been a pattern of economic development in contemporary North Carolina characterized by low wages, violent discouragement of unionization by the state officials as well as employers, enduring racial inequalities, little protective legislation for workers, transfer payments to the poor lower than the national averages, and fewer controls over business activity than found in many other states.

The political apparatus of the State of North Carolina not only has allowed this pattern to develop, it has also played an active role in creating and maintaining it. As Wood (1986:1) argued, the government of North Carolina

> played a decisive role in attracting "external" capital by providing the social, political and economic conditions required to facilitate exploitation and capital accumulation; by containing class conflict; and by limiting the possibility of "external" intervention

either in the form of the unionization of the state's workers, or in the form of Federal social and economic regulation.

These conditions created a labor force that in some ways offers the benefits of industrial investment in Third World countries, but without Third World liabilities. As Robert C. Holland, a business consultant and President of the Washington, D.C.–based Committee for Economic Development explained:

> I see the Southeast as the major area for business relocations. Labor and land are cheap in this region, and the uncertainties about government instabilities are not found here (quoted in SWEC, 1986:11).

In recent years, in pursuit of investment, North Carolina's state government has developed a wide number of agencies, divisions, departments, and programs whose purpose is to attract "external" capital to the state by publicizing North Carolina as a "promised land" for high-yield capital investment. The Industrial Development Division of the State of North Carolina, which was established in the late 1970s, employed sixteen full-time industrial recruiters whose role was to "sell" North Carolina to corporate executives outside the state. Wood (1986:164) argues that these recruiters are not pursuing *all* industries, but specifically those that would be best suited to and attracted by North Carolina's labor climate—that is, labor intensive, low-wage industries seeking to escape unionization, labor market competition, and higher wages in other regions.

It is important to note that the kinds of industries that fit this description, and which North Carolina has actively recruited and attracted, are most heavily concentrated in the competitive sector of the economy. Industries in this sector find it more difficult to pass on every increase in wages, taxes, or regulatory costs to consumers as easily as businesses in the oligpopolistic sector such as automobiles, metals, rubber, and petroleum production. Thus, competitive-sector industries frequently operate on a narrow margin of profitability. For this reason they are particularly attracted to states that can promise reduced labor, regulatory, and tax costs. As a relatively small, family-run operation, Imperial Foods was an ideal target for North Carolina's industrial recruitment. In 1980, Imperial responded to the attraction of a nonunionized labor force that enjoyed few labor market options, and that would consequently be willing to accept low wages and marginal working conditions, by moving its operation from Pennsylvania to North Carolina.

North Carolina's public industrial policy is not merely a passive one, promising a hands-off attitude toward business and business regulation. The State is also proactive in providing businesses special benefits. North Carolina state laws allow local city and county governments to issue revenue bonds to finance branch plant recruitment, and allows counties to negotiate property tax abatements with potential industrial recruits (Tomaskovic-Devey, 1991:15). As one example of the extremes to which the state will go to attract low-wage industry, in 1989 John Martin, Governor of North Carolina, eliminated the inventory tax on *all* manufacturers in order to lure a *single* cookie plant to the state (Tomaskovic-Devey, 1991:16).

Altogether, these forces have produced a form of growth with only limited benefit for workers. Wood (1986), however, suggests that there were two key institutions that might have placed pressure on North Carolina's political establishment in ways that would have resulted in a closer linkage between economic growth and economic advancement for workers. The first of these is unionization, and the second is Federal regulation. Both of these mechanisms for improving wage and working conditions, however, have been effectively blocked by the political-economic arrangements within North Carolina.

Blocking Worker Organization

The most consistent specific vehicle by which unions have been undercut in North Carolina is the state's right-to-work law. This law hinders the ability of unions to organize, and legally limits the strength of unions by outlawing union shops. Under the right-to-work law, which is more appropriately named a "right-not-to-unionize law," if a union wins the right to represent a plant, only those workers who wish to join the union, pay union dues and abide by union decisions, such as a strike vote, do so. In states without such laws, when a union wins recognition, all of the workers in the plant must join the union, pay dues and abide by union decisions.

Because it is a right-to-work state, even a unionized plant in North Carolina may have up to 49 percent of its work force who are not union members. Consequently, the economic strength of the union is diminished because not all workers pay dues, and its bargaining strength is substantially weakened because employers know that even if there is a strike vote, only the union members will walk out. Thus, while strikes may be an inconvenience, in many plants they do not threaten a total shutdown of operations. Moreover, in a plant that is significantly split between unionized and nonunionized workers, managers have to employ far fewer strike breakers in order to maintain near-full levels of operation than they would if they were faced by a union-shop strike.

When right-to-work laws are coupled with the willingness of North Carolina's government to use the police power of the state to arrest or otherwise control striking workers, the ability of workers to improve their bargaining position through strikes—which in the final analysis are the basis of organized labor's power—has been seriously damaged. One of the most notorious modern examples of this was the 1958 strike at the Harriet-Henderson mills in Henderson, North Carolina. One of the longest and most violent strikes in U.S. history, this struggle involved over one thousand workers, open violence against the strikers, including the bombing of workers' homes, and at times, nearly one-fifth of the state's entire police force.

> The state police and units of the National Guard, reinforced on occasion by regular army units, maintained fixed bayonets and were given authority by the state legislature to arrest without warrant, to protect strikebreakers imported from Virginia, and to enforce injunctions against picketing. In addition, a special judge

and prosecutor were sent to establish a strike court at which
unionists and sympathizers were sentenced to hard labor on road
gangs and to heavy fines (Wood, 1986:160–161).

The Henderson strike provides a dramatic example of direct
state action against workers' organizations in the postwar period,
but it is far from the only one (Koeppel 1976). "Intimidation of
strikers by sheriffs, local police, and state troopers remains a
characteristic of North Carolina's strikebreaking apparatus" (Wood,
1986:161).

In North Carolina not only are unions kept from organizing by
the combined efforts of state government and industry, but already
organized companies are kept out by a similar constellation of
forces. In order to insure North Carolina remains an employers'
paradise, members of the business community have often actively
worked to discourage investment that they felt might raise the value
of labor by creating too many job opportunities, or by establishing
a higher wage scale, particularly if the industry seeking relocation to
North Carolina was a unionized one. In one instance, in 1976 the
owners of Cannon Mills sought to keep a Philip Morris plant from
being built in their county because they feared it would create
competition for workers and would drive up the price of labor
(Luebke, 1990). In another instance, the Raleigh Chamber of
Commerce has a written policy against recruiting companies that
do not agree to resist unionization, and throughout the 1970s and
1980s they have rejected companies such as the Miller Brewing
Company, Brockway Glass, and Xerox because they would bring
union jobs (Wood, 1986:163). "As recently as 1991 groups of
businessmen actively discouraged United Airlines from locating a
major maintenance facility in Greensboro, North Carolina, for fear
that the 1,500 unionized high skill jobs would drive up wages and
increase unionization" (Tomaskovic-Devey, 1991:24).

This climate of state-sponsored or state-tolerated opposition to
unionization and intimidation of already unionized workers in
North Carolina was part of the experience of workers at the
Imperial plant in Hamlet. After the fire, Valerie Ervin, an organizer

for the United Food and Commercial Workers who had been working in North Carolina, said she had never feared for her life before she came to Hamlet. After the fire, workers were threatened with reprisals for speaking out about unsafe conditions at the plant. Ervin said:

> The toughest state I've ever worked is in North Carolina. . . .
> People are afraid for us to come to their homes. They feel that
> there's going to be violence (quoted in Trevor, 1991:B1).

As a result of this political-economic history, North Carolina has, despite its demonstrable economic growth, failed to provide significant advancement for the majority of the industrial labor force that has been the backbone of this growth.

In recent years a new problem has emerged, the problem of sustaining the rate of growth the state enjoyed throughout the Sunbelt boom of the 1970s and 1980s. Some authors have likened the attraction of outside investment into the state to a great buffalo hunt. As one report observed:

> The stampede of plants to the South is definitely over—especially
> for the rural areas that lack a skilled workforce, transportation,
> infrastructure, and cultural amenities (MDC, 1986).

This slow-down of economic growth has been reflected in lessened growth in state revenue. Among other things, this has meant that the state has had to make cutbacks in its already low level of public service, and has felt a need to intensify its pro-business/anti-labor stance in order to compete for the remaining few domestic industries that might relocate to North Carolina.

What all of this means for industrial workers, as well as other working people in North Carolina, is that they operate in a societal context hostile to worker protection, a context created by a state that has actively blocked the ability of workers to make their collective voices heard through effective labor organization, and which additionally is now facing a fiscal crisis that threatens to exacerbate these conditions.

Blocking Worker Safety: The Case of NC-OSHA

The second factor Wood (1986) suggests might be an avenue
for North Carolina workers to improve their situation is through
Federal regulation. In the case of workplace safety, a relatively
strong Federal law has been in place since 1970 in the form of the
Occupational Safety and Health Act. The act's stated goal is "to
assure as far as possible every working man and woman in the
Nation safe and healthful working conditions." The Act requires
that each employer furnish each employee "a place of employment
which is free from recognized hazards that are causing or likely to
cause death or serious physical harm" to employees (Public Law
91–596, quoted in Noble, 1986:3).

The law gives impressive rights to American workers. First it
obliges companies to reduce the risks in the workplace. While other
labor laws limit businesses from preventing efforts by workers to
make improvements in the safety of their workplace, the OSH Act
not only allows workers to fight for safety and health, it places the
burden of responsibility on the employer, demanding that the
company take action to improve the workplace in ways that benefit
the worker. The second way in which the Act is impressive is in its
breadth of coverage compared to other protective legislation. Nearly
all workers are protected by the OSH Act. Public-sector employees
are the only group of workers who are not protected by the Act
(Noble, 1986).

The OSH Act was not the first attempt to protect American
workers' health and safety. Massachusetts passed the first worker
safety law in 1877 and all other states eventually had some kind of
legal protection of at least some workers. The OSH Act, however,
was the first Federal law to protect workers' health and safety, and
it was the first law to require Federal inspectors and a Federal
system of fines. The OSH Act also differs from all previous worker
health and safety legislation because it gives employees the right to
participate in agency inspections (Noble, 1986).

Despite its positive potential for American workers, the OSH
Act is not as progressive as similar legislation in other countries. For
example, U.S. employers, unlike those in some other nations, are

not required to establish health and safety committees, nor are they required to involve workers in decision making about health and safety issues. In addition, some property rights of the employer are protected through an appeal system that facilitates employer challenges to cited violations (Noble, 1986).

The establishment of OSHA, nevertheless, threatens the interests of investors because it can make inroads into profits. In order to maintain profit levels employers need to either keep their production costs low, or be able to pass on any increase in costs to consumers. Profit pressures can inhibit the development of a safe workplace because minimizing costs usually means foregoing the establishment of safety measures that absorb workers' time or the company's money (Noble, 1986). The OSH Act, which insists that safe practices be implemented, even if they have a negative impact on profits, is particularly threatening to competitive-sector industries, which as previously mentioned, are less able to pass on the cost of a safe workplace to consumers.

The OSH Act potentially restructures the relations between workers and managers of capital by insisting that profits are not the only standard by which businesses will be judged. It creates new rights to health and safety for employees and empowers the Federal government to enforce them.

Many employers have seen the OSH Act as an unwelcome intrusion on the rights of investors in a private production system, have fought vigorously against its implementation, and in many cases sought to circumvent its requirements. Especially after the economic downturn of the mid-1970s, investors and capital managers have worked particularly hard to neutralize the effects of the OSH Act. Employers have found support for these efforts in the Federal executive branch. Every president since the mid-1970s has sought support from the business community by backing their demands that economic costs be weighed when any new worker safety or health standards are considered. This includes, for example, supporting the right of employers to claim economic hardship as an acceptable reason for not implementing health and safety standards.

In addition, Congress sought to appease states'-rights advocates by allowing states to create their own version of OSHA that was to be controlled by the state rather than the Federal government. In a last minute compromise during the passage of the bill, state governments successfully lobbied for this joint program. According to the hearings held by the Committee on Education and Labor of the House of Representatives to inquire into the Hamlet fire (hereinafter designated as CEL, 1991), North Carolina was one of the 23 states to opt for a state-run program. By establishing the North Carolina Occupational Safety and Health Administration (NC-OSHA) in 1974, North Carolina become one of 23 states with their own OSHA program. Of these 23, 10 have only been conditionally approved because they are not in compliance with Federal OSHA regulations. North Carolina is one of these ten on probation. No state OSHA, however, has ever been decertified and placed under Federal control because of non-compliance, regardless of their performance record, and no specific criteria have been established to determine whether or not a state should be decertified (CEL, 1991:104).

If a state chooses to establish its own OSHA operation, it has the option of setting its own penalties and priorities. NC-OSHA has used this prerogative to minimize the effect of penalties for violations of safety and health standards. In 1991, for instance, North Carolina increased the fines for OSHA violations for the *first time* since the establishment of NC-OSHA in 1974. The current maximum fine in North Carolina (and by no means the most common one) is $14,000, just a fraction of the Federal maximum fine of $70,000 (Parker, Menn and O'Brien, 1991).

Workers in North Carolina, like other American workers could be protected by Federal regulation under the OSH Act. The implementation of the OSH Act, however, has been diluted at the Federal level by the executive branch. In addition, the option of states' rights has allowed the state of North Carolina to organize its own version of OSHA, one that is even less effective than the Federal version. In this way, the potential for protection of North Carolina workers by Federal regulation has been successfully blocked in North Carolina by the mutual efforts of business and government in North Carolina. These efforts frequently intersect in significant ways as businesses, particularly competitive sector industrial operations, pursue their profit goals through limiting worker power, and the State pursues its development goals by offering a haven for industries fleeing more unionized states with more stringently enforced occupational health and safety regulations.

Institutional Context

The history of North Carolina's political economy reveals a state in which workers have been most often blocked in their efforts to control their work environment by a business-government coalition favoring a relatively *laissez faire* industrial policy. But this political-economic climate alone does not explain the complex dynamics that led to the fire at Hamlet. Word *could* have reached authorities about the unsafe practices in the plant, and NC-OSHA *did have* the legal authority to unlock the doors. What then kept these things from happening? This question is partially answered by examining the institutional context in which the fire took place, and by delineating the specific pattern of industrial relations among Imperial's management, workers and NC-OSHA.

By the late 1980s Imperial Foods was under considerable pressure because of the general economic decline and because of specific fiscal problems within the corporation. Even before the fire in Hamlet, it appears that Emmett Roe, the owner of Imperial Foods, was facing financial difficulty. In 1990 he had closed a plant in Alabama without giving his employees proper notice. The courts had awarded the laid-off workers $250,000 in severance pay, although by the time of the fire no payments on this obligation to the Alabama workers had been made. Roe was facing suits for $350,000 in debts owed to his creditors and a $24,000 bill for unpaid taxes (Greif and Garfield, 1991). The financial difficulty which Roe faced may have increased the likelihood of decisions that placed profitability ahead of the health or safety costs to workers.

This interpretation would be consistent with the findings of Clinard and Yeager (1980) which suggest that the greater the financial strain faced by businesses, the greater the likelihood that they will engage in regulatory violations.

Regardless of what decisions Roe's financial pressures or management policies may have provoked, NC-OSHA could have intervened in a way that would have ultimately protected the workers in Hamlet. What were the factors that disrupted the ability of NC-OSHA to regulate the conditions at Hamlet? Two issues stand out. First, there is some evidence to suggest that workers who recognized hazards at the plant found it difficult to make their concerns for a safe workplace heard. Second, NC-OSHA failed to effectively regulate Imperial's safety practices because it was not adequately funded, and because, at least according to some observers, it was not efficiently organized.

Unheeded Warnings

In order for workers to be protected from dangerous work environments, at least in any work environment where they are not empowered to alter their own work conditions, someone must recognize the problems and make them known to those who *do have* the power to alter the hazardous conditions. There is evidence that the workers at the Hamlet plant were aware of safety problems and that they attempted to make their voices heard.

At the hearings on the fire, Mr. Bobby Quick, an employee at the plant, was asked if any fellow employee had made a complaint about the locked doors. Mr. Quick said his immediate co-workers knew about the problem although they had not gone to management:

> The maintenance [workers] talked about it amongst ourselves. We never took it to the office. We said amongst ourselves we hope a fire doesn't break out (CEL, 1991:55).

Among other departments in the plant, however, people did complain to management, although their efforts apparently did not lead to any changes in the hazardous conditions. Quick testified that:

> A lot of people talked about it catching on fire and killing people. I recall one day Brad [plant supervisor and the son of its owner Emmett Roe] was there. I think it was a white lady who told him, it was the day that it smoked up. She said "This thing is going to kill somebody." Brad did not pay her no attention. He was always rushing the maintenance men to fix something so they would not lose money and product. All they cared about was the product, getting it out (CEL, 1991:55).

At the Congressional hearings, representatives asked why more people did not question the safety of the plant, or why they were not more persistent in their complaints. Mr. Quick was asked if people were fearful of making a complaint. He answered by saying:

> If you try to make a statement to Brad he did not want to hear it. What you said did not matter. He was running the show. If you keep making a stink, he will fire you, you know (CEL, 1991:55).

The threat of firing in response to voicing concerns about safety was also revealed in the testimony of North Carolina's governor before the Hearings Committee. Governor Martin referred committee members to Alfred Anderson whose wife had died in the fire. Martin said that prior to the fire Mr. Anderson had accompanied his wife to talk to her boss about conditions at the plant. She was reprimanded for taking her complaint outside of the plant, even to her husband (CEL, 1991:122).

And another witness, Dr. Fred McQueen, a local physician who examined the 25 bodies, indicated that Mrs. Anderson's experience was not unusual. Dr. McQueen said that a system should be designed to allow workers to make anonymous complaints. He wrote:

Many workers present me, a physician, with complaints but do not want to follow through with their complaints because of the fear of losing their jobs (CEL, 1991:122).

Overall, the testimony that has come forth in this case suggests that there were workers who recognized safety hazards in the plant and in its method of operation, and who did try to have them remedied. Their expressions of concerns, however, did not result in any changes. Additionally, the evidence suggests that many other workers at Imperial felt they inhabited a chilling climate when it came to suggesting safety problems to management. The perception among workers that there are costs attached to making complaints regarding job safety, perhaps costs as high as losing one's job, represents a critical institutional flaw in any work setting where the only power workers have to rectify unsafe conditions is through appeals to management. In the case of Imperial, this flaw was a significant factor in the loss of 25 lives.

The Failure of OSHA

Had the concerned workers at Imperial chosen to contact OSHA instead of bringing their complaints directly to the plant's management, they, like many other workers in North Carolina, would not likely have met with success. First of all, they would have been informed by a poster in the plant to call an 800 number. Three-fourths of the 160,000 workplace posters publicizing the phone number for safety complaints, including the posters at Imperial, listed a number that had been disconnected, with no forwarding number. Thus, the basic requirement of being able to contact the safety agency could not be met. Certainly, a highly motivated worker, familiar with the process of hunting through a bureaucratic tangle of phone numbers and disconnected lines, might have reached OSHA. But the more likely response of the average worker who called the NC-OSHA number only to be told it was disconnected would be to conclude that the office was no longer in operation. At the very least, the incorrect posters, and the failure to replace them with correct ones, constituted a serious limitation on the accessibility of OSHA to the workers at Imperial and elsewhere in North Carolina.

The incorrect posters and other problems faced by NC-OSHA reflect in part the organization's inadequate level of funding. Nationally, OSHA is seriously underfunded, and NC-OSHA is comparatively even less well funded. North Carolina Governor James Martin testified before Congress that although a minimum of 64 safety inspectors were required to be working in the state according to Federal OSHA guidelines, the legislature had authorized only 34. He went on to say that in January of 1991 he attempted to have 19 more inspectors authorized, but that the legislature had denied his request. Even if Martin's request had been granted, however, North Carolina would have remained 11 short of the minimum number of required OSHA inspectors. Only nine states in the United States have fewer inspectors than is recommended by Federal OSHA regulations. Of these nine, North Carolina falls the farthest below the recommended number, funding only 53% of the total number of inspectors required. As a consequence, for instance, although North Carolina has 83 poultry plants, only half of them have ever been inspected since the inception of NC-OSHA.

In 1980 North Carolina had 1.9 million workers and 47 OSHA safety inspectors. Ten years later, when North Carolina's work force had grown by 37 percent, to a total of 2.6 million, the number of OSHA inspectors had declined by 12 percent, to 42 inspectors. According to the Bureau of Labor Statistics, between 1977 when John Brooks, Commissioner of the Department of Labor and head of the NC-OSHA, first took office, and 1988, the number of North Carolina workplace injuries grew from 120,000 a year to 177,300 (Menn, 1991). This rate of growth in workplace injuries outstripped the growth in the actual number of workers, suggesting that between 1977 and 1988 North Carolina actually lost ground in workplace safety despite the fact that the purpose of the OSH Act was to ensure just the opposite. The record of NC-OSHA in improving worker safety in North Carolina is not commendable.

In addition to the inadequate numbers of inspectors, Brooks reported to the Congressional committee that until late in 1991 the inspectors NC-OSHA did have were able to work in the field only four days a week because the department lacked sufficient travel funds. Since then they have been able to work in the field only three days a week because of further cuts in NC-OSHA funding. Brooks also noted that even if he hired additional staff there would be difficulty training them because the closest training center is in Chicago and it is constantly booked up (CEL, 1991:168).

At the Congressional hearings on the fire it was also revealed that $453,000 which could have been used for salaries for OSHA inspectors in North Carolina was returned to the Federal government in 1991 (CEL, 1991:129). Moreover, this was not a one-time budgetary aberration. According to testimony, in five of the six years preceding the Imperial fire, Federal OSHA money had been returned to Washington by NC-OSHA. These funds were returned to the Federal government because in order to accept them, the state would have been required to match them. For example, in 1991, because the state legislature was unwilling to provide the state OSHA with $243,000, they were unable to accept the matching $453,000 from the Federal government (CEL, 1991: 223).

Brooks also explained that another reason the money was not accepted is because it was stipulated for salaries only. Because there is a hiring freeze on state jobs in North Carolina, according to Brooks, it would be illegal to spend the money to hire additional safety inspectors (CEL, 1991:225). This particular explanation seems somewhat disingenuous because it is not true that under the state hiring freeze *no one* is ever hired. Cases are often made that certain positions are of such crucial importance that they must be filled. Insofar as we have personally witnessed continued hiring in universities in North Carolina while the state was under a "hiring freeze," it is difficult to believe that had there been significant political will to bring NC-OSHA up to standards it could not have been done. But then that is the point, since the inception of NC-OSHA, there has been little political will in North Carolina to make it a powerful agency actually capable of protecting workers to the full extent envisioned by the Federal OSHA Act. NC-OSHA has been budgetarily strangled and bureaucratically stymied since its inception, a pattern that is consistent with the goal of North Carolina's political leadership of ensuring a business investment climate relatively unimpeded by so-called "burdensome regulation."

In the final analysis, the lack of personnel and funding resulted in a seriously inadequate state-run OSHA program in North Carolina. This conclusion is perhaps best demonstrated by Representative Kildee's (D. Michigan) detailing of an evaluation made by Federal OSHA of the OSHA program in North Carolina. He said:

> I am looking at your evaluation of North Carolina OSHA Mr. Scannel, and I read, "North Carolina OSHA conducted only five general schedule health inspections during 1990, all of which involved trenching." That means, no inspections were conducted to identify worker overexposure to toxic substances. Later it says, "North Carolina OSHA does not inspect in response to complaints within a reasonable time frame, no imminent danger complaints, and fewer than 10 percent of serious complaints are inspected within OSHA's recommended time frames." In North Carolina when workers report safety problems, it may be 2 years before an inspection occurs. North Carolina has complaints from 1984 that have not yet been inspected (CEL, 1991:222).

Failure of Controls in Context

A competitive economy dominated by profit-seeking investors, a government committed to offering an attractive profit-making climate and consequently far from aggressive in protecting the health and safety of workers, and workers with very limited ability to shape the safety and health conditions of their work place, all contributed to the fire in Hamlet. These things alone, however, did not cause the tragedy at Imperial. In order to understand how these things interacted to produce the outcome they did, it is important to examine the ways in which the activities of government regulatory agencies intersected with the activities of the management of Imperial. The fire and the locked doors may have resulted from actions taken by management at Imperial, but those actions were made possible by the failure of several control agencies.

Kramer and Michalowski (1991) suggest that state-corporate crime can be understood as the result of an interaction between elements of government and elements of the private-production system. They offer the destruction of the space shuttle Challenger as a prototypical example of state corporate crime, emphasizing the relationship between several governmental units (NASA, Congress, and the Administration), and a private corporation, Morton Thiokol, the builder of Challenger's rocket motors. We argue that the Hamlet fire was likewise a case of state-corporate crime. But unlike the prototype offered by Kramer and Michalowski, the events leading to the Hamlet fire were more the consequences of socially injurious omissions on the part of governmental agencies, rather than direct consequences of the pursuit of specific goals, as was the case with governmental actions surrounding the building and launching of the ill-fated Challenger.

In the case of the Hamlet disaster, the critical intersections were between a private business, Imperial Foods, and several government agencies at the Federal level (US-OSHA and the USDA), at the state level (NC-OSHA, the office of the governor, and the state legislature), and at the local level (the county building inspectors and the city of Hamlet fire department). For a variety of reasons each of these agencies, by omission—that is, by failing to perform the control functions assigned to them—made possible the continuation of the hazardous conditions at the Imperial plant in Hamlet that led to the deaths of 25 workers. To unravel this skein of ultimately destructive decisions and omissions we will first examine the specifics of the fire and then discuss the ways in which each of the controls failed within the specific context of Imperial's operation in Hamlet.

The Imperial Fire

The accumulated evidence in the Hamlet fire indicates that the single most important factor leading to the 25 deaths was the lack of readily accessible routes to safety. All but 1 of the 25 deaths resulted from smoke inhalation. Only one person died of extensive burns (CEL, 1991:233). The fire itself and the heat it produced was not large enough within the 30,000 square foot building Imperial occupied to kill the number of people it did. Rather, people died because they could not escape the smoke the fire produced. Particularly telling is the fact that a number of the dead were found in a large freezer where they had retreated to escape the fire. Once inside the freezer they were protected from the heat and fire, but unfortunately they were unable to close the door tightly enough to keep out the toxic smoke (CEL, 1991:118). Considering that these workers had sufficient time to reach the freezer, in all likelihood they would also have had sufficient time to escape the building, *if* there been adequate pathways to safety. This point is underscored by the example of one woman who survived because, although she could not get out of a blocked door, she was able to put her face out of the door where a friend who was outside fanned away the smoke with his baseball cap.

There were eight entrances to the building. Four were locked from the outside and one other was probably locked from the outside. Three doors were not locked. One was the main plant entrance which is where most of the employees who did escape exited, and which was the only door marked with an exit sign. One door was blocked by the fire. And one door, that could only be reached by walking through a freezer, was unmarked and unknown to most employees because they were not allowed in the freezer unless that was their work station (CEL, 1991:102).

Workers testified that most employees assumed that the doors were not locked because of fire laws (CEL, 1991:52). And in fact that is the law. The OSHA law reads, "Every exit must be well lit. Door passages and stairways that might be mistaken for access should be so marked. Doors should be unobstructed so that employees can always get out" (CEL, 1991:100).

There were two reasons given for why the doors were locked; one was that it was to keep the flies out, and one was that it was to keep the employees from stealing the chicken.

Approximately a dozen current and former plant workers told news reporters that doors were routinely locked to keep employees from stealing chicken nuggets. Police records show the company reported employee thefts three times in recent years. "Hamlet police records show Imperial employees stole chicken valued at between $24 and $245 (Drescher and Garfield, 1991). If the theft of chicken was, in fact, the reason for locking the doors, it suggests that Imperial management operated according to a frightening calculus wherein preventing the theft of several hundred dollars worth of chicken parts justified risking human lives by cutting off what would be escape routes in case of fire, and doing so in violation of the law. It is also disturbing that in all of the discussion and reportage about the locking of the doors, there appears little evidence that the simple solution of installing fire doors with alarms that sound whenever the door is opened, a commonplace installation in many buildings and a solution that would have both insured safe exits *and* minimized the use of these doors for illicit commerce, was ever seriously considered.

In addition to locked doors, exits were unmarked and employees were not made aware of where exits were and whether they were locked or not. There had never been a fire drill in the plant nor any fire safety instruction of employees.

The fire itself started because of the unsafe practice of repairing hoses carrying hydraulic fuel while continuing to maintain cooking temperatures with gas flames under large vats of oil. To minimize down-time, Imperial Food Products routinely left its gas-fired chicken fryer on while repairing adjacent hoses carrying flammable hydraulic fluid, a maintenance worker testified (Trevor and Williams, 1991). Bobby Quick testified at the Congressional hearings that on the day of the fire he heard Brad Roe tell a maintenance worker to hurry repairs to the line in order to avoid down-time (Trevor and Perlmutt, 1991).

The vats of oil are 27 feet by 4 feet and are kept at 390–405 degrees. The flash point of cooking oil is 460 degrees (CEL, 1991:49). On the day of the fire, repairs were being made on hoses carrying hydraulic fuel to the cooking vats. The cooking was not stopped as the repairs were made. The insurance department of the state of North Carolina filed a report describing how the fire started.

> The cause of the fire was determined to be the ignition of hydraulic oil from a ruptured line only a few feet from a natural-gas-fueled cooker used in preparation of the chicken. Investigators determined that during a repair operation, the incoming hydraulic line separated from its coupling at a point approximately 60 inches above the concrete floor and began to discharge the fluid at high pressure. This high pressure and subsequent flow resulted in the hydraulic fluid being sprayed against the floor and onto the nearby cooker. Ignition of the fuel was immediate; likely from the nearby gas burners. . . . The intense fire also impinged upon a natural gas regulator (located directly above the ruptured hydraulic line) on the supply line to the burners which soon failed and added to the fuels being consumed (CEL, 1991:112).

To make matters worse, there were no automatic cutoffs on the hydraulic or gas lines, there was only one fire extinguisher in the plant, and there were no working telephones to call the fire department when the fire broke out. An employee had to drive several blocks to the fire station to inform them that there was a serious fire at the plant (CEL, 1991:57).

How did these conditions come about, and what were the acts of omission on the part of governmental agencies that helped make it possible?

Omission by the Federal Government

Two Federal agencies failed the workers at Hamlet in important ways. The first of these is OSHA. OSHA was statutorily responsible for insuring the quality of services provided by state-run

NC-OSHA. As previously discussed, while Federal OSHA had known for quite some time about the inadequacy and ineffectiveness of the North Carolina agency's operations, no effective effort was taken to remedy the situation, except to file a report.

The second agency that could have, but did not act to prevent the disaster in Hamlet came as a surprise to most people—the United States Department of Agriculture (USDA). Because Imperial Foods in Hamlet is a meat-processing plant, a USDA agent visited the plant *daily* in order to make sure that the meat was being handled properly.

Kenneth Booker, the regular inspector for the USDA, told a congressional panel that he knew about the locked doors because workers had complained to him, and that he had talked with plant managers about the problem. He did not do anything further because he believed he lacked authority, and because Imperial management told him the door could be quickly unlocked in an emergency (Davis 1991). Booker's failure to pursue the matter is yet another omission that helped make the Hamlet tragedy possible. USDA's involvement in the deaths at Hamlet, however, is not limited to Booker's inaction. A USDA agent also was responsible for the locking of at least one of the doors in question.

The summer before the fire, on June 19, 1991, Grady Hussey, a USDA inspector, who sometimes substituted for the regular inspector, Booker, cited Imperial Foods for allowing flies to enter the plant and for leaving two doors open to a trash bin. An Imperial official, Joseph Kelly, responded to the citation writing on it that he had solved the problem stating, "Inside door closed and outside door closed and locked. Outside door to this area will be locked at all times unless for an emergency." Hussey signed his name on the citation noting that "corrective action has taken place" (Drescher, 1991b:A1).

The USDA claimed that it had no responsibility in the case. Carol Foreman, former assistant U.S. Agriculture secretary who supervised meat and poultry inspections from 1977 to 1981 disagreed stating, "Every USDA inspector is a law enforcement officer, they carry a badge and they are sworn to uphold all laws of the United States." She said the inspector should have noticed locked doors. "This inspector had time to pick up a telephone and call the N.C. Department of Labor and say there's a serious hazard here. If the inspector saw somebody get raped or murdered in that plant, would he say that wasn't his responsibility too?" (Drescher and Perlmutt, 1991b). Again, it appears that the simple solution of requiring automatically closing doors, rather than signing off on the solution of locking the door, a patently illegal option, was not considered by either the USDA inspector or by Imperial management. As in the case of the other doors, the simplest and least costly option—locking the doors—was the route taken.

The Failure of North Carolina State Government

Three components of the state government in North Carolina contributed to the circumstances that led to the fire and deaths at the Imperial plant. First of all, the state legislature refused to match funds with the Federal OSHA. The actual decision-making process of the individual legislators who voted not to fund OSHA to the required level is difficult to know for sure. The general political climate of North Carolina suggests, however, that probably some combination of four views on worker safety—(1) expanding NC-OSHA would contradict the interests of key constituents in the business community, (2) mandatory safety inspections are an unacceptable intrusion of the state into the rights of private enterprise, (3) inspections are not worth the money they would cost in the light of North Carolina's budget crisis, or (4) expanding NC-OSHA would give the wrong signal to industries that might relocate in North Carolina—played a role in the history of the North Carolina legislature's refusal to adequately fund NC-OSHA. Not only did the legislature fail to fund NC-OSHA's inspector staff to required levels, but it even failed to provide adequate travel and training funds for the limited number of NC-OSHA inspectors it did authorize. In addition, the state legislature was apparently quick to interpret the state's hiring freeze as an absolute barrier to the expansion of NC-OSHA's staff of inspectors, when exceptions to this freeze were allowed in other areas deemed "critical." Additionally, the Governor appeared to be reluctant to use the weight of his office to pressure the legislature toward expanding the number of NC-OSHA inspectors. While the Governor did request funds from the legislature in 1991 for additional inspectors, this was the first time in six years he had done so. In the previous five years of his tenure in office he took no lead in attempting to bring NC-OSHA up to Federal standards.

The internal operations of NC-OSHA itself may have also contributed to the situation in Hamlet in ways that are not entirely attributable to the lack of financial support NC-OSHA received from the state. While the underfunding of NC-OSHA was undoubtedly the critical factor in limiting its effectiveness, employees of NC-OSHA have also suggested that the management style of John Brooks, its director, may have been a contributing factor. Four current safety inspectors and five recent retirees from NC-OSHA discussed Brooks with news reporters. All expressed frustration with the department's performance over the past 10 years. "A lot of people have come in, seen what was going on, and left," said Bryan McGlohon, who retired in 1987 after 14 years as a safety inspector and consultant. McGlohon said he left in part because of Brooks' "lack of skill in human resources. I can't put up with bureaucracy and inefficiency." Each of the other eight inspectors said he knew of at least one person he considered qualified rejected by Brooks for a job in the past few years (Menn, 1991b). It is difficult to know to what extent internal management difficulties further limited NC-OSHA's effectiveness, or to what extent these difficulties were themselves the consequence of the stress resulting from an inadequate budget, but the testimony of current and former NC-OSHA workers suggests that the organization may not have been functioning as effectively as it might have, even in the face of its limited budget.

Taken together, these factors suggest that the State of North Carolina, for a variety of reasons, simply did not take the issue of worker health and safety seriously, or at least did not take them seriously enough to insure that NC-OSHA was adequately funded and effectively run.

Local Government

The operations of local government agencies also played their part in contributing to the Hamlet fire. Hamlet is located in Richmond County, which is responsible for regularly conducting inspections to identify unsafe or unlawful buildings in the county. According to the North Carolina Insurance Department, the Hamlet plant was in violation of building codes because it did not have a sprinkler system, did not have enough doors, workers had to walk more than the allowable 150 feet to exit the building, one door opened to the inside, four doors were locked, and there were no exit signs. Some of these violations were a result of Imperial management having made changes in the building without requesting inspections and without obtaining building permits.

Another issue regarding local inspection concerns the question of whether or not the building code violations at Imperial were inappropriately "grandfathered" as permissible under Richmond county law. According to this law the Building Code Council cannot require existing buildings to meet new and tougher codes unless the building is substantially renovated. In 1983 a new $125,000 roof was put on the building after a fire damaged the plant, an expenditure that could have been viewed as a substantial renovation. The Richmond County inspector, under the wide latitude provided by the building code, however, chose to conclude that despite the new roof, the Imperial plant had not been substantially renovated, and that it did not have to bring the entire building up to code (Drescher, 1991a).

Richmond building inspector Jack Thompson examined the new roof put on in 1983 but not the building. "I just figured the roof wouldn't be more than 50 percent of the property's value." He said he did not check property value records and only guessed at Imperial's worth. "I did look around but as far as digging around looking to see what was holding the building up, I didn't do that. Didn't nothing stand out to me that wouldn't meet the code"

(Williams and Drescher, 1991). What can be said of Thompson's
testimony is that it is relatively clear he did not take a proactive
stance toward building safety. This minimalist approach to building
safety inspections is consistent with the climate of business
regulation in North Carolina generally, and in industry-hungry
Richmond county in particular, and is another example of the
velvet-glove treatment given to industry in North Carolina.

The other local government agency that played a role in the
deaths of the 25 workers, although perhaps a minor one, was the
Hamlet Fire Department. Here the story takes a racial twist. The
town of Hamlet is predominately white, and its fire department is
all white. Although Hamlet is a small town, it has a suburb—the
town of Dobbins—which, as a reflection of the continuing patterns
of residential racial segregation in North Carolina, is predominately
black and has a black fire department. When the fire at the plant
started, the Dobbins Fire Department arrived at the scene. They
were not, however, allowed to assist in the rescue and were asked to
leave. Members of the Dobbins Fire Department claim they were
asked to leave for racial reasons. Specifically, they contend that
members of the Hamlet Fire Department believe that because the
members of the Dobbins Fire Department are black, they are not
qualified fire fighters (*Charlotte Observer*, 1991). It will never be
known for sure whether or not the added aid of the Dobbins Fire
Department might have saved additional lives, but the simple fact
that they were not allowed to assist in the rescue raises serious
questions about the relative priorities that guided the Hamlet Fire
Department in attempting to assist the workers trapped inside the
Hamlet plant.

Conclusion

The fire in Hamlet was caused by an array of actors, actions,
omissions, and social circumstances that surrounded the workers in
concentric circles from the closest supervisors and owners to local,
state and Federal agencies, and finally to the organization of both
the North Carolina and the U.S. political economy itself. Like a

noose, these concentric circles closed around Hamlet and interacted in a way that brought about the death of 25 workers. When the list of factors arrayed against worker safety in North Carolina are tallied, it is surprising that there are not more workplace disasters such as the one at Imperial. It also suggests that many other industrial employees in North Carolina work on the fine edge of potential disaster. The Hamlet fire was not an aberration. It was almost predictable. In fact, it had been predicted by some workers.

In the final analysis, what is particularly disturbing and particularly telling is that *so many* components of the system designed to protect the health and safety of workers, from Federal OSHA, to NC-OSHA, to local inspectors *had to fail* in order for this killing fire to have occurred. The deaths in Hamlet are clear evidence that laws alone are not sufficient to protect worker safety. They require political will for their effective enforcement. Without this will, they become more symbolic than real. The Hamlet fire constitutes a clear instance of state-corporate crime precisely because it was the absence of this *political will* and the omissions on the part of *politically constituted agencies* that enabled the management of Imperial to continue violating basic safety requirements at the plant in its pursuit of private profit.

REFERENCES

Bloom, Jack. 1987. *Class, Race and the Civil Rights Movement.* Bloomington: Indiana University Press.

Chambliss, William. 1989. "State-Organized Crime." *Criminology* 27:183–208.

Charlotte Observer. 1991. "Firefighters Near Plant Not Called: Chief Cites Racism." September 6, 4a.

Clinard, Marshall and Peter Yeager. 1980. *Corporate Crime.* New York: The Free Press.

Committee on Education and Labor, House of Representatives. 1991. *Hearing on H.R. 3160, Comprehensive OSHA Reform Act, and the fire at the Imperial Food Products Plant in Hamlet, North Carolina* Serial

No. 102–47, September 12, Washington, D.C.: U.S. Government Printing Office.

Crow, Jeffrey. 1984. "Cracking the Solid South: Populism and the Fusionist Interlude." In L. Butler and A. Watson (eds.) *The North Carolina Experience: an Interpretive and Documentary History.* Chapel Hill: University of North Carolina Press.

Davis, Matthew. 1991. "Inspector: Managers Were Warned." *Charlotte Observer*, November 13, A 6.

Drescher, John. 1991a. "In Hamlet Fire Government Safety Nets Gave Away." *Charlotte Observer*, September 22, A1, 7.

———. 1991b. "USDA Inspector Ok'd Locking of Door in Hamlet Plant." *Charlotte Observer*, November 13, A1, 6.

———. 1991c. "Hamlet Plant Violated Code." *Charlotte Observer*, November 15 A1, 9.

Drescher, John and Ken Garfield. 1991. "Workers: Doors Kept Locked." *Charlotte Observer*, September 12, A1, 11.

Ermann, M. David and Richard J. Lundman. 1987. *Corporate and Governmental Deviance: Problems of Organizational Behavior in Contemporary Society.* Third Edition. New York: Oxford University Press.

Greif, James and Ken Garfield. 1991. "Debt Dogged Imperial's Owner— Then the Fire." *Charlotte Observer*, September 15, A1, 12.

Hagan, John. 1988. *Structural Criminology.* Cambridge: Polity Press.

Kauzlarich, David and Ronald Kramer. 1993. "State-Corporate Crime in the U.S. Nuclear Weapons Facilities." *Humanity and Society* (forthcoming).

Key, V.O. 1950. *Southern Politics in State and Nation.* New York: Alfred A. Knopf.

Koeppel, Barbara. 1976. "Something Could be Finer than to Be in Carolina." *The Progressive* 40 (June): 21–22.

Kramer, Ronald C. 1982. "Corporate crime: An Organizational Perspective." Pp. 75–94 in Peter Wickman and Timothy Daily (eds.) *White Collar and Economic Crime.* Lexington: Lexington Books.

Kramer, Ronald and Raymond Michalowski. 1990. "State-Corporate Crime." Paper presented at the American Society of Criminology, November.

Luebke, Paul. 1990. *Tar Heel Politics: Myths and Realities.* Chapel Hill: University of North Carolina Press.

MDC. 1986. *Shadows in the Sunbelt: Developing the Rural South in an Era of Economic Change.* Chapel Hill: MDC, Inc.

Menn, Joseph. 1991. "North Carolina Official Puts Blame on Legislature." *Charlotte Observer,* September 6, A1, 4.

Myerson, Michael. 1982. *Nothing Could be Finer.* New York: International Publishers.

Offe, Claus and Volker Ronge. 1982. "Theses on the Theory of the State" in Anthony Giddens and David Held (eds.) *Classes, Power and Conflict.* Berkeley: University of California Press, pp. 249–56.

Noble, Charles. 1986. *Liberalism at Work: The Rise and Fall of OSHA.* Philadelphia: Temple University Press.

Parker, Jennifer, Joseph Menn, and Kevin O'Brien. 1991. "North Carolina Inspection Program Ranks Last in U.S." *Charlotte Observer,* September 5, A1.

Pope, Liston. 1942. *Millhands and Preachers.* New Haven: Yale University Press.

Roebuck, Julian and Stanley Weber. 1978. *Political Crime in the United States.* New York: Praeger.

Simon, David R. and D. Stanley Eitzen. 1990. *Elite Deviance.* (3rd edition.) Boston: Allyn and Bacon.

Sklar, Martin J. 1988. *The Corporate Reconstruction of American Capitalism: 1890–1916.* New York: Cambridge University Press.

Southern Women's Employment Coalition (SWEC). 1986. *Women of the Rural South: Economic Status and Prospects.* Lexington, Ky.: SWEC.

Sutherland, Edwin H. 1940. "White-collar Criminality." *American Sociological Review* 5 (February): 1–12.

Tomaskovic-Devey, Donald. 1991. *Sundown on the Sunbelt? Growth Without Development in the Rural South, A Report to the Ford Foundation.* Raleigh: North Carolina State University Press.

Trevor, Greg. 1991. "Work-safety Advocates Buck Anti-union Sentiment." *Charlotte Observer,* October 27, pp. B1, 4.

Trevor, Greg and David Perlmutt. 1991. "Worker to Testify of Order to Rush Repair." *Charlotte Observer,* September 12, A1, 10.

Trevor, Greg and Paige Williams. 1991. "Worker: Repairers Left Fryer On." *Charlotte Observer*, September 10, A1, 9.

Vaughn, Diane. 1983. *Controlling Unlawful Organizational Behavior: Social Structure and Corporate Misconduct.* Chicago: University of Chicago Press.

Williams, Paige and John Drescher. 1991. "Plant Not Inspected as Authorized." *Charlotte Observer*, September 21, C1.

Wood, Phillip. 1986. *Southern Capitalism: The Political Economy of North Carolina, 1880–1980.* Durham, N.C.: Duke University Press.

GREGG BARAK

Crime, Criminology and Human Rights:
Toward an Understanding of State Criminality[1]

"State criminality" or the harms illegally or legally organized and inflicted upon people by their own governments or the governments of others, have skimpily but increasingly been documented by social scientists/criminologists (Schwendinger and Schwendinger, 1970; Block and Chambliss, 1981; Falk, 1988a; Block, 1989; Chambliss, 1989; Luyt, 1989; Scott, 1989; Zwerman, 1989; and Barak, 1991b). Nevertheless, it is still safe to argue that after some twenty years of recognizing state criminality as a concept, little progress has been made in either precisely specifying what the various forms of "state criminality" are, or, in analyzing such case studies as those which present themselves, for example, before the United Nations Human Rights Commission. In other words, despite the many mass mediated discussions of these "crimes against humanity" as found in publications like *Newsweek, Time, and The Wall Street Journal,* or in those more critically-oriented discussions as found in such publications as *Mother Jones, The Nation, and In These Times,* one still observes a scarcity of scholarship by criminologists on this topic. Until such time as this scarcity is removed, or until such time as there is serious development in the study of state criminality, there will remain significant gaps in the study of crime and in the study of the state and social control.

More specifically, the relationship between state criminality and social control requires recognition by criminologists that we, too, play a role in not only defining the boundaries of the discipline, but in helping to create what constitutes "crime" in the real world. It is important, therefore, that as critical criminologists, we develop ways of communicating progressive prospectives on crime and social justice to popular audiences (Barak, 1988). It is my further contention that the study of state criminality must become central to the study of crime and social control, if we are to develop a left realist critical criminology that is capable of intersecting with the common-sense social reality of crime and violence. Efforts at developing an understanding of these relationships have been occurring for the past couple of decades. Beginning in the late 1960s and early 1970s, revisionist historians and critical sociologists alike were starting to focus attention on the interrelationships between the modern state and the various systems of social control (Cohen and Scull, 1985).

Out of this work there has reemerged the macro or classical 19th-century socio-historical interest in the importance of the connections between questions of order, authority, power, legitimization, hegemony, organization, and change. These questions of social control have gone well beyond the micro or predominant 20th-century questions which merely created various typologies of the means and processes involved in the socialization of conformity. The abandonment of a social-psychological perspective on a social control divorced from the history and the politics of individual, group, and class struggles, and the preference for a social control grounded in the interplay of cultural production, ideological construction, and political economy, has served to resurrect the role of the state as central to each of these areas of social control.

It was precisely these macro political and economic relations, ignored by traditional or positivist criminology during most of the 20th century, that has historically limited the scope of the field to the study of the criminal behavior of the powerless. Gradually, however, over the past fifty years there has been an expansion over the "acceptable" boundaries of criminological focus to include the criminal behavior of the powerful, beginning with the professional, white-collar, organized, and most recently, corporate criminals.

During this shifting in criminological paradigms, the establishment of a critical criminology reunited the study of the state with the study of crime which had previously been separated by positivist criminology. Although progress has been made in describing the integral connections between class, race, gender, crime, social control, and the state, very little light has been shed upon understanding the role and the development of state organized criminality in the reproduction of both the crimes of the powerful and the powerless. Before such an understanding can come about there must first be a development of state criminality and its legitimation within the field of criminology.

Toward an Understanding of State Criminality

Is it not an ultimate contradiction that the state has been both a crime-regulating and crime-generating institution? That is to say, the state through its formal and informal policies not only engages in crime control, but it also engages in the development of crime, its own and others. As a criminogenic institution, the state not only violates the rights of individuals, but it contributes to the production of other forms of criminality as well. From the perspective of critical criminology, these injuries or harms ("crimes") may or may not violate law per se.

The criminological journey toward the development of a criminology of state criminality will not be accomplished without resistance from both inside and outside the boundaries of academic criminology. Simply put, there are a number of disciplinary biases and political obstacles to overcome. To begin with, the study of state criminality is problematic because the very concept itself is controversial. This is due, in part, to the debate over whether or not one should define "crime" in terms other than the law codes of individual nations.

Traditional criminology has always ascribed to the legalistic state definition of crime, and confined investigation and analysis to legally proscribed behavior and its control (Schwendinger and Schwendinger, 1970; Platt, 1974; Michalowski, 1985). Outside of the conventional confines of criminology have been those acts such as imperialism, exploitation, racism, and sexism, or those acts not typically prosecuted such as tax-evasion, consumer fraud, government corruption, and state violence. Critical criminology, accordingly, has not confined itself to studying legally defined crime. Utilizing other definitions, such as crimes against humanity or politically defined crime, critical criminology has studied harmful and injurious behavior which may or may not be sanctioned by particular nation-states' definitions of illegality, but which are recognized in the "higher" criteria established in various international treaties, covenants, or laws. Therefore, for the purposes of this discussion, crimes by and of the state, like those crimes against the state, may be viewed similarly as involving exploits of both a violent and nonviolent nature. They may, in fact, involve violations of the same established legal relations or prohibitions, including but not limited to such behaviors as: murder, rape, espionage, cover-up, burglary, illegal wiretapping, illegal break-in, disinformation, kidnapping, theft, assassination, terrorism, secrecy, unaccountability, corruption, exporting arms and importing drugs illegally, obstruction of justice, perjury, deception, fraud, and conspiracy. In addition, state criminality may include the more general transgression of both domestic and international laws, not to mention the more subtle institutional relations or behaviors which cause social injury, such as the bankrupting and the destroying of whole economies or the violation of universally shared notions of fundamental human rights.

Now then, these critical definitions of crime which have opened up the scope of "criminality" have certainly not as yet been adopted by conventional criminologists nor even considered by the general public. In fact, both leftists and rightists, inside and outside of criminology, have found such conceptualizations of crime to be unreal, unnatural, idealistic, impractical, or irrelevant. The point, however, is that for those critical criminologists who think otherwise, the time is long past due for the serious development of the substantive areas of state criminality. Through this type of critical development within criminology there stands the possibility of transforming the very nature of the study of criminality from the individual to the political.

In order to carry out such a criminological agenda, investigators cannot be deterred in their study of state criminality by the lack or failure of the state to adjudicate itself or its agents as criminals. After all, just because it has been the case that states have chosen to ignore, dismiss, or down play their own criminality, it does not follow that we criminologists should do the same. Similarly, criminologists should extricate themselves from the trap of viewing state crime within the old political double standard: treating the phenomenon as though it involves the behavior of certain designated "bad guys" states and not the behavior of so-called "good guys" states.

For example, the case of terrorism presents much theoretical, strategic, and ideological work to be done. Scholarly interest in this area, especially as conducted by students of criminology and criminal justice, has been highly focused or selected on some but not all terrorist acts. This selectivity refers not only to countries emphasized and neglected, but to the various forms of terrorism committed. By most legally-defined or state-based notions of terrorism, the typically incorporated crimes include those "retail" terrorist acts committed by groups or individuals against agents or symbolic representatives of a real or imaginary enemy state. Typically omitted from most discussions are those "wholesale" acts of terrorism waged by state-supported networks against various independence or national revolutionary movements (Chomsky and Herman, 1979; Herman, 1982).

Or what about the role of covert and overt aid in the domestic affairs of developing nations, especially in trying to affect the outcomes of elections? It used to be, in the glory days of the American empire, that neither the President, the Congress, nor the people considered whether we had a right to intervene in the domestic affairs of another nation. U.S. aid in those days, mostly covert, "was routine, and so pervasive as to be immune to political criticism" (Weinstein, 1989:14). But with respect to the practicalities, if not the underlying principles, U.S. foreign policies are now beginning to be publicly questioned. At the same time, however, for example, the Bush administration during its first year in office, attempted to redefine the term assassination in an effort to circumvent President Ford's 1975 executive order formally banning U.S. assassinations of foreign officials. According to a recent "memorandum of law," the original order has not been changed, only watered down to exclude the possibility of assassination without premeditation (Wright, 1989:1C). Whatever the state finally decides about these "murders," elections, and other forms of covert and overt intervention, criminologists should not be precluded from exploring and examining these actions as state crimes against humanity.

Like the study of corporate crime, the study of state crime is problematic because it involves examining behaviors engaged in by agents and organizations which are both socially and politically acceptable (Clinard and Yeager, 1980; Ermann and Lundman, 1982). Access to studying the politically powerful, especially with respect to deviant behavior, has always been difficult. While both corporate and state criminality have the potential for undermining the very stability of the system that the corporate-state strives to protect, it is the latter crimes by the state which pose the greater threat to the political legitimation of the system as a whole. State criminality, in other words, provides the type of inherent contradictions which simultaneously challenge the prevailing political ideology yet accommodate the same behavior in the name of greater common interests or national security. The political repression or governmental crimes committed against the Chinese demonstrators in 1989 was an excellent example of this point. To label and to study such behavior as criminal was to participate in a delegitimation of the Chinese state; one can well imagine the consequences for any Chinese criminologist who would have attempted to examine this form of state criminality.

Analysis of state criminality is further complicated because it involves not only the overlapping activities of "criminal" and "noncriminal" organizations, but also because it involves the study of state-supported corruption and violence which never can be totally separated from individual acts of criminality and terrorism; each is somehow related to the inequitable distribution of economic wealth and legal-juridical privileges. Concerning the former set of relationships, Block (1986:59) summarized the situation nicely when he argued that traditionally organized crime and state organized crime are inseparable in many cases because

> organized crime has been and continues to be inextricably linked to transnational political movements and to that segment of the American political establishment known as the espionage community or more aptly, the transnational police force.

He further concluded (1986:76) that this kind of interplay between organized and state criminality results in the situation where

> it may very well be the case that certain political assassinations or other intelligence moves may be done not in the interests of foreign policy carried out by hired goons and thugs, but rather in the interest of drug smugglers and international gamblers carried out by their clients in the intelligence services.

As for the connections between individual criminality and state criminality, Dieterich (1986:50) has argued, for example, that the material debasement of the "majority of the Latin American peoples is an inevitable consequence of the current capitalist accumulation model" and the physical and psychological submission of these peoples "into a state of apathy and fear is a functional prerequisite for that accumulation model." On the U.S. domestic front, Henry (1991) has already demonstrated the relationship between a "free market" economy and street criminality, as both are tied to policies of omission and marginality and to the viability of informal economic activity as an alternative response to legitimate work. Therefore, the ability of criminology to recognize not only the criminal content and the criminogenic nature of various forms of state intervention into the affairs of other countries, but also the criminality and the crime-producing influences of domestic policies of noninterventionist omission, becomes a necessary prerequisite for the development of the serious study of state crimes.

In sum, the development of a criminology of state criminality requires that criminologists move way beyond the rather one-dimensional media portrayals and political discourse associated with the selectively chosen crimes by the state. In order to establish a criminology of the structural and etiological reasons (causes) of state criminality, criminologists and other legal and political scientists must first present the kinds of conceptual frameworks which not only incorporate the full array of state crimes, but which can aid us in understanding the relative harm and injury inflicted by the behaviors and policies of nation-states.

State Criminality and the U.S. Experience

It should be pointed out that state criminality is not indigenous or symptomatic of any particular socio-economic formation, including precapitalist, capitalist, or socialist. As far back as the fifth century A.D., for example, state criminality had been acknowledged in the course of realizing that the actions of pirate bands were essentially the same as those actions of states and empires. That is to say, both pirates and empires had the capacity to seize property by force or violence. The only real difference between the two was the scale of their endeavors, and the success of pre-states or empires to impose a justifying rhetoric or ideology for their theft of land, property, and people (Jenkins, 1988; Chambliss, 1989). In the contemporary world, of course, regardless of the particular socio-economic and state formation, crimes by and of the state can be found globally. In other words, historically it has been the case that both democratic and undemocratic regimes have engaged in state criminality. It may very well be the case that political repression and state crime have less to do with the democratic or undemocratic nature of the government per se, and more to do with the power of a particular state regime such as the U.S. or the U.S.S.R., for example.

A glance at the "democratic" history of the United States reveals the patterned actions of state criminality. Whether we are discussing the 19th-century crimes of the U.S. government which were in violation of the fundamental rights of Native and African American peoples, or we are examining those state crimes which have violated the legal and civil rights of workers, minorities, and dissidents over the past century, the evidence clearly demonstrates that these crimes were not accidental or due to some kind of negligence. On the contrary, those state actions engaged in and/or the consequences of the policies of a developing political economy were the outcome of premeditated and intentional decisions. In fact, some of these "crimes against humanity," such as slavery, were in full compliance with the supreme laws of the land.

In light of these historical realities, the student of 20th-century U.S. state criminality, for example, when studying the role of the Federal Bureau of Investigation as a formal institution of social control, should strive for an integration of the dual-sided nature of state "crime-fighting" and "political-policing." The Palmer Raids and the Red Scare of 1919, the McCarthyism of the early 1950s, and the counter-insurgency campaigns of the late 1960s and early 1970s used against those citizens protesting the involvement of the United States in Southeast Asia, reveal a domestic history of extraordinary political repression or state criminality against those who have seriously challenged or posed any kind of threat to the status quo (Glick, 1989). Such activities, covert and overt, have not been limited to domestic enemies alone, but have included foreign political enemies as well. Since it was established in the late 1940s, the Central Intelligence Agency has had a rather consistent history of supporting repressive dictators in such countries as Cuba, Iran, the Philippines, Nicaragua, Brazil, South Korea, and Argentina, and of overthrowing or destabilizing democratically elected governments in Guatemala, Chile, Jamaica, and Nicaragua—to name only a few (Bodenheimer and Gould, 1989). Here again, as with the domestic state crimes these international state crimes, would appear to select their victims in response to the needs of *laissez faire* or the free market economy, consistent with the real or the perceived needs of capital accumulation.

What these domestic and international examples of state crime have shared in common has been their ongoing series of legal and illegal clandestine operations used against those politically labelled deviants. Within the United States, the FBI's Cointelpro, or counterintelligence programs of the 1960s and 1970s used against the Black Panther Party for Self-Defense, the anti-war movement, and the American Indian Movement, included a variety of illegal and unconstitutional techniques to delegitimate or to otherwise criminalize lawful organizations (Churchill and Wall, 1988). These state crimes have involved such everyday illegal activities as surveilling, burglarizing, and tampering with the mail. In addition, there have been the more exotic forms of state criminality such as employing propaganda to smear progressive organizations, or sending out disruptive *agents provocateurs* (Wolfe, 1973; U.S. Congress, 1976; Caute, 1978; and Churchill and Wall, 1988).

The study of state criminality, more so than the study of any other form of criminality, is by definition a highly politicized undertaking. In other words, the study of state crimes cannot be separated from the emotionally-charged landscape of a changing political economy, which involves among other things, the study of law, power, and ideology as well as the study of public policy, foreign and domestic. A case in point is the study of terrorism where one person's "terrorist" has been another person's "freedom fighter." For example, with respect to U.S. supported state terrorism, it should be recognized that such forms of state criminality as the involvement in systematic counterrevolutionary warfare, pro-insurgency, or interventionism, are responsible for all kinds of human casualties. The tens of thousands of lost lives and an even larger number of permanently injured citizens of Latin American countries over the past few decades reveals just some of the harm done by international state criminality. I refer specifically to the illegal detentions and the mass torturing, murdering, and kidnapping by U.S. trained secret police and militia in such countries as Guatemala and El Salvador (Nelson-Pallmeyer, 1989).

This kind of U.S. state-engaged criminality, or what has otherwise euphemistically been referred to by the military, the U.S. State Department, and the mass media as "low-intensity" conflict or warfare, has been virtually ignored by students of governmental or organizational crime. Such state policies have been designed "not only to defend the U.S. empire against the rising challenges from the poor but also to conceal from U.S. citizens the unpleasant consequences of empire" (Nelson-Pallmeyer, 1989:2). These low-intensity activities have involved an unprecedented degree of coordination among the White House, the National Security Council, the Central Intelligence Agency, the State Department, the Agency for International Development, conservative private aid groups, and a semi-private network of drug-runners, arms merchants, and assassins (Nelson-Pallmeyer, 1989). The "secret" crimes of low-intensity conflict have striven to integrate the more traditional military, political, economic, and psychological aspects of warfare with the more modern, technological aspects of mass communications, private consumption, and social control. Such interventionism, for example, into the affairs of Nicaragua eventually wore the people down and contributed to the defeat of the Sandanistas in the elections of 1990.

The study of U.S. state criminality should not only include those "proactive" crimes of the state, at home or abroad, such as the Iran-Contra Affair and the subsequent behaviors of the Contras and Sandinistas or the recent invasion of Panama, but they should also include the crimes by state "omission" such as the denial of the fundamental right to work for an adequate income or the right to be permanently free of homelessness in a society as rich as the United States. With respect to the former crimes by the state, the syndicated columnist, David Broder, has drawn out the important parallels between Oliver North and Manuel Noriega. In response to an editorial which appeared in *The Wall Street Journal* shortly after General Noriega and his people stole the results of the May 1989 election in Panama, Broder maintained that the correct lesson to learn was the one concerning U.S. hypocrisy in relationship to

Noriega in particular and to the crimes against the people of
Nicaragua in general. He wrote (Broder, 1989:2B):

> When the executive branch of the U.S. government evades laws
> passed by Congress, when it brushes aside the verdict of the
> World Court on its illegal mining of Nicaraguan harbors, then it
> cannot be surprised when the head (Noriega) of a client
> government decides to ignore the election returns.

With respect to the crimes of omission, it is precisely those state
domestic and economic policies of noninterventionism and deregulation which have combined not only to deny people of their
basic human needs, but which have also helped to contribute to the
production of the more traditional forms of criminality (Henry,
1991; Barak, 1991a).

In the context of human rights for the people of both
developed and developing countries, it is my contention that the
study of state criminality should be connected to those struggles
which have historically attempted to expand the notions of
fundamental justice for all. In the next section, I will attempt to
show the linkages between crime, criminology, and human rights
and the worldwide effort of the United Nations Human Rights
Commission to challenge some of the more commonly experienced
state crimes against humanity.

The Politics of Human Rights Violations

The politics of struggling for worldwide social justice and the
politics of condemning the human rights abuses of nation-states by
such organizations as Amnesty International or the United Nations
Human Rights Commission (UNHRC) will now put an end to the
global spectacle of human rights violations and to the suffering of
millions of people any time in the near future. More likely, the
politics of condemning human rights violations will continue to
"heat up" as the strength of the various geographical blocs continue
to increase. Most recently, for example, regional blocs involving
nations from Latin America, Africa, and the Middle East have

begun to "rival" the blocs of the two superpowers and the older European nations. For example, at the 1990 UNHRC meetings in Geneva, resolutions were passed against human rights abuses during the Israeli resettlement of Soviet Jews in the occupied territories and the U.S invasion of Panama. At the same time, the Commission rejected a loosening of the sanctions on South Africa. China, however, despite the massacre at Tiananmen Square, managed to escape an official sanction from UNHRC. Also escaping sanction were the 1989 human rights abuses which occurred in such other countries as Guatemala, Iraq, Sri Lanka, Cambodia and the Philippines. What effects the current democratic revolutions in Eastern Europe and the Soviet Union will have on the centuries-old struggle for social justice is still too early to discern.

The problem in studying the politics of human rights violations cannot be separated from the problem of studying state criminality because they are both related to the basic issue of confronting the fundamental and irreconcilable differences between empire and social justice. Countries which have lived under the "sphere of influence" of the U.S.S.R. or the U.S. have experienced various forms of exploitation and domination. Neither superpower has been very likely to admit to its own crimes against humanity. In fact, both countries have gone to great lengths to rationalize and justify their politically necessary behavior. Through propaganda and disinformation efforts, each of the superpowers have attempted to suppress or to put a noble label around their seamy and contradictory behavior as they have been in conflict with the professed ideals of each country.

The principles for addressing human rights abuses globally have been evolving at least since the French and American revolutions. Today the means for addressing these violations include the shaping of world opinion and the holding of nation-states accountable to edicts of international law, to global treaties and declarations, and to universal concepts of human rights, in short, supporting those worldwide efforts aimed at achieving self-determination and independent development for all peoples on the earth. The role of the United States in the domestic and international affairs of

developing nations serves as an example. Since 1945, U.S. foreign
intervention in places like Africa and Asia have certainly served
more as a deterrent than as a facilitator of the materialization of
human rights for Third World people. And for the past two
decades, of all governments in the West, it has been the United
States that has most consistently opposed the realization of the right
of self-determinism by the peoples of developing nations. As Falk
(1989) has argued, it comes as no surprise, therefore, that the
United States has been the nation consistently portrayed as an
implacable foe of the rights of people. This hegemonic resistance by
the U.S. places both ideological and physical obstacles in the way of
maximizing human rights worldwide.

When it has come to the ratification of the major multi-lateral
human rights agreements or instruments, the United States has one
of the very worst records among Western liberal democracies. By
refusing to sign and recognize these various documents, the United
States has, at least indirectly, contributed to the worldwide abuse of
human rights. For example, it was not until 1988 that the United
States finally ratified the Prevention and Punishment of the Crime
of Genocide which was opened for signature in 1948. As of 1989
the U.S. had still failed to ratify such human rights documents as
the Convention on the Reduction of Statelessness (1961), the
International Convention on the Elimination of All Forms of
Racial Discrimination (1965), the American Convention on
Human Rights (1965), the International Covenant on Economic,
Social and Cultural Rights (1966) the International Covenant on
Civil and Political Rights (1966), the International Convention on
the Suppression and Punishment of the Crime of Apartheid (1973),
and the Convention on the Elimination of All Forms of
Discrimination Against Women (1979).

Naturally, signing and enforcing any of the documents that
have identified and attempted to delegitimate those public and
private policies, domestic and foreign, which have helped to
reproduce crimes against humanity, have often been correctly
viewed as impediments to capital accumulation. This is true
whether we are discussing developed or developing nations. With

regard to the post-1945 construction of a U.S. foreign policy based
on isolationism and interventionism, the international recognition
of "human rights" as legally binding, would certainly help to alter
the philosophy of a leadership that has never truly "trusted law or
morality or international institutions as the basis for maintaining
international security" (Falk, 1988b:4). Grounded in the failures of
Wilsonian idealism and the inter-war diplomacy, U.S. post-World
War II diplomacy, policy, and ideology has always been based on
the belief that the way to peace (and "democracy") was through
superior military power and the contradictory preparation for war
as the only basis for peace. Perhaps, in light of the current thawing
of the Cold War, and in response to the Soviet Union, the United
States may be "forced" to rethink its policies, for example, on low
intensity conflict.

The mere rejection of low-intensity conflict as business as usual
or its recognition as a form of state criminality vis-a-vis the
internationalization of human rights law, would, in effect, outlaw
such behaviors as counter-revolutionary terrorism and structural
violence that afflicts the poor and underdeveloped peoples of the
world. Accordingly, Falk (1989:68) has stressed that

> the rights of peoples can be undertook at its deepest level as a
> counter-terrorist code of rights and duties, especially directed
> against state terrorism of the sort associated with foreign policies
> of leading imperial governments.

More generally, resisting all forms of state criminality is no simple
enterprise as it calls for challenging the prevailing ideologies of
militarism, nationalism, and regionalism. The struggle for world
peace, social justice, and the reduction in the crimes of and by the
state also necessitates, on the one side, a decreasing role of the
national police apparatuses and, on the other side, an increasing
role of multilateral cooperation among nations. To put it simply,
this utopian world vision requires that peoples of the global
community understand that "no problem we face, not the nuclear
one, not the ecological one, not the economic one, can possibly be

handled, even addressed, on a unilateral national basis" (Ellsberg, 1988:18).

Nevertheless, some people have argued that it is simply naive to believe that these kinds of agreements are going to eliminate the state criminality of human rights abuses. After all, as they say, these agreements have no teeth. Others, however, have argued that it is just as naive to dismiss these efforts simply because of the politicization of the process itself. In other words, since the end of World War II the struggle for social justice in general and the work of the UNHRC in particular has minimally functioned to successfully

> establish norms and goals for the international community. The growing consensus on an expanded definition of fundamental human rights can be linked to the existence of U.N. covenants and the efforts of the Commission (Allen, 1990:12).

Karel Vasak, former UNESCO legal advisor, has called on nation-states worldwide to sign on to what has been termed the "third generation of rights." The third generation of rights goes further in its attempts than the first and second generation of rights did in their attempts to maximize the realization of human rights for all the people of the world. Each generation of politically evolved human rights violations has been the product of different historical struggles waged by people without rights to obtain them. With each passing historical period, there has been the expansion of both the notions associated with fundamental rights and with respect to whom those rights pertained.

The first generation of rights has been referred to as "negative rights" in that they have called for restraint from the state. These rights were derived from the American and French revolutions and the struggle to gain liberty from arbitrary state action. These rights can be found in the Civil and Political Rights of the International Bill of Rights. The second generation of rights has been referred to as "positive rights" in that they have required affirmative action on the part of the state. These rights can be found in the Economic, Social, and Cultural Rights of the International Bill of Rights. They emerged from the experiences of the Soviet Union and they also resonate in the welfare state policies of the West.

Finally, the third generation of rights has called for international cooperation. These rights are currently evolving out of the condition of global interdependence confronting the earth today. For example, in 1990, UNHRC members introduced a resolution that "encouraged an expanding role for the world body in defining the relationship among technology, development and the ecological integrity of the planet" (Adler, 1990:13). The UNHRC resolution, while not recommending any action at this time, has gone on record to say that

> the preservation of life-sustaining ecosystems under conditions of rapid scientific and technological development is of vital importance to the protection of the human species and the promotion of human rights (quoted in Allen, 1990:13).

Such a resolution, of course, recognizes that human rights obligations can no longer be satisfied within the boundaries of individual nations. Therefore, the rights of people independent of states are required, not only for a reduction in state organized violence and the maintenance of world peace, but for the protection of the environment and for a massive scale of global development (Crawford, 1988).

Putting human rights into practice by all types of universal agreements reached by both state and non-state representatives, is certainly one of the prerequisites for a reduction in all forms of state criminality, especially the more blatant forms often ignored by even the most democratic of nations like the United States. The argument here is that a recognition of these critical relationships by criminology and the adoption of basic human rights obligations as a part and parcel of a progressive criminological practice, are absolutely essential for the establishment of a criminology of state criminality. Moreover, without the legitimation of the study of state criminality both inside and outside of our academic discipline, criminology will remain captive to the prevailing social and moral contexts of legally defined state crime.

Conclusion

This essay has implicitly argued that state criminality is
ubiquitous. It has also been explicitly argued that state criminality is
victim-producing and criminogenic. Consequently, crimes by and
of the state are responsible for much of the global crime, injury,
harm, violence, and injustice. Historically, it has been suggested
that we are in an emerging period of the third generation of rights
as evidenced by various declarations and the expanding movement
or struggle on behalf of universal human rights. Accordingly, I have
contended that the time has come for criminologists to devote
serious time to the study of state-organized crime.

If such work is finally emerging, then the lag in time between
the introduction of the concept "state" to the field of criminology
and the actual practice of studying state criminality, may be roughly
parallel to the time lag between the introduction of white
collar/corporate crime as a concept and the actual practice of
studying this form of criminality. That is to say, it took some two
decades after Sutherland first introduced "white collar crime"
before criminologists were seriously engaged in studying the crimes
of the "privately" powerful. It now appears that it may have also
taken about two decades between the time when radical
criminologists of the late 1960s first introduced the concept of state
criminality to the discipline, and the time when criminologists
finally began to seriously examine the crimes of the "publicly"
powerful.

To reiterate, whether the study of state criminality involves the
detailed investigation of agents or organizations violating the rights
of its own citizens, or whether it involves the examination of
interstate terrorism, or whether it involves exploring the patterned
interaction between the two, analysis requires that criminologists
and others appreciate the two-sided and often hypocritical nature of
this form of political deviance. A case in point would demand the
unraveling of the connections between the U.S. Savings and Loan
(S&L) scandal and the involvement of known CIA agents and
members of organized crime. Of course, with respect to these S&L

state-organized thefts, what laid the foundation or groundwork was the federal deregulation of the S&L industry passed into law by a bi-partisan Congress during Ronald Reagan's first term as president. Without this change in the legal structure and in the policies controlling the operations of the individual savings and loans, there would not have been the institutionalized opportunity for the biggest theft in U.S. history. A theft which is currently being estimated, at a cost to the American taxpayers, of something on the order of $500 billion to one trillion dollars (Reeves, 1990).

Moreover, with respect to the study of state criminality and crime in general, both the S&L thefts and the S&L back-outs as well as the deregulation itself, cannot be divorced from the underlying changes in the political economy which were creating economic dilemmas that deregulation sought to obviate. Failure to develop such macro-level analyses and criminological constructs of the crimes of the powerful typically results in very unsatisfying and highly reductionist analyses about individual greed and organizational survival divorced from the political economy itself. Such contradictory analyses, which are perhaps better than no analyses at all, may help explain to some degree why it has often been the case that these allegedly unacceptable behaviors can be so easily swept under the political and criminological carpets.

In *Revolutionaries and Functionaries: The Dual Face of Terrorism,* Falk (1988a) has underscored this point with respect to state terrorism in particular. He has argued persuasively that unless there is the development of both objective and neutral scholarship and action, then the chances are strong that the study and transformation of political violence and state criminality will fall victim to the often employed double standard of justice. This kind of victimization can come about by the unscientific and uncritical acceptance of the language and discourse used to describe politically deviant global behavior. As criminologists, therefore, not only should we be involved in the process of demystifying political deviance, but we should also be on the look-out for all forms of state criminality brought about by anti-democratic and repressive forces, whether they operate at home or abroad.

I know that there are skeptical criminologists out there, consisting of both the sympathetic left and the adversarial right, who question not only the value of a criminology of state criminality, but of an expanded definition of "criminality" in the first place. These criminologists and others have asked me, for instance, what kinds of contributions criminologists can make to the study of crimes by and of the state that the other social scientists and even journalists could not make? Let me briefly respond to each of these concerns.

Regarding the appropriateness of a criminology of state criminality and the expanded definition of crime: First, I believe that both are consistent with the more critical trends in criminology as represented traditionally by arguments advanced by Sellin and Sutherland in the 1930s and 1940s, and more recently by the radical arguments advanced by Chambliss, Quinney, Platt, and others beginning in 1970 with the Schwendingers' classic statement: "Defenders of Order or Guardians of Human Rights." Second, as I have argued throughout this essay and elsewhere, the serious study of the systems of exploitation, including state policy as a crime-producing institution, have yet to be considered, especially as these are related to the processes of both victimization and criminalization.

As for the critical contributions that I believe could be made by the scientific study of state criminality as opposed to the traditionally "noncriminological" study of crime by the other social scientists, or by those treatments of the mass-mediated or even the alternatively mediated discussions of crime by journalists, they appear to me to be self-evident. As students of the convergence of crime, law, justice, control, politics, and change, criminologists are in the unique position of having a focus on the interaction of the dynamics of these properties as they have shaped the development of crime, criminology, and social control. Bringing this kind of "special" knowledge to the study of state criminality presupposes having undergone the type of demystification of crime and justice not typically experienced by either social scientists in general or journalists in particular. And, I would argue that while this will vary by degree, it is still equally true of bourgeois or critical social scientists and of mainstream or alternative journalists.

In the end, if criminology does not become engaged in the serious study of crimes by and of the state, then this omission will not only have stood in the way of criminology providing the complete picture of crime, but it will have been partially responsible for the reproduction of the ongoing criminalization and victimization of people around the globe. Stated differently, the lines of inquiry pertaining to the theoretical questions posed by the crimes of the powerful and by the relationships between social control and social justice, require that the examination of state criminality be central to this whole area of investigation. Finally, to confront state criminality as a legitimate enemy of civil society is to join the struggle for universal human rights and social justice.

NOTE

1. This essay is reprinted with permission from *The Journal of the Human Justice*, Volume 2, Number 1, Autumn, 1990.

REFERENCES

Allen, Terry. 1990. "The Politics of Human Rights." *In These Times*, April 25–May 1, pp. 12–13.

Barak, Gregg. 1991a. *Gimme Shelter: A Social History of Homelessness in Contemporary America.* New York: Prager.

———— (ed.). 1991b. *Crimes by the Capitalist State: An Introduction to State Criminality.* Albany: State University of New York Press,

————. 1988. "Newsmaking Criminology: Reflections on the Media, Intellectuals, and Crime." *Justice Quarterly* 5:565–587.

Block, Alan. 1989. "Violence, Corruption, and Clientelism: The Assassination of Jesus de Galindez, 1956." *Social Justice* 16:64–88.

————. 1986. "A Modern Marriage of Convenience: A Collaboration Between Organized Crime and U.S. Intelligence." Robert J. Kelly, (ed.), *Organized Crime: A Global Perspective.* Totowa, N.J.:Rowman and Littlefield, 1986.

Block, Alan and William Chambliss. 1981. *Organizing Crime.* New York: Elsevier.

Bodenheimer, Thomas and Robert Gould. 1989. *Rollback! Right-wing Power in U.S. Foreign Policy.* Boston: South End Press.

Broder, David. 1989. "Lawlessness At Home Invites Defiance." *The Montgomery Advertiser and The Alabama Journal,* Sunday, May 14.

Caute, David. 1978. *The Great Fear: The Anti-Communist Purge Under Truman and Eisenhower.* New York: Simon and Schuster.

Chambliss, William. 1989. "State-Organized Crime." *Criminology* 27: 183–208.

Chomsky, Noam and Edward S. Herman. 1979. *The Washington Connection and Third World Fascism.* Boston: South End Press.

Churchill, Ward and Jim Vander Wall. 1988. *Agents of Repression: The FBI's Secret Wars Against The Black Panther Party and The American Indian Movement.* Boston: South End Press.

Clinard, Marshall and Peter Yeager. 1980. *Corporate Crime.* New York: The Free Press.

Cohen, Stanley and Andrew Scull (eds.). 1985. *Social Control and the State.* Oxford: Basil Blackwell.

Crawford, James. 1988. *The Rights of Peoples.* Oxford: Oxford University Press.

Dieterich, Heinz. 1986. "Enforced Disappearances and Corruption in Latin America." *Crime and Social Justice* 25:40–54.

Ellsberg, Daniel. 1988. Remarks presented at the session, "The Growth of the National Security State," at the conference on *Anti-Communism and the U.S.: History and Consequences,* sponsored by the Institute for Media Analysis, Inc., Harvard University, November 11–13.

Ermann, David and Richard Lundman. 1982. *Corporate and Governmental Deviance: Problems of Organizational Behavior in Contemporary Society.* New York:Oxford University Press.

Falk, Richard. 1989. "United States Foreign Policy as an Obstacle to the Rights of People." *Social Justice* 16:57–70.

————. 1988a. *Revolutionaries and Functionaries: The Dual Face of Terrorism.* New York: E.P. Dutton.

————. 1988b. Remarks presented at the session, "The Growth of the National Security State," at the conference on *Anti-Communism and the U.S.: History and Consequences,* sponsored by the Institute for Media Analysis, Inc., Harvard University, Nov. 11–13.

Glick, Brian. 1989. *War At Home: Covert Action Against U.S. Activists and What We Can Do About It.* Boston: South End Press.

Henry, Stuart. 1991. "The Informal Economy: A Crime of Omission by the State?" in G. Barak (ed.), *Crimes by the Capitalist State: An Introduction to State Criminality.* Albany: State University of New York Press.

Herman, Edward. 1982. *The Real Terror Network: Terrorism in Fact and Propaganda.* Boston: South End Press.

Jenkins, Philip. 1988. "Whose Terrorists? Libya and State Criminality." *Contemporary Crises* 12:1–11.

Luyt, Clifford. 1989. "The Killing Fields: South Africa's Human Rights Record in Southern Africa." *Social Justice* 16:89–115.

Michalowski, Raymond. 1985. *Order, Law, and Crime: An Introduction to Criminology.* New York: Random House.

Nelson-Pallmeyer, Jack. 1989. *War Against the Poor: Low-Intensity Conflict and Christian Faith.* Maryknoll, N.Y.: Orbis Books.

Platt, Tony. 1974. "Prospects for a Radical Criminology in the United States." *Crime and Social Justice* (Spring-Summer), pp. 2–10.

Schwendinger, Herman and Julia Schwendinger. 1970. "Defenders of Order or Guardians of Human Rights?" *Issues in Criminology* 5:123–157.

Scott, Peter. 1989. "Northwards Without North: Bush, Counterterrorism, and the Continuation of Secret Power." *Social Justice* 16:1–30.

U.S. Congress Senate Select Committee to Study Governmental Operations with Respect to Intelligence Activities, Vol. 6, *Intelligence Activities: Senate Resolution 21*, Washington, D.C.: Government Printing Office, 1976.

Weinstein, James. 1989. "Now That It's Out in The Open, The Underlying Principles Should Be Debated." *In These Times* October 11–17.

Wolfe, Alan. 1973. *Repression: The Seamy Side of Democracy*. New York: McKay and Company.

Wright, Robin. 1989. "U.S. Redefining Ban on Assassinations." *The Montgomery Advertiser and Alabama Review Journal* October 15.

Zwerman, Gilda. 1989. "Domestic Counterterrorism: U.S. Government Response to Political Violence on the Left in the Reagan Era." *Social Justice* 16:31–63.

About the Authors

Judy Root Aulette is an Assistant Professor in the Department of Sociology at the University of North Carolina at Charlotte, where she teaches courses in gender and women's studies. The poultry industry in North Carolina has recently been the central focus of her research. Based on interviews with poultry workers, union organizers and feminist organizations in North Carolina, she has written a number of papers on the oppression of workers in chicken and turkey processing plants, most of whom are African American women. In addition to her scholarly work, Aulette has also played an activist role, writing and speaking to promote both union organization in the poultry industry and an end to the horrific conditions of work in the processing plants.

Gregg Barak is Professor and Head of the Department of Sociology, Anthropology, and Criminology at Eastern Michigan University. He is the author of *In Defense of Whom? A Critique of Criminal Justice Reform* (1980) and *Gimme Shelter: A Social History of Homelessness in Contemporary America* (1991), and the editor of *Crimes by the Capitalist State: An Introduction to State Criminality* (1991).

Robert M. Bohm is a Professor in the Department of Criminal Justice at the University of North Carolina at Charlotte. He received his Ph.D. in Criminology from Florida State University in 1980. His research interests are diverse, but recently have focused on the death penalty in the United States, especially death penalty opinion. Bohm is the current president of the Academy of Criminal Justice Sciences.

231

Susan L. Caulfield, who received her Ph.D. in Criminal Justice from the State University of New York at Albany, in 1988, is an Assistant Professor of Sociology at Western Michigan University. Her recent publications concentrate on the perpetuation of violence through both criminological theory and agents of the state apparatus. Lately, her work concentrates on ways in which feminist methodology can be integrated into the study of "crime."

Kimberly J. Cook received her B.A. in Sociology at the University of Maine, M.A. at the University of New Hampshire, and is currently pursuing her Ph.D. in sociology at the University of New Hampshire. Areas of research interest, in addition to abortion and the death penalty, include violence against women, women in poverty and welfare policies, the feminization of poverty, and public policy. She is a single mother and social activist firmly believing that the personal is political.

Drew Humphries is currently writing about maternal crack/cocaine use, but has published in the areas of female victimization, crime and the media, the political economy of crime, and the history of social control. She is an Associate Professor of Sociology at Rutgers University, Camden, New Jersey.

Raymond Michalowski is currently Chair of the Department of Criminal Justice and Adjunct Professor of Sociology at Northern Arizona University. His published works include *Order, Law, and Crime, Radickale Kriminologie*, and articles on a diverse array of topics, including vehicular homicide, criminological theory, corporate crime by transnationals, the second economy and black markets in Cuba, state-corporate crime, and the political economy of imprisonment. He is currently working on an ethnography of a Cuban law collective and wishing that Arizona had an ocean.

Wayman C. Mullins received his Ph.D. in Psychology from the University of Arkansas. He taught at Hofstra University before joining the Criminal Justice faculty at Southwest Texas State University in 1984. He has published extensively in the area of right-wing terrorism, including a book with Charles C. Thomas, publisher. He is also editor of the *Journal of Police and Criminal Psychology*.

Jeffrey Ian Ross is an Assistant Professor at the University of Lethbridge. He has conducted research, written, and lectured on political and criminal violence and policing for close to a decade. His articles have appeared in *The Blackwell Encyclopedia of Political Institutions, The World Encyclopedia of Peace*, academic journals such as *Conflict Quarterly, Terrorism, Comparative Politics*, and a variety of popular magazines in Canada and the United States. In 1986 Ross was the lead expert witness for the senate of Canada's Special Committee on Terrorism and Public Safety.

Kenneth D. Tunnell is an Associate Professor at Eastern Kentucky University. He received his Ph.D. in Sociology at the University of Tennessee in 1988. He is the author of the recent *Choosing Crime: The Criminal Calculus of Property Offenders*, published by Nelson-Hall. His continuing research interests are in qualitative approaches to understanding crime and criminals and the political economy of crime and social control.

Nancy A. Wonders is an Assistant Professor of Criminal Justice at Northern Arizona University. She received her doctorate in Sociology from Rutgers University in 1990. Her scholarship explores the link between criminology and political sociology, with special emphasis on the relationship between social inequality, law and justice.